An Introduction to

Design and Culture

Second Edition

The design of everyday goods, images and environments plays an increasingly large part in our lives today. The impact of new materials and production processes, together with the changing nature of society and the consumption choices we make, present designers with considerable challenges. Now in a completely new and updated edition, this book provides a history of the development of modern (and postmodern) design within its international cultural, social and economic context.

This revised edition explores new themes of postmodernism and design, the alliance between technology and design, and the relationship between identity and design. A key theme is the development of a discourse on design that can be traced through different social periods, movements and cycles.

The author draws on a wealth of mass-produced artefacts, images and environments to illustrate the discussion, including sewing machines, cars, chairs, televisions, fashion items, interiors, graphic communications, electronic and branded goods, and exhibitions. She includes a full guide to further reading which will be of particular value to students.

An Introduction to Design and Culture will be ideal reading for all students of art and design, art and design history, and media and cultural studies; it also contains much of interest to social historians.

Penny Sparke is the Dean of and a Professor of Design History in the Faculty of Art, Design and Music of Kingston University. She has published a number of books about twentieth-century design, including books on Italian design, Japanese design, car design, and gender issues in design.

AN INTRODUCTION TO
Design and Culture
1900 to the Present

Second Edition

Penny Sparke

LONDON AND NEW YORK

First published 1986 by
Unwin Hyman Ltd
Third impression 1989

Reprinted 1992, 1994, 1995, 1998, 2000

Second edition published 2004
by Routledge
2 Park Square, Milton Park, Abingdon, Oxon, OX14 4RN

Simultaneously published in the USA and Canada
by Routledge
270 Madison Avenue, New York, NY 10016

Reprinted 2005

Routledge is an imprint of the Taylor & Francis Group

© 1986 Penny Sparke
© 2004 Penny Sparke

Typeset in Perpetua and Bell Gothic by
Bookcraft Ltd, Stroud, Gloucestershire
Printed and bound in Great Britain by
MPG Books Ltd, Bodmin

British Library Cataloguing in Publication Data
A catalogue record for this book is available from the British Library

Library of Congress Cataloging in Publication Data
Sparke, Penny.
An introduction to design and culture : 1900 to the present /
Penny Sparke.– 2nd ed.
p. cm.
1. Design–History–20th century. 2. Design–History–21st century.
3. Design, Industrial. I. Title.
NK1390.S63 2004
745.4'09'04–dc22   2003025080

ISBN 0-415-26335-2 (hbk)
ISBN 0-415-26336-0 (pbk)

CONTENTS

PART TWO
DESIGN AND POSTMODERNITY, 1940 TO THE PRESENT 115

ILLUSTRATIONS

ACKNOWLEDGEMENTS

This book could not have been written without all the support and stimulation I received over eighteen years spent teaching on the joint Royal College of Art/ Victoria and Albert Museum History of Design Programme. My thanks go to all the staff I worked with there, among them Dr Gillian Naylor, Professor Jeremy Aynsley, Professor Christopher Breward, John Styles, Marta Ajmar and Helen Clifford. Special thanks go to the many visiting scholars – too numerous to list here – who presented seminars over the years and opened my eyes to new ideas emanating from a number of disciplines hitherto unfamiliar to me and which changed the way I thought about design. Above all it is to the students – at both MA and PhD levels (especially, in the latter category, Quintin Colville, Trevor Keeble, Susie McKellar, Nik Maffei and Viviana Narotzky) – that I owe the greatest thanks, as it is they who are pushing the boundaries forward through their research, continually challenging my assumptions. I continue to be challenged by the PhD students I am supervising at Kingston University, as well as by the staff who teach Design History at that institution. My contact with design tutors and students across a range of disciplines, both at the Royal College of Art and subsequently at Kingston University, has also ensured that I understand not only where design is coming from but also, I hope, where it is going.

At Routledge I would like to thank Rebecca Barden, Julene Knox (for energetic picture research) and Helen Faulkner. Above all I must thank John, Molly, Nancy and Celia for putting up with my spending too many holidays and weekends working on my laptop.

INTRODUCTION
Twentieth-century design and culture revisited

Perhaps we should speak of a 'political economy of design'.[1]

This book is an almost completely rewritten version of one I wrote back in the early 1980s, entitled *An Introduction to Design and Culture in the Twentieth Century*. Sitting down to rewrite it I initially set out with the idea that I would simply add a new section to accommodate the events of the intervening years. Very swiftly, however, I realised that that was not going to be possible. Not only had many more things happened in the world of design since the 1980s, my perspective on the subject had also been utterly transformed by the vast amount of theoretical literature that had emerged since then. While the broad themes that directed the earlier text remained valid, something very substantial had happened in the intervening years which meant that, if the new text was going to constitute a valid contribution from the perspective of the early twenty-first century, a much more radical overhaul was going to be needed.

The essential story of design's passage through the twentieth century had, of course, not changed substantially from the earlier account. However, the vast amount of new primary research and intellectual debate that had emerged between the mid-1980s and the present day under the umbrella heading of 'postmodernism', relating in particular to the general area of 'the culture of consumption', required the context of design to be approached quite differently. Back in 1986 I had written that

> Within the framework of industrial capitalism, which created it and continues to dominate it in contemporary society, design is characterised by a dual alliance with both mass production and mass consumption and these two phenomena have determined nearly all its manifestations. *Like Janus, design looks in two directions at the same time: as a silent quality of all mass-produced goods it plays*

a generally unacknowledged but vital role in all our lives. As a named concept within the mass media it is, however, much more visible and gener-ally recognised.

That same statement still holds true for this later study. The difference between then and now, however, is that while the 1986 text acknowledged design's important role within consumption, it paid little more than lip-service to the ways in which designed artefacts and images negotiated the arenas of the social and the cultural through the mediation of consumption. This was not because it didn't deem it important, but rather because, at that time, there was little research available with which to demonstrate the depth of that relationship, the extent to which, that is, the modern concept of design was born of market demand and facilitated by mass manufacturing industry, designers, and their institutional support structure in the public and private sectors. Material relating to these last three areas filled the majority of the pages of the last book, but little detail was presented with which to illuminate the first. As this book will demonstrate in some detail, however, design's relationship with production and the world of professional practice should not, as it is in so many studies emanating from the field of 'cultural studies', be ignored. Without it, none of the complex contradictions that are the very stuff of design can be adequately engaged with.

Having said that, if the rapidly changing society that characterised the era of modernity had not required a visual and material means of expressing its aspi-rations and its identities, design, and by implication designers, would not have played such a prominent role in modern life. Design and designers are, and have been for many years, a *sine qua non* of the modern commercial system ensuring, through the activities of production and consumption, that people's needs and desires (whether consciously acknowledged or not) are met by the visual and material images and artefacts that enter the marketplace and help us define who we are.

This simple idea provided the starting point for this new introductory study of the relationship between design and culture since 1900. The structure of the book divides the twentieth century into two main periods – 1900 to 1939, and 1940 to the present. They correspond, in broad terms, to the historical periods of 'modernity' and 'postmodernity' (even though there is not a sudden transition from one to other but, rather, a considerable overlap). Each of the ten chapters is divided into two sections to allow a broad chronology to guide the narrative. The first sections in the first five chapters of the book cover the years 1900 to 1914, while their second sections deal with the period 1915 to 1939. In the second part of the book the first sections of the next five chapters cover the period 1940 to 1969, while the second sections of those chapters provide an account of design's trajectory over the period 1970 to the present day. Because design's role in the marketplace is deemed to be so fundamental to its 'acculturisation', the first chapters of each of the two main parts of the book focus on the broad context of the 'culture of consumption'. Much writing related to this subject has emerged since the 1980s focusing on subjects and themes as diverse as department stores, shopping, the city, spectacle, gender, ethnicity, class, taste, and the influence of the mass media, not to mention the vast amount of theoretical work emanating from such diverse disciplines as history (including the history of religion), social history, cultural history, art history, decorative arts history, architectural history, design history, visual culture, material culture, American studies, Italian studies, gender studies, cultural studies, media studies, sociology, anthropology, social psychology and cultural geography. This broad-based body of literature has positioned design, whether overtly or by implication, as a cultural phenomenon. At the same time design's inherent multi-disciplinarity is such that it has also been continuously dependent for its changing self-definition over the period in question, on its close links with the worlds of economics, technology, art and politics. However, by the end of the twentieth century it had become clear that design's main imperative was to create and reflect meaning in the context of everyday life. Back in the early 1980s that had not been quite so evident.

In my earlier book I failed to provide any useful working definitions or defining frameworks for the two main concepts – design and culture – that I was at pains to document. This is still a daunting task as they are both difficult, complex concepts which have transformed themselves significantly over time and which have been defined by different people at different times in different ways. However, there are some useful defining characteristics which are worth mentioning, if only tentatively. In linguistic terms, for example, the word 'design', with its obvious (although misleading) roots in the Italian '*disegno*' and French '*dessin*', can be used both verbally ('to design') and substantively ('design'), the latter deriving as a direct result of the former. This allows one the freedom to treat it ambiguously both as a process and as the result of that process. From the perspective of this study, therefore, it was deemed important to discuss both 'designing' and 'design' – and their interface with culture. This double level of meaning imbues the concept with an appropriate richness. The word 'culture' is even harder to define, denoting, as it can, so many different things, from its normative meaning, when it is used to describe highly valued, highly aestheticised activities – such as opera, poetry, theatre, and fine art – which are believed, by many people, to represent the greatest of human achievements, to its anthropological sense in which it refers, more simply, to 'a way of life'. Interestingly, like 'design' the word 'culture' also has a verbal derivation, linked to the idea of 'growing' or 'nurturing'. In recent times the word has been transformed into a noun denoting the result of the above activity. Putting the two words design and culture together immediately compounds their complexities, and they impact upon each other in interesting ways. Design's relationship with culture is, for example, significant at both of the latter's levels, whether 'high' or 'popular'. Indeed this dualism constitutes an important leitmotif in this text. The tension between the high-minded idealism underpinning modernist design ideas and the value-free approach of the postmodernists who embraced the importance of cultural 'difference' can be seen as one of the dominant themes of the period, and the one which stimulated the strongest design debates. In its visual and material incarnations, design embodied that tension.

The structure of this book reflects the multiple contexts of design as it evolved through the twentieth century, and the text emphasises the ways in which it has been both an agent and a mirror of change. While many other accounts of design and material culture see them performing a primarily 'illustrative' role, this study credits design with having a formative function within society and culture, believing that, through its visual and material language and the ideological values and messages it carries within it, it can communicate complex messages. In turn these can be negotiated and transformed, but they are difficult to ignore. In this sense design is seen as being part of the dynamic process through which culture is actually constructed, not merely reflected.

If the culture of consumption makes design necessary, technological progress makes it possible. Engendered as a process by the division of labour which played a part in the development of a model of industrial production, design carries technology's messages with it into the sociocultural context. It both mediates the philosophical underpinnings of industrial manufacturing – its essential rationality for example – and the cultural messages of the materials of manufacture, transferring them into the arena of consumption. The second chapters in the two main parts of this book address design's relationship with the culture of technology. In determining production technologies and specifying materials the designer plays a key part within the production process of goods and images. In essence design acts as a bridge between the worlds of production and consumption as the process of 'designing' is transformed into the sociocultural concept 'design'. Materials are of special significance in this context. Until they have been 'designed' and have become material 'somethings' they have minimal cultural content. The designer holds enormous power in this respect and can manipulate materials to create multiple meaning, in spite of the fact that they will, inevitably, subsequently be transformed within the contexts of consumption and use.

The third chapters in each section of the book turn from the worlds of consumption and production to that of the designer whose primary function is to act as a bridge between the two distinct spheres. It is not the intention here to suggest that he/she (mostly he) is a monolithic, heroic figure, but rather to demonstrate the fact that design is a practice as well as an abstract concept, and that the cultural context of that practice is part of the bigger picture. Design practice has always been fragmented and diverse with enormous chasms separating its specialist fields – the fashion designer and the car designer, for example, have always inhabited different universes. It is also a moving target, constantly transforming itself to suit the economic, technological, political and cultural climate within which it functions at any one time. Due to the fact that twentieth-century professional design practice emanated from two main roots, however, there have always been areas of commonality across some specialised design fields. While one face of modern design originated within a commercial tradition, manifesting itself either in two-dimensional graphic advertising or in various kinds of display or 'spectacle' which overtly set out to promote consumption in various ways, its other important face emerged as an extension of the work of architects, who believed they could control the whole visual and material environment and make the world a better place to live in. These chapters document the evolving, complex and overlapping routes taken by these two traditions and the design practices they engendered. They also track the emergence and development of 'designer-culture', one of design's most potent contributions to twentieth-century cultural life, which is predicated on the need, at one level of the market, for design to maintain a link with fine art in order to imbue it with a high level of cultural significance and to distinguish certain products from other, more mundane, goods in the marketplace. Most significantly, perhaps, this strategic cultural referencing also enabled goods with an overt 'design' content, frequently made manifest by a marketing or branding link with a designer's name, to command higher prices than 'anonymous' products.

The fourth chapters in each section of the text focus on the ideas and discourses that underpinned design practice since 1900. As a set of ideas which emerged in the years between 1900 and 1939 and formed an ideological baseline for design practice, and as an aesthetic ideal which influenced a new generation of designers as well as the many nations which sought to distinguish themselves as 'modern' after the Second World War, modernism dominates the picture, even though the period of its demise, which began in the 1960s, has been almost as long as the one in which it was hegemonic. In the final analysis, modernism's impact was felt most acutely by those cultural institutions – museums and educational establishments among them – which embraced its ideology most fully. However, the concept of 'modernity', or rather the multiple 'modernities' experienced by the mass of consumers, had an enormous effect on everyday life as it was lived by vast numbers of people during the twentieth century. Designed goods and images played a key role in providing them with access to those 'modernities'.

The last chapters in both sections of the book take as their subject the ways in which, once its key contexts and discourses were established, design has been used by powerful political and economic groupings, nations and corporations in particular, both to define and express their identities and to empower themselves. In this context design's ability to embody and express the idea of international modernity was especially meaningful, although local inflections were inevitably developed to reflect the special features of the nations and corporations which used design as an intrinsic feature of their modernising strategies. These chapters demonstrate the power of design both to form and to express identities, whether for political or commercial ends. They also touch on its capacity to construct and represent the stereotypical characteristics of a range of culturally defined categories, such as class, gender and ethnicity, offered up by individuals for negotiation in the marketplace.

These ten chapters offer a picture of design as it relates to culture from a number of key perspectives, and describe different facets of that complex relationship. As we have seen, 'design' and 'culture' are both complex phenomena. If there is one concept which lies at the heart of their relationship in the twentieth century and which holds this study together, however, it is that of 'identity' or 'identities'. The way in which individuals and groups depend upon the mass media as a means of defining themselves in groups is a key characteristic of modern life. Increasingly through the twentieth century values were communicated to people less and less through interaction with their local communities, and more and more through the media. Through its inherent relationship with industrial production, a key agent of mass mediation, and its presence in the mass-disseminated goods, images and services that resulted from that process, design became a key component of all the messages that were communicated. To extend Marshall McLuhan's analysis of the mass media, not only is the 'medium' the 'message'; it is the *design* of the medium which is crucial in this context as it determines the way in which the message is read and negotiated. Arguably, by the late twentieth century design had become more significant than the medium itself as it played an increasingly ubiquitous role in influencing the ways in which individuals and groups defined themselves. In other words the lifestyle references in the media became the most significant communicators of their messages.

Design expresses itself visually and materially, primarily (although not exclusively) in the context of consumption, and it is negotiated through the agency of 'taste', which underpins consumer choice. It is a complex language, however, which can operate simultaneously as representation and as materiaity. This way of thinking about design prioritises its role within identity formation. In the words of the cultural critic Grant McCracken, 'without consumer goods, certain acts of self-definition and collective definition in this culture would be impossible'.[2] Those definitions are, inevitably, as numerous as the individuals and the groups that relate to them. At the same time, however, a number of key overarching identities emerged in the twentieth century, notable among them one we call 'modern'. The visual style developed by the modernists – simple, undecorated, etc. – was one way of recognising the 'modern', but the definition of 'modernity' went beyond that to include the experience of engaging in a lifestyle which embraced all that modern life had to offer, from technologically sophisticated goods to access, for women, to the public sphere. Inevitably, that experience varied according to the situations of individuals or groups dependent upon the vagaries of class, gender and race. Design became everyone's bridge to their own brand of modernity.

In the first half of the twentieth century the term 'design' can be understood as being synonymous with 'modern' design, although its characteristics varied according to whose 'modernity' was in question, and in certain instances 'modern' could even be expressed by the adoption of a historical style. The latter half of the century presents a more complex picture, one which, in this book, is characterised by the umbrella term 'postmodernism', used as a catch-all to describe the pluralistic cultures that emerged in those years. Within postmodernity, arguably, design had an even more integrated role, its very existence being one of the prerequisites of the 'condition'. However, even with postmodernity, on one level the concepts of 'design' and 'modernity' continued to be linked, and it remained very hard to disengage them from each other.

This text is dependent upon a number of theoretical texts, and situates itself within the body of literature relating to the subject of the 'culture of consumption' which emerged in the 1980s and 90s. Feminist ideas developed in the same decade have also been a strong influence. It is especially indebted to two texts published in 1986. The first of these is Andreas Huyssen's *After the Great Divide: Modernism, Mass Culture and Postmodernism*. The ideas articulated in that book can be seen to relate directly to design, even though Huyssen stopped short of pushing very hard in that direction himself as it was not the focus of his study. The second text – Pierre Bourdieu's *Distinction: A Social Critique of the Judgement of Taste*, written first in the 1970s but translated into English in the mid-1980s – also provided an important framework for this study of design and culture.[3] This text positioned design within a sociocultural framework which made sense of it and which took Thorstein

Veblen's innovative ideas of the late nineteenth century forward several stages. Although much of the material in Bourdieu's book is dated now, and the case studies were very specifically French, his proposition that the exercising of taste underpins both the shape and the dynamic of modern society and culture is one which has still not been fully acknowledged, so preoccupied have historians and theorists been until recently with post-Marxist ideas and with prioritising production over consumption. Bourdieu's ideas help challenge the modernist framework which has tended to dominate most accounts of design to date.

In trying to encompass a wider spectrum of design activities and objects, this text is more ambitious than its 1986 predecessor. The primary focus on product design remains, but more effort has been made to include fashion, graphic, interior, environmental and virtual design where appropriate. This is not simply for inclusiveness for its own sake but rather because the author has come to understand that modes of professional practice and ideas flowed from one area to another through the twentieth century, and that consumers and users do not compartmentalise designed goods and images in the same way as manufacturing industry. Over a period of time ideas generated within specialised design fields went on to influence others. The role played by 'identity' within fashion design, for example, permeated the world of interior decoration in the early century and subsequently went on to play a role within car design in the 1990s. Similarly the emphasis on 'spectacle', visible in the early twentieth-century shop window display, moved into objects themselves through the agency of industrial designers in the 1930s. Also, the aesthetic relationship that consumers have long had with decorative art objects – ceramics, glass and textiles among them – has finally been transferred to computer-generated images. These are just some of the insights that it has been possible to gain by considering design across a range of media and within a historical context.

Most importantly, however, this text sets out to avoid the historicising tendencies of its predecessor. In spite of efforts to withstand their often strident claims, the dominance of modernist texts in the early 1980s was such that the 1986 study was inevitably influenced by them and unwittingly reproduced their rhetoric and their tendency to reductivism to some extent. All that has changed since the maturation of the disciplines of cultural and media studies, and the impact of postmodern ideas in the broadest sense. It is now much easier to understand that design had, and continues to have, no fixed definition or meanings, nor one ideal path to follow. Rather it is a constantly transforming concept, reflected in a set of practices and influenced by a broad context of changing ideologies and discourses which have affected its shifting parameters. If a discourse of design can be developed it must be one which recognises the high level of relativism, pragmatism and contextualisation that has determined the concept's past and which will undoubtedly continue to affect its future. Design will continue to be influenced by consumption, the fashion system, identities of all kinds, and production, whether industrial or craft-based, as well as by broader ideologies and discourses outside its control. It is a constantly moving target, although its future is, like everything else, significantly influenced by its past. In short, the picture of design and designers is constantly being repainted. This book can only, therefore, present a sketch of it, as the colours will constantly change.

PART ONE

Design and modernity, 1900–1939

Chapter 1

CONSUMING MODERNITY

Conspicuous consumption and the expansion of taste

> The department stores had fostered an extravagant taste not only for clothes
> but also for 'things one might do without'.[1]

Although the modern concept of 'design' did not have any common currency
until the middle years of the twentieth century, the idea of goods and images
being imbued with aesthetic and functional characteristics as a means of
attracting and meeting the needs of consumers and users has a long history
and is intrinsically linked to the development of what has been called 'modern' society. In brief, it developed as a direct result of the expansion of the
market for consumer goods and the democratisation of taste. As modernity
impacted upon the lives of ever larger numbers of people, design – the visual
and conceptual component of the mass-produced goods and images that
accompanied people's everyday lives and helped to give them meaning – took
on the role that had hitherto been performed for the social elite by the decorative arts. For centuries hand-made furnishings, ceramics, glass, metalwork,
dress, printed artefacts and even carriages had played many roles within the
lives of the members of the upper classes, acting as providers of comfort; as
markers of propriety; as the glue of social, family and gender relations; and,
as social mobility increased, as visible signs of fashionability, taste and
aspiration.

From the eighteenth century onwards, in both Europe and the USA, industrialisation began to create new levels of social upheaval as increased access to
goods started to blur traditional class distinctions. New classes emerged as
increasing numbers of consumers embraced goods which played more than a

mere utilitarian role in their lives. Within this context of enhanced social mobility the link between the decorative arts and taste was reinforced and became a key social indicator. As in later years industrially produced goods gradually became accessible to more and more levels of society, designed goods and images took over from the decorative arts the task of demarcating social difference, becoming a means through which large numbers of consumers could express their social aspirations and achievements. They also, significantly, took on the task of messengers of fashionability and modernity. In the years leading up to 1914, the products and images being consumed in ever increasing numbers were not always characterised by what we would now understand as a 'modern' aesthetic, but the experience of living in the modern world was well established and understood.

There has been much debate about the moment at which the process of modernisation first came to be expressed through material culture. Studies have been undertaken, for example, which have documented 'conspicuous consumption' as a sixteenth-century phenomenon, and several social historians have studied the changing patterns of consumption in the eighteenth century and their relationship with material culture.[2] Lorna Weatherill, for example, has demonstrated the way in which, in Britain, the levels of ownership of new goods varied considerably in urban and rural areas. 'Saucepans,' she explained, 'associated with cookery on enclosed stoves, were four times as common in London and in other towns as they were in the countryside, where about only one in twenty households used them. Earthenware, although used in farming as well as in households, was more common in London than in provincial towns'.[3] Her groundbreaking study, which set out to substantiate the claim that 'mass' demand preceded, and indeed helped bring about, the changes in manufacturing techniques associated with the 'Industrial Revolution', provided data relating to both aristocratic and demotic consumption, and to the ways in which certain goods – textiles, ceramics and metal goods in particular – played key social and cultural roles for new consumers.

Through the nineteenth century the middle classes continued to expand in number, and their capacity to consume increased. Studies of the patterns of their consumption in Britain in the nineteenth century are few and far between, however and the picture presented by historians to date has tended to focus on goods destined for the private, domestic arena.[4] Work is being undertaken on the customers of high-end manufacturers, such as the furniture making and interior decorating firm of Holland and Sons, but there is still much more work to be done on the consumption patterns of people inhabiting the other end of the social spectrum.[5] W. Hamish Fraser has provided an overview of the way in which the expansion of the nineteenth-century British market for manufactured goods was a direct result of the growth in the population, an increase in spending power, and shifts in taste which encouraged people to transfer their spending from one set of goods to another. In the 1860s, he explained, more gas cookers became available as a result of a fall in the price of gas; by 1914 new household objects, such as the US Bissell carpet sweeper, came on to the British market; following its success in the US marketplace the domestic vacuum cleaner made its appearance in Britain at the turn of the century; and by the first decade of the new century the bicycle and the automobile had become common appendages of the urban scene. The strategies involved in catering for, sustaining and expanding this new mass market subsumed the question of design through its role growing within advertising, marketing and retailing.[6] Visual elaboration was also a component of the appeal of the new goods themselves, albeit to a limited extent, as technological novelty tended to play a key role in most consumer choices. Sometimes aesthetic decisions were taken to conceal the novelty that was perceived by some consumers as a threat rather than a bonus. This was especially the case in some of the new domestic electrical products, which featured rococo patterns on their metal body-shells in order to enhance familiarity and relieve anxiety.

Great Britain was the first country to witness the advent of mass consumption, but the same phenomenon became visible very soon afterwards in a number of other European countries, as well as in the USA. Although it took longer than Britain to make demands of its manufacturers to produce more goods, when it finally did so the USA saw a much more dramatic and rapid growth of consumer activity and a more forward-looking approach towards the development of new technological products destined for both the public and the private spheres. In his study of the changing nature of the American middle classes the historian Richard L. Bushman has shown how they achieved refinement by the mid-nineteenth century as a direct result of material and environmental developments. Gentility, he argued, went hand in hand with the sophistication of a model of domesticity, the growth of cities and the acquisition of taste.[7] Focusing more specifically upon changing consumption patterns and their relationship with material culture, S.J. Bronner's collection of essays, *Consuming Visions: Accumulation and Display of Goods in America 1880–1920*, documented the impact of the concept of modernity on American society in these years as expressed through consumers' choices of the material environments they either selected for themselves or had created for them.[8] Karen Hultenen's essay, for example, described the subtle transformation of the parlour into the living room, and the modernising effect of the intensification of the female inhabitant's association with that newly defined space.[9] In Bronner's book, design was defined by its link with the concept of modernity. The growth of consumption – especially at its most conspicuous, which accelerated to include participation by sectors of society that had not hitherto been involved in that activity at a significant scale – was understood as a key feature of the emerging modern world.

Consumption had a material face which was visible in both the public and private spheres. Although historians have tended to move away from the idea that these spheres were entirely separate – men inhabiting the former, that is, and women being confined to the latter – the changing material culture of the two different spheres was largely specific to each in the years leading up to 1914.[10] Cultural historians have devoted many pages to discussions about the public sphere, in particular the expansion of city culture in the late nineteenth and early twentieth centuries, although they have focused less on the concept of design than upon the impact of modernity in general on people's changing experience of everyday life. However, the material environment, and the new objects within it, undoubtedly played a key role within those transformations. The extensive work on the concept of the *flâneur* – Baudelaire's term for the city 'wanderer' – and on Walter Benjamin's writings about the commercial face of the city, has explored the new experience of the city and equated it with the concept of 'modernity'.[11] Elizabeth Wilson, for example, has concentrated on women's experience of the city in this period, seeing it as an escape from domesticity and the private sphere.[12] While the modern urban experience has been described in terms of the high level of 'spectacle' that was visible to city dwellers, to date accounts of it have emphasised their reception of it and have not focused on the production of spectacle nor upon its designed components in any detail.

The idea of modernity undoubtedly existed before architects and designers created a visual/material equivalent for it in the early twentieth century. There were, however, many signs of a manmade shift in the look of the city itself – whether London, Paris, Vienna or New York – at the end of the nineteenth century. The impact first of gas and then of electric lighting, for example, transformed the city into a very different night-time environment, while the advent of new retailing outlets, department stores in particular, transformed the act of shopping and, perhaps more significantly, that of window shopping. New objects of transportation, trains and cars among them, also contributed to the new 'feel' of everyday life. Technology and design worked hand in hand to facilitate a transformation of the visual impact and the material fabric of the urban environment, which in turn had a transforming effect upon those who experienced them.

The American cultural historian William Leach has written at length about the way in which the impact of the enormous sheets of plate glass which suddenly entered the environment as store windows created a new level of spectacle for the city dweller or visitor.[13] Seen from the street itself, the illuminated contents of these public 'theatres' provided a new and dramatic form of popular entertainment. Most significantly for the emergence of a concept of design defined by its role in the formation of modernity, these new spectacular displays were created by a new visualiser, the show window display artist, whose job it was to create a dramatic visual focus, a frame for consumer goods which were as yet less overtly modern in their appearance, for the numerous *flâneurs* whose presence transformed the streets of the city. The overtly commercial role of this form of display provided a foretaste for what later came to be called 'design for industry', and the nineteenth-century store display artist can be seen as a fore-runner of the inter-war creative artists, known as industrial designers, who went on to transform the appearance of goods.

Many accounts of the birth of the department store have been written by literary historians, social and economic historians and architectural historians, among others.[14] The fascination with the subject derives from a desire to capture the heart of early modernity as it affected consumers; to uncover the roots of contemporary consumer and commodity culture; and to understand more fully the nature of the 'modern' experience. Feminist historians have been particularly active in this field, seeing the department store as a site of women's first encounter with the public sphere and commercial culture. Of relevance to this account of the emergence of a concept called 'modern design' is the fact that the department stores of the second half of the nineteenth century marked the consolidation of an emphasis on the experience of 'seeing' and the marginalisation of the functions of the other senses. In sharp contrast to the act of buying goods from a market stall, an activity which involves touch and smell as much as sight, the dominance of the eye characterised the modern way of shopping and of interacting with the modern world.[15] This shift marked a moment when the visual appearance of the goods and environments that consti-tuted the material culture of modernity took on an extra level of potency and became the key characteristic of the increasingly visual world as experienced by modern consumers and created by modern 'designers'.

Within the public sphere numerous visual, material and environmental markers of modernity – from the new objects of public and private transport, through dress, posters and other public signs, to spaces within public buildings – were in evidence in the late nineteenth century.[16] So novel was the appear-ance of many of the new objects of transportation – bicycles, railway trains, transatlantic liners and early aeroplanes – that their engineered forms took on an iconic significance. So powerful was their visual and symbolic impact that a little later, in the first decades of the twentieth century, architects and designers were to take their aesthetic lead from them when designing their 'modern' buildings and objects. The 'rational' kitchen, for example, took its inspiration from Pullman trains and liners where space was at a premium.[17] In the years leading up to 1914 designers began to borrow from one new form to create

Figure 1.1   The Dickens and Jones department store in Regent Street, London, in the early twentieth century. Such stores marked women's early entrance into the public sphere.

another, the smooth, aerodynamic forms of early automobiles, for example, taking their lead from the bulbous shapes of the prows of boats and the fuselages of aeroplanes.[18] In such a way was the self-referential aesthetic of modernity created, the early product designers borrowing forms from their immediate predecessors in this role, the engineers. Most significantly, the creators of material culture at the turn of the century refused to look backwards for models as their Victorian antecedents had done. They felt impelled, rather, to look sideways to contemporary sources. Alternatively they looked beyond culture to nature in order to start afresh, as manifested in the sensuous forms of Art Nouveau, the first of the international modern decorative styles.[19]

While the material culture of the public sphere openly embraced modernity, welcoming the influence of new materials and the visualising skills of the creative engineers, quickly coming both to represent and embody it, the private sphere was slower to respond to the same impetus. Nowhere was this more apparent than in the domestic interior, especially in those areas of the home where everyday life and its accompanying rituals were visibly enacted. In the USA at the turn of the century, for example, following the advice of Edith Wharton and Ogden Codman in their book on the subject, the interior

Figure 1.2   The parlour in the Curtis family's residence in Beaumont Street, Dorchester, Massachusetts, USA. The abundance of rugs, textiles and patterned surfaces typified the high-Victorian search for comfort in the domestic interior.

fashion of the day favoured the French eighteenth-century style, understood to be the perfect messenger of 'good taste', especially for that newly rich sector of society which had not been brought up in 'tasteful' environments and which was, as a result, reluctant to take risks in the game of social display.[20] Even in this most conservative of arenas, however, a level of modernisation gradually became apparent as new technologies, such as gas and electric lighting and heating, began to make an impact.[21] While not every aspect of material culture moved at an equal pace towards modernity there was an overall sense at the turn of the century that, in a variety of ways, important transformations were taking place which were changing the experience of everyday life for expanding numbers of people.

Dress, or fashion as it had become for the majority of people by this time, played a key role within both the private and the public spheres. A number of studies have looked in detail at the cultural impact of men and women's clothing in relation to the concept of modernity in this period. Elizabeth Wilson, for example, has shown how fashion and modernity developed hand in hand with each other, especially in their negotiation with identity and urban life, while Christopher Breward's account of male clothing in the period has demonstrated that men were not, as has frequently been claimed, operating outside the fashion cycle, nor were they absent from the picture of consumption.[22] Indeed the claim of standardisation in men's dress can be seen to indicate an ideological position rather than a reality. Just as Henry Ford subtly modified the 'Model T' automobile according to changing tastes while claiming that it remained unchanged, the early twentieth-century party line in relation to men's dress was controlled by the modernist belief that men were governed by rationality rather than desire, and that they resisted the urge to join the fashion cycle. As Roland Barthes was to explain later, the language of material culture in the context of consumption operated simultaneously on two levels. In order to follow the 'logic' of the capitalist economy it had to depend upon the irrationality of 'desire' – the emotion underpinning many consumption choices – but it also articulated the rationality of the production system.[23] From the outset design was characterised by this dual alliance, its main *raison d'être* being its role within industrial production but its primary function being that of stimulating desire. Nowhere was this more overt than in the gap between the reality of everyday consumption and the rhetoric surrounding early modernism, which claimed a rational underpinning for design.

In 1899 the social scientist Thorsten Veblen published his seminal text *The Theory of the Leisure Class*, one of the first attempts to understand the system underpinning conspicuous consumption.[24] Later Georg Simmel also set out to unravel the same conundrum.[25] Veblen focused his study on the way in which society was driven by conspicuous consumption and leisure. In the consumption of women's fashionable dress he saw the existence of a social process which could be used to describe the consumption of other kinds of goods as well, although with less intensity. The situation he observed was characterised by fashionably dressed women acting as markers of their husbands' social position and continually seeking new, ever more fashionable clothes in emulation of those whom they saw as their immediate social superiors. The concept of 'upward emulation' was his way of describing the mechanism that underpinned the continual process of 'conspicuous consumption' and fashion change. Although Veblen did not focus his attention on design – that is, on the second-level process which made fashionable dress attractive to consumers in the first place, and which imbued the objects themselves with a level of 'added value' – it was clearly an inherent, albeit unacknowledged, component of the social process he had observed.

Veblen was more interested in the sociocultural function of dress than he was in the characteristics of the dress itself. For the designers who supplied the dress – among them the French couturiers Worth, Doucet and Paquin – and who were kept in business by the continual demand for novelty, detail

of Kay's Indian muslin and Nonpareil velveteen; the style and the work were due to the pretty young wearer, who had well earned the success

was a narrow panel of the velveteen.   The tunic was bordered like the skirt with a hem over velveteen, very gracefully draped without bows,

No. 446. THE COURANCE AND DESGOFFE TOILETTES.
Made-up Models, trimmed, 5s. 6d.; untrimmed, 2s. 9d.; Flat Patterns only, 1s.; of Madame MYRA, 39 and 40, Bedford Street, Covent Garden.

she and her dress met with. The pleated skirt of cream muslin was hemmed at the edge over a band of green velveteen, and on each side

and pleated into a pointed velveteen band. The pointed plastrons, with the muslin gathered on each side of them (there were plastrons

Figure 1.3   An illustration from *Myra's Journal of Dress and Fashion*, September 1885. Increasingly, women from a broad spectrum of society sought to express their fashion awareness and social aspirations through dress.

was everything and their task was continually to refine the language of dress – new colours, decorative details, shapes, levels of elaboration – such that they retained their desirability. The system Veblen described with reference to dress was equally relevant to a range of other visual and material artefacts which also experienced stylistic redundancy: interiors, furnishings, toasters, knives and forks, and eventually automobiles, amongst the wide range of items on the almost endless list of consumable goods available at the turn of the century. So fundamental was the role of material culture in maintaining the stability of a society of which the main characteristic was continuous change that the dependency upon visually skilled individuals to conceptualise and continually renew the visual appearance of the consumable 'signs' available to an ever goods-hungry population was paramount.

In these formative years the signs in question continued to include the traditional decorative arts, which contained within them the safety of familiarity and were therefore 'risk-free' for consumers who were uncertain of their taste. As the importance of fashionability and of modernity began to take over from the role of tradition for increasing numbers of people, however, material culture began to reflect that fact. This was most apparent, in the first instance, in the two-dimensional world of commercial promotions, which embraced advertisements, magazines, and the packages created for branded goods. The development of a system of visual information and mediation surrounding goods made consumers aware of what was available to them and helped to plant in their minds the idealised images on which their aspirations could be based. The growth of modern advertising and the modern mass media magazine, aimed in the first instance at women, served to create new levels of desire and accelerate the growth of consumer culture, which was predicated upon the idea of modernity.

In this context the expansion of women's magazines, especially those focusing on fashion and the elaboration of the home, was significant in the second half of the nineteenth century. Margaret Beetham has provided an account of the growth of these magazines in Britain in the years in question, while Jennifer Scanlon has documented the development of the American woman's magazine *The Ladies' Home Journal*.[26] Both studies emphasised the ways in which these publications served to position women at the heart of consumer culture. As well as acting as consumer guides, most importantly these magazines contained advertisements for the countless consumer goods on offer, thereby providing an important information source for shoppers. In tandem with the growth of magazines the number of household advice books also expanded in these years on both sides of the Atlantic, offering yet another source of information for housewives keen to perform their tasks properly and depicting yet another idealised image of domesticity for female consumers.

One of the subtlest ways in which advertising and marketing penetrated the consciousness of consumers was through the use of brands. Changes in retailing from market stalls to fixed shops and urban department stores put a greater emphasis on the roles of packaging and branding. Rather than buying foodstuffs loose, shoppers increasing bought pre-packed goods which had been prepared in factories and distributed in bulk to retail outlets.[27] Susan Strasser has described the changes that took place in retailing in these years

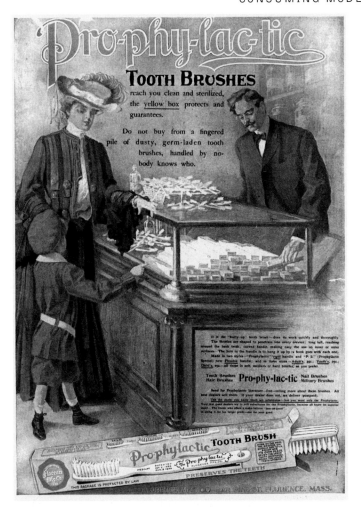

Figure 1.4   The *Pro-phy-lac-tic* toothbrush, pictured here in Colliers, 1905, was one of the early branded and packaged goods to be retailed in fixed shops in the USA in the early twentieth century.

and the accompanying rise of branding as a means of identifying goods in the minds of consumers.[28] This was the era in which the names of companies, used as brands – Kelloggs and Hoover among them – came to replace the name of the commodities themselves in the minds of consumers. Packaging and branding necessitated the emergence of another group of 'visualisers' whose role was to create attractive, memorable images which would promote the brand over the product. Although brand names were often visible on packets – especially of food products – they were in essence immaterial concepts which sold products through their appeal to a desirable lifestyle.

The rise of branded goods in the USA represented a major shift in the way in which goods were bought and sold, as well as creating a new link between design and marketing that was to become increasingly complex over the next century. Companies found names for their products which were not simply their own but which evoked a particular 'lifestyle'. The Pittsburgh Reduction Company, for example, which produced aluminium kitchenware items, coined the name 'Wearever' for its range of products. It was intended to describe its pots and pans for their potential consumers, who were perceived as rational beings who wanted value for money. The company employed artists to develop a range of magazine advertisements to promote its 'Wearever' range and shops were encouraged to use a banner in their shop windows with the name emblazoned on it. A sophisticated visual promotional framework was developed around the campaign to sell aluminium pots and pans involving designers of different kinds – graphic artists, packaging artists and show window display artists among them. In the years before 1914, however, no attempt was made to make the goods themselves look attractive. Their desirability was communicated through all their accompanying visual information rather than through the aesthetic language of the pots and pans themselves. This means of conveying 'added value' represented a first stage in the process that ended up, in the inter-war years, as industrial design, when manufacturers finally realised that the visual impact of goods themselves gave them a competitive edge that advertisements, packaging and shop window displays could not achieve on their own.

By the early years of the twentieth century, in its attempt to stimulate and requite consumer desire, the commercial world had developed a set of sophisticated marketing strategies involving a wide range of visualising and conceptualising practices. In conjunction with each other the expanded market, the emergence of a new technologically oriented concept of modernity, the phenomenon of new consumers using material culture as a means of defining and communicating their identities and aspirations, and the availability of more and more goods, images and services in the marketplace, created the necessary backcloth for the emergence of a concept of modern design which began to pull all these strands together. Most significantly that concept of design was characterised by its unique position at the interface between consumption and production, and its ability to relate to both the irrational behaviour of consumers and the increasingly rational process of mass manufacturing. Above all its ability to represent modernity – the key aspiration and ideal for new consumers – made it one of the key cultural and commercial forces of the early twentieth century. By 1914 the framework was in place for a new, modern visual and material culture – not yet called 'design' – which was defined to a significant extent by its role within conspicuous consumption and the sociocultural requirements of the marketplace.

Consumer culture and modernity

Consumer culture is in important respects *the* culture of the modern west.[29]

In the years between the two world wars, modernity entered into the lives of large sections of the populations of the western industrialised world in a multitude of ways. Sometimes, as the social historian Sally Alexander has so evocatively shown, it was expressed by a touch of lipstick or the puff of a cigarette.[30] At other times it was represented by the wholesale reinvention and reshaping of the material environment, as seen, for example, by visitors to New York's World Fair in 1939.[31] Modernity was a limitless concept. It existed to the extent to which people could imagine the future and bring that vision to bear on the present. It was frequently experienced as an aspirational concept – something which promised a level of 'added value' in people's lives, which went beyond 'need' into the world of 'desire'. Presented to them through the mass mediation of industrial manufactured goods, magazines, films and advertisements, it had something of the unattainable about it while it was still, to a limited extent, attainable. Luxurious, it was also democratic. Perhaps modernity's key characteristic, as it was presented to the consumers of the industrialised world, was its inbuilt ambivalence and contradictions. Inevitably designers, paid to be imaginative and visually innovative, played a key part in this process of envisioning various models of modernity and of ensuring that, by being constantly renewable and renewed, it remained just out of reach.

In the inter-war years the outward signs of modernity continued to be most obviously visible in the public arena. Europe and the USA witnessed the arrival of mass urbanisation and increasing levels of wealth. As a result the graph of mass consumption rose dramatically with far-reaching effects on the mass environment, which was transformed beyond all recognition. As car ownership grew, for example, an enhanced roadside material culture of motels, drive-in cinemas and petrol stations developed to support it. Also in the public arena, the increased consumption of goods for personal embellishment – from frocks to make-up – and the enhanced visibility of women in public spaces were such that city life was visually transformed. The ever-increasing impact of graphic advertising and commercial display added to that effect, creating a mass environment which, in urban and increasingly in suburban centres, was visually transformed. These changes did not happen by

Figure 1.5 A Texaco gas station, designed by Walter Dorwin Teague Associates, *c.*1934. Modern-style gas stations constituted one face of the enormous impact made by the advent of the most modern of all material cultural artefacts, the automobile.

themselves, of course, but were driven by the commercial machine that underpinned the expansion of consumer culture at this time. This was especially apparent in the USA, where the art of marketing was at its most sophisticated. Much has been written about the new processes that were put in place. Susan Strasser and R.S. Tedlow, for example, have documented the rise of mass marketing in the USA, showing the complex way in which it developed.[32] Case studies have contributed to this picture, showing how marketing ensured that mass-produced goods reached a large-scale audience of consumers. In her essay 'Celluloid Dreams: The Marketing of Cutex in America, 1916–1935', Kate Forde has shown how the J. Walter Thompson Advertising Company set about selling nail varnish to a female mass market.[33] The Cutex brand was heavily advertised through women's magazines, the readership of which was expanding exponentially at this time.[34] Forde explained how JWT's strategy was to sell the name of Cutex as if it were a kind of deity, in line with a range of other modern hygiene products, among them Borax, Kleenex, Lux and Pyrex.[35] The utilisation of strikingly modernist packaging was also an important selling point. The importance of the detail of this and other studies – among them Kathy Peiss's *Hope in a Jar: The Making of*

America's Beauty Culture – is crucial to an understanding of the way in which consumer fantasies were to a significant extent created, controlled and fulfilled by the commercial system, which embraced design.[36]

Even with the hardships of the 1930s the desire to consume a particular range of goods – cars, refrigerators and other domestic appliances among them – did not abate. These new products of the technological industries came with a vision of modernity built into them. Cars, for example, were manufactured by new techniques and, from the late 1920s, were styled to appeal across a spectrum of consumers. General Motors' range of cars, for example, included its up-market Cadillac and its down-market Buick.[37] The market segmentation of goods not only reflected consumer difference, but also played a key role in creating it. The result was the emergence of a subtle consumer–design relationship that applied right across society not, as previously, only for the wealthy sector which had been able to demonstrate its 'taste' through the acquisition of goods. Sally Clarke has described the way in which, inasmuch as it was not possible for GM to predict consumer tastes, its venture into industrial design constituted a business risk which it was, nevertheless, willing to take.[38] It was undoubtedly a risk that paid off.

The democratisation of taste and luxury brought about by design's alliance with mass production industry was intensified through the inter-war years across the industrialised world, and brought into being a new sensitivity to stylistic change on a mass basis. The fashion cycle that Veblen had analysed some decades earlier became a widespread reality, fuelled by those areas of material culture – fashionable dress and motor cars in particular – which were most susceptible to this kind of change. Arguably a gendering of material culture was put in place whereby women used their dress, their beauty products and their interiors to express their level of fashion awareness, and therefore of their real or aspired-to social standing, whereas men were beginning to invest their status and identities in their own range of consumer machines. The fact that the car was a visual sign located primarily in the public sphere confirmed its essential masculinity.

Much has been written about the female consumer in the inter-war years. Indeed, even within the period it was widely acknowledged that women were the key consumers. In *Selling Mrs Consumer*, the household management expert Christine Frederick described what she believed to be the characteristics of 'feminine consumption'.[39] In a section entitled 'Guessing at Mrs Consumer's Character' she explained that 'Mrs Consumer habitually proceeds more along the lines of instinct than upon theory or reason and accommodates herself more readily to practical realities. Man is more thoroughly theoretical'.[40] In an article entitled 'Consuming Brotherhood: Men's Culture, Style and Recreation as Consumer Culture, 1880–1930', Mark A. Swiencicki claimed,

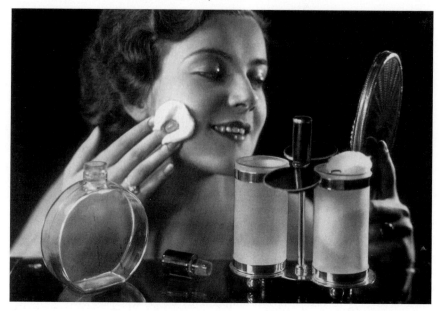

Figure 1.6   One of the ways in which women entered modernity was through the embellishment and streamlining of their bodies, as evidenced by this application of make-up in the inter-war years.

however, that, 'men were indeed a very large and important consuming constituency.'[41] The evidence he provided indicated that men were indeed significant consumers in that period, with their range of possible consumables including ready-to-wear clothing, sports equipment and recreational activities. Unlike women, he argued, men did not acquire their goods from shops and department stores but rather from a range of non-retail outlets such as saloons, lodges, clubs, barbershops and dime theatres.[42] What is clear from all the literature dedicated to gendered consumption in this period is that designed goods, images and services played an important role in motivating sales and meeting the needs and desires of both men and women, albeit perhaps in different ways.

In his book *Auto Opium* the sociologist David Gartman argued that what has been described as the 'feminisation of the automobile' – the emphasis upon colour and appearance in consumer decision-making in relation to this product – was in fact a means of men not having to admit that they, as much as women, participated in the fashion cycle and were equally interested in the process of the aestheticisation of everyday life, which was being intensified at an enormous speed. With the advent of mass manufacture the worlds of production and consumption became increasingly intertwined, Gartman also explained, as the makers of products such as cars also became their consumers. The car industry was the classic example of this phenomenon, as the workers who assembled the cars manufactured by Ford and GM also constituted a large section of the market for the end product. Gartman described this as a form of compensation through consumption for the loss incurred by their labour being sold to the capitalist system.[43]

The effects of cars on the urban and rural landscape were seen not only in the fact of their presence but also in the other environmental elements that naturally accompanied them. New road systems crisscrossed the countryside; petrol stations became familiar features of the town and countryside, and in the USA roadside cinemas, restaurants and motels proliferated. Not only the buildings but also their graphic advertising appealed to a world on wheels and were designed accordingly. The design historian David Jeremiah has researched the expansion of petrol stations in Britain in the years in question, showing how they 'irreversibly changed the shape of the rural and urban landscape'.[44] His essay explained how this change did not come about without resistance, and that a sector of the population saw this as a regrettable American influence which was ruining the environment. Indeed, from the outset the advent of consumer culture had its aggressive opponents who did not want the natural landscape polluted by 'unnatural' constructions and 'garish' graphics. A level of conservatism always accompanied the more accepting face of consumer culture, and resistance was felt at many moments. Aluminium cooking pots were, for example, believed to spread disease, and new chemical substances, such as the nitrocellulose in nail polish, were also seen as a danger. Design, whether in the form of advertisements, packaging, or as part of goods themselves, played an important role in offsetting such anxieties and appeasing consumers through an appeal to their needs and wants, and an evocation of a pleasant, beautiful world in which progress was always seen as benevolent.

Arguably the advent of the motor car was the most radical modernising material cultural force of the inter-war years, most dramatically in the USA but also significantly in Europe. This has been recognised by a number of studies which have focused on the automobile's cultural impact. In their preface to *The Automobile and American Culture* the editors, David L. Lewis and Laurence Goldstein, noted society's ambivalent relationship with the automobile. 'We still complain', they wrote, 'that vehicles disturb tranquillity, pollute the environment, kill us off in large numbers, and strain our pocketbooks. But only a handful of us have traded motor vehicles for mopeds, much less bicycles.'[45] In his study of the influence of the motor car on British society in the period in question, Sean O'Connell concentrated on the artefact's powerful relationship with class and gender, emphasising its inherent masculinity which, he argued, 'has ultimately prevented millions of women from taking to the driving seat.'[46]

Other designed public environments played a key role within the formation of urban modernity, especially those linked to work, shared leisure, and shopping. In all the modern metropolises of the western industrialised world, shops and the experience of shopping were important agents of modernisation for large sections of society. Building on pre-1914 innovations when the modes of selling to a mass market were first put in place, shops took on the visual symbolism of that novelty by presenting themselves through a set of visual languages which were overtly modern. The effect was circular in that these new environments simultaneously reflected and created a modern consumer culture. Indeed, shops were among the first buildings and interior spaces to be influenced by the modern styles available on the marketplace, from the austere forms of high modernism in the most up-market stores (Simpsons of Piccadilly in London, for example) to the more decorative, American-influenced curved forms of streamlining, sometimes referred to as 'modernistic', and the French-derived 'moderne' style.

French designers played a special role in the modernisation of the shopping environment. In that country manufacturing was dominated by the luxury trades – those of haute couture, perfumes, interior decoration and craft-made furniture among them. Shopping was therefore geared on the one hand to the socially and financially privileged who purchased their goods from elite outlets while, on the other, it promised a level of new level of accessibility to a luxurious lifestyle for aspiring consumers who could experience the modernity of the department store and the 'boutique'. In her study of 1920s Paris, Tag Gronberg explained how the *devanture de boutique* (shop front) was 'frequently cited as the most appropriate means of modernising Paris'.[47] This was described as a feminised modernity, strongly bound up with the concepts of fashion and luxury.

Modernity was especially evident in post-war dress. After the First World War a revolution occurred in women's dress and general profile such that the soft flowing forms of the early century were replaced by a more linear, angular silhouette. On one level, the idealised body was dramatically transformed as fashionable women increasingly aspired to a look which was much nearer to the modernist 'machine aesthetic'. Men's idealised bodies also changed to reflect a changed image of modernity. Transformations in hairstyling were particularly apparent, new technology enabling women to curl their new short hair and present it in the fashionable styles of the day. Innovative hairdressers, such as Antoine of Paris, turned hairdressing into an art form which was emulated in urban centres across the globe. The spaces in which such activities took place were hybrid in nature, reflecting both the advances made possible by technology and the traditionally private and intimate process of having one's hair dressed at home.[48]

Even within the private arena of the home, the bastion of traditional values, modernity was making its mark in these years. This was especially noticeable in the kitchen and the bathroom where new technologies were having an impact and where there was less resistance (than in the living room) to the improvements that could be made. The kitchen was affected by advances in organisation, inspired by the work of the household management expert Christine Frederick and others in the early century, such that continuous work surfaces were increasingly in evidence for those consumers who could afford them. The new labour-saving appliances were consumed in large numbers, their impact being as much as status objects as time-savers. The refrigerator, in particular, took on an iconic significance in the 1930s, representing the arrival of modernity in countless kitchens across the globe.

The entry of modernity into the domestic arena in these years went hand in hand with the housewife's changing role and status. From a rational scientist, in charge of her laboratory, she was increasingly depicted as a caring wife, mother and consumer and by the 1930s also as a charming hostess, minus her apron, inviting visitors into her home and showing them her modern goods.[49] Inevitably for large sections of the population this was an idealised shifting image rather than a lived one. It was created for the most part by manufacturers and their advertisers in order to convince women that they should identity themselves as consumers first and foremost and define both themselves and the social status of their families through consumption.

In spite of the efforts made by manufacturing industry to introduce modernity into the domestic arena in order to sell its goods, the home retained a predominantly traditional face. This was especially apparent in the living areas where familial values were located and which depended upon the role of memory for their continuity. Thus, in addition to a wide range of material references to the past and artefacts which, while frequently mass-produced, had historical references built into them, the souvenir and the inherited object continued to play the same important role they had performed for many years. Nonetheless, many signs of an encroaching modernity were also in evidence. The claustrophobic Victorian parlour, for example, was gradually being replaced by lighter, brighter living rooms containing fewer pieces of furniture and less clutter. This cautious, evolutionary approach to an acceptance of a transformed environment has been described by the literary historian Alison Light as being characteristic of a preference for a 'conservative modernity'.[50] A number of historians have demonstrated that the path to modernity was not the same for everyone; that cultural categories such as gender, class, age and ethnicity, affected the way in which it was negotiated.[51] Women, perceived by many as the key consumers of the period, seem to have accepted modernity into their midst in the inter-war years, albeit rather slowly. In all but the most affluent of homes, interior decoration was not undertaken by professionals but by housewives themselves, aided by consumption and tradesmen. Domestic modernisation was therefore largely in the hands of consumers themselves, aided by the mass dissemination of models available to them in magazines, shop windows and films. Indeed, it has been argued that Hollywood films played a key role in these years, influencing both interior décor and dress.[52] The private sphere was slower than its public equivalent to embrace modernity.

Nowhere was this mediated modernity more apparent than in the new suburban residential areas that developed around the key cities both in the USA and Europe. Inhabited for the most part by the new upper-working class and middle class, these areas represented the other face of the sophisticated metropolises of these years – New York, London, Paris, Berlin, Stockholm and Vienna among them. The social and cultural geography that separated the city from the suburb was fairly uniform across the industrialised world, albeit with inevitable local variations, and it served to set up distinctive taste cultures. On one level the suburbs now consumed what the cities had consumed some time earlier and had since rejected as being unfashionable. On another level the suburbs and the cities supported completely different systems of production and consumption which did not touch each other but which, nonetheless, had some things in common. It became apparent that it was possible within mass production and consumption to have distinctive taste cultures, all of which were perceived as modern according to their own defi- nition of the term, but which had little in common with each other. This can be explained, in part, by Ben Fine and Ellen Leopold's theory of 'systems of provision', which suggests that people's tastes are formed only in the economic context of the particular system of provision which is available to them.[53] While the theory is partially valid, it ignores the importance of the role played by the nationally and globally distributed media to which, in the twentieth century, most people had access, and which were as powerful agents of taste formation as what was available in the local shops.

By the late 1930s a concept of modernity had penetrated the worlds of most people living in the western industrialised world to some extent or other. The effects of marketing, advertising and branding were widespread and there was an increased level of self-consciousness about the stylistic languages of mass- produced goods, images and spaces. Self and group identities were increasingly being negotiated through consumption, the meanings of which were injected into material and visual culture, not only at the time of the manufacture and sale of goods and images, but also as they moved into social and cultural circula- tion. Once modernity was negotiated by the consumers and users of material

Figure 1.7   Xanti Schawinsky's calendar for the Olivetti Company, created in 1934, showed how graphic designers could reinforce the modernity of products by visually linking them with the image of a fashionable woman.

and visual culture, desires were stimulated which, in turn, required the creators of goods and images to supply the necessary objects of those desires. Thus was the fashion cycle fuelled.

Consuming designed visual and material culture, and thereby embracing modernity, had, by the inter-war years, become one of the primary means through which the majority of the inhabitants of the industrialised world acquired their identities and positioned themselves in society. Such was the intensification and expansion of this process that designers found themselves no longer at the margins but at the very epicentre of modern consumer culture.

Chapter 2

THE IMPACT OF TECHNOLOGY

New production methods, new materials

> Mass production is the focussing upon a manufacturing project of the principles of power, accuracy, economy, system, continuity, and speed.[1]

While one face of modern design was defined by its sociocultural role within the expanded picture of consumption and the newly defined marketplace – an area of modern life which could not be easily rationalised and systematised – its other important defining context was the much more rationally based world of mass manufacturing and technological innovation. Indeed, the story of expanded consumption and market demand cannot, on its own, account for the development of a concept of modern design; it was also defined by its key role within the manufacture of large numbers of standardised goods which were produced to meet expanding market demand but which, because of the high investment costs needed to produce them in large numbers, had to be sold aggressively. Design crossed the technology/culture divide: as a process which was intrinsic to mass manufacturing, as well as a phenomenon which communicated sociocultural values, it was embedded equally firmly within the worlds of consumption and production. Indeed, it was one of the key forces which helped to link those two worlds together and make a seamless connection between them.[2]

In addition to understanding design's role within the sociocultural context of consumption it is also important to appreciate its position within the story of technological change as it affected, and was affected by, manufacturing and the world of materials. Technological innovation underpinned the manufacture of the vast number of newly conceived products that came into being from the late nineteenth century onwards. They challenged and excited designers' imaginations as well as constituting a whole new area of material culture which complemented the more traditional arena of the decorative arts. The wide availability of such novel goods as vacuum cleaners and electrical appliances and new modes of transportation, as well as the new forms of advertising and retail display which were developed in these years, provided the means through which both existing and new consumers could create new identities for themselves and negotiate their entry into modern life.

The modern concept of design, and the process that underpinned it, superseded the traditional decorative arts, and the craft process that had generated them, as a direct result of the development of the division of labour within industrial manufacturing. This new means of producing goods caused the work of the traditional artisans to become fragmented into a number of new, differentiated tasks. The advent of mass consumer culture also required that new commercial tasks were undertaken by designers who had a unique perspective on the market. As a result, designing emerged as a new activity, or rather as a new combination of activities. In response to the social transformations that industrialisation brought with it, and the ensuing need for material culture to carry new sociocultural meanings, designing combined a new set of activities which crossed the production/consumption divide. Consequently, it was uniquely placed to represent the notion of 'modernity' as it related to both arenas.

Industrialisation was one of the key defining features of the modern world. In Britain the discovery of steam-power inspired the invention of numerous new machine tools and production techniques.[3] In turn these new tools facilitated the manufacture of new consumer machines. New materials, cast iron among them – the result of the work of the steam-pump – were responsible for dramatic changes in the design of products and of the environment, making possible new kinds of architectural and product decoration. These discoveries transformed the production of the traditional decorative arts: in textile production, for example, the Spinning Jenny and the Jacquard loom revolutionised the ways in which textiles were both conceived and made and caused the designer, unlike craft weavers who had been able to make decisions as they went along, to have to make aesthetic choices in advance of manufacture. The need to make decisions earlier represented an important paradigm shift from the working process of the artisan, who had depended upon tacit skills, to that of the designer for industry, who had to undertake more self-conscious, rational planning. This was echoed in many nineteenth-century industries, among them fabric printing, where a mechanical roller was used, and in ceramics production, which made an increasing use of moulds. In the nineteenth century this divided labour process created a multitude of new 'art workers' whose jobs involved translating the ideas of fine artists into mass manufactured goods.[4]

While Britain transformed the manufacturing methods of the decorative art industries, creating large numbers of goods for the new consumers, the USA made huge advances in the efficient organisation of labour and production in the new, technologically oriented industries; in the development of highly specialised machine tools; and in the manufacture of new goods with a technological bias. Much has been written about what was dubbed 'the American System of Manufacture'. H.J. Habakkuk, for example, has described the differences between the developments in Britain and the USA, showing that mechanisation was much more advanced in the latter because, given the greater availability of farming land in that country, manual labour was in short supply.[5] Siegfried Giedion's seminal text, *Mechanisation Takes Command* of 1948, focused on the theme of the importance of the machine to American culture and to that country's pre-eminence in modern, functional design.[6] Indeed modernism – the prevailing design philosophy of the mid-twentieth

Figure 2.1 Ford 'Model T' automobiles on the 'Body Chute' at the Highland Park Factory, 1915. Ford's production system at this time represented a pure model of mass production. It was modified later by General Motor's model of 'flexible' mass production.

century – considered the machine, with its links with function and rationality, to be the key metaphor and source of aesthetic inspiration for modern design.

David A. Hounshell's study of America's technological progress, published in 1984, focused on the fundamental continuities within the story of American manufacturing in this period.[7] He outlined a story which began with the changes that took place in American arms production in the nineteenth century, and moved through to automobile manufacturing in the 1920s. His narrative took in clocks, sewing machines, bicycles, agricultural machinery and automobiles along the way. Hounshell maintained that each industry learnt from the one before it, and that continuity existed in the use of steel as a basic material, in the development of standardised components, and in the use of specialist machine tools. By Henry Ford's time, Hounshell argued, with the production of the 'Model T' 'pure' mass production had been achieved. It was however, in his view, only to last twelve years, as 'flexible mass production', spearheaded by Alfred P. Sloan at General Motors, superseded Ford's ideal of completely standardised manufacture. Sloan's 'impure' model, Hounshell argued, could be explained as a response to the demands of the market which, for sociocultural reasons, required product differentiation. Hounshell's text concluded, in fact, just at the point when the 'designer' (in the form of Harley Earl at General Motors, who was followed by others performing similar roles appointed by other manufacturing companies) was catapulted into industry to create that level of differentiation. By the 1920s, Hounshell argued, the existence of a second-hand car market, the urbanisation of the mass of the American population, and the importance to the consumer of buying a second car which was not black and which was more impressive than his/her neighbour's equivalent, meant that, while pure standardisation was a technological possibility, it was not a commercial reality. Hounshell emphasised an important moment in the early part of the story of modern design, the one in which technology and culture came directly into conflict with each other. In the event culture won the day and 'design' provided the means by which the two forces could achieve a new harmony with each other. In essence, from that point onwards the products of the new mass production industries became as sensitive as the decorative arts had long been to non-technological issues, such as stylistic and fashion change. In addition the role of the visualiser became highly valued by industries which acknowledged that they were forced to accommodate an element of 'art' within their otherwise highly efficient, rational operations.

While shifts within mass manufacturing created a gap which was filled by design, other areas of technological innovation helped to transform the nature and appearance of the modern environment as well as providing new challenges for the designer. The impact of plate glass windows on the cityscape, for example, mentioned in the previous chapter, was matched by the presence of other new materials, such as cast and wrought iron and concrete, which also helped to articulate the language of modernity to inhabitants of the modern material world. Architects and designers were keen to exploit the symbolic potential of the new materials in order to create a visual and material modernity. In Vienna, for example, the architect Otto Wagner was quick to use the new material aluminium in two of his projects.[8] As the design historian Judy Attfield explained, cultural historians and critics have tended to present analyses of representations of material culture rather than its actual materiality which, she argued, is experienced in a way that it is difficult to discuss.[9] In an exploration of the cultural impact of materials, designers have inevitably played a key role as they have created the world that people, however tacitly, have encountered and come to understand.

The architects and designers associated with the Art Nouveau movement, who sought to create a new style with no historical baggage attached to it, inevitably looked to new materials as a means of achieving that ambition. As Helen Clifford and Eric Turner explained, 'Metal architecture stood for modernism. Cast iron was employed by Art Nouveau designers and architects for its practical qualities and aesthetic possibilities ... cast iron ... was particularly suitable for the expression of the suppleness and tensile strength of the Art Nouveau "whiplash curve".'[10] Blending together the achievements of the engineers with a new language of modern decoration, the Art Nouveau designers self-consciously created an aesthetic modernity with the help of new materials which had not yet acquired any cultural baggage.

While technology made new materials available it could not, on its own, ensure either their application or their acceptance in the marketplace. Designers played a key role in gauging popular taste and aspirations and in transforming new materials into desirable goods. That was sometimes a relatively easy task, as in the case of celluloid which, because it could be used as substitute for more expensive, highly desirable materials, including jet, ebony, coral, amber and ivory, found immediate acceptance. Aluminium proved much more challenging to designers. Indeed it wasn't until the turn of the century, when that new metal could be produced cheaply and had begun to replace enamel and brass as materials for cooking pots, that it was able to play a substitute role, although even then it was regarded with some suspicion. Only in the inter-war years were designers were able to create a new aluminium aesthetic and visualise aluminium products as modern objects in their own right.

This sense of a new material modernity was, inevitably, most visible in the public sphere in these years. Within the more traditional context of domesticity there was however also a growing level of acceptance. The gradual absorption of new materials into the home occurred through the acceptance in the early century, for example, of items made of pressed glass, a replacement for more expensive cut crystal, and others made of the new plastic – Bakelite – which was used for electrical accessories such as plugs and switches.[11] A number of other materials that had traditionally been used within the domestic sphere found themselves used in new ways in order to create a sense of modernity. In the USA, for example, the renewed use of chintz in interior furnishings came into fashion in the early twentieth century, replacing the earlier heavy velvets and brocades and ushering in a new feeling of lightness which was perceived as decidedly modern.[12]

Although the home was slower than the public arena to rise to the challenge of new technologies in this period, the effects of gas and electricity were transforming both the public and the domestic spheres. By the late nineteenth century the flavour of rationality which pervaded the factory and the office also began to permeate the home. A search for rationalism and increased efficiency underpinned factory practice in the last years of the nineteenth and the early years of the twentieth century. In the factory and the office this had been achieved through the application of Taylorism and by the increasing modifications made to what has been called the 'American System of Manufacture' – the production of standardised interchangeable parts combined with the moving assembly line.[13] The system was demonstrated at its most refined at Henry Ford's Highland Park Factory, where the 'Model T' automobile was first manufactured in 1913. The thinking that led to the use of the moving assembly line and the use of standardised parts was reflected in the design of the automobile, visually characterised by the multiplicity of its components which failed to add up to a unified whole. In spite of its overtly engineered, rather than designed, aesthetic, the Model T had strong consumer appeal as it was marketed at first-time buyers whose preoccupations were with low price and reliability, qualities which Ford was able to provide. Mere ownership was, in itself, a mark of social distinction for the members of the rural population at whom the car was targeted and who, up until that time, had had to make do with horses. As Hounshell has shown us, however, it was a marketing strategy which had a limited life, as the product was unable to continue to stimulate desire once it was no longer a question of first-time ownership and competition had entered the marketplace.

Taylorism, a scientific measuring system which analysed ways in which tasks were carried out and which suggested more efficient time-saving alternatives, was in evidence in the office and the factory, imposing a strong ethos of rationalism in the workplace. The desire for rationality in this context as a means of enhancing productive efficiency was transferred from the factory and office into the domestic arena a few years later. The impetus to rationalise housework was also an extension of the tradition of household advice which had begun with the writings of Catherine Beecher and her sister Harriet Beecher Stowe back in 1869.[14] In order to demonstrate that a history of woman's labour could be documented as fully as that of male labour in the public workplace Ruth Schwartz Cowan and Susan Strasser, among others, have charted the development of this advice literature.[15] Both their books emphasised the importance of the concept of the so-called 'labour-saving' home of the late nineteenth and early twentieth centuries and set out to show that, as it is not clear what the home is meant to produce, the concept of 'efficient production' was ultimately less relevant in the domestic context than in the factory. With much productive work – preserving fruit, sewing clothes, etc. – having been transferred to the factory, they both explained, the

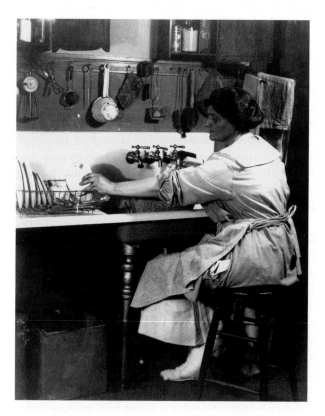

Figure 2.2   A photo from the Agricultural Extension Department of the International Harvester Corporation in Chicago, showing how rational planning in the kitchen required all 'tools' to be within an arm's reach, for maximum efficiency.

emphasis in housework had moved to nurturing and consuming rather than producing. In this new context the introduction of efficiency into the household was a more complex proposition with a less obvious purpose.

As in the factory, reorganisation preceded mechanisation in the implementation of efficient practice in the home. Christine Frederick's book of 1913, which had been serialised a little earlier in the pages of the *Ladies' Home Journal*, outlined the ways in which tasks could be simplified by a reorganisation of the elements in the kitchen in order to reduce the number of steps that were needed to prepare a meal; the professionalisation of the housewife by giving her a white gown, in emulation of a laboratory technician; and the re-positioning of food preparation tools in emulation of an artisan's workplace.[16] In essence this attempt to bring rationality into the feminine sphere, hitherto perceived as an arena dominated by emotional values and consumer desire, meant a transformation of the existing elements of the home rather than the introduction into it of new, technologically innovative domestic tools. Through the absorption of her ideas into modernist kitchen planning and design, the impact of Frederick's work was greatest in the years after the First World War. In the years before 1914, in the USA, it was paralleled by another movement known as 'Home Economics'.[17] Like Frederick, Ellen H. Richards was a prime mover, aiming to make housework more efficient by focusing on the elimination of germs and sanitation and to gain more respect for housewives. Both home economics and Frederick's ideas were formulated in the context of what has been called 'The Servant Problem', the shortage of servants for middle-class households which resulted in housewives having to undertake their own housework. The same phenomenon was also in evidence in Europe, although unlike the USA, where it had been taken up by the servantless middle classes; in Germany, for example, it was part of a programme of paternalistic social reform directed at the wives of working men.[18]

The promotion of a culture of rational planning entered the home through architectural thinking. Although in the pre-war years the labour-saving concept had only in the first instance envisaged a reorganisation of simple, traditional tools, it nonetheless encouraged manufacturers to approach housewives as 'rational beings' for the first time, and stimulated consumers to think in terms of 'rational consumption'. It also put housewives in the right frame of mind to accept the new domestic tools – electrically powered ones in particular – when they became available in the marketplace by the end of the first decade of the twentieth century. Indeed, when the newly formed electrical companies – General Electric and Westinghouse in particular – and the smaller domestic appliance manufacturers – Hoover and Sunbeam among them – set out to produce and market their new products, they were quick to develop a marketing strategy that stressed the importance, to the housewife, of using the new appliances as a means both of professionalising her role and of making her life easier. Producers of aluminium pans, for example, set up experimental kitchens in department stores where home economics experts demonstrated the benefits of using their products, thereby preparing the housewife to accept such goods rather than to reject them out of hand as might have been the case if she still had assistance from servants.[19] One historian has suggested that they were also purchased by women who had been lucky enough to retain their servants as a means of encouraging them to stay.[20] Although their beneficial properties represented an entry into modernity for the progressive housewife, prior to 1914 the small household tools that were manufactured and sold – toasters, electric frying pans, electric chafing dishes and food heaters among them – were presented as crude, engineered, mechanical devices rather than as tamed, visually attractive, domestic goods. Like the 'Model T' they sold on the basis of their use-value, and their novelty and ownership alone were sufficient to suggest the social status of their consumers.

The distinction between invention and design was very clear. While the inventor's role was to create new applications for available technologies, the designer acted as the interface between these applications, manufacturing industry and consumers. In the late nineteenth and early twentieth centuries new concept followed new concept such that the consumer machines we are all now so familiar with – the sewing machine, the telephone, the refrigerator, the bicycle and the automobile – were all born in this fruitful period, in which everything seemed possible. The greatest quantity of new products was conceived in the USA. In Europe, given the abundance of manual labour, the push to create new machines was less energetic.[21]

Once invented, these new goods had to be manufactured and sold in the open market place, and it was the designer's task to ensure that they could be made at an affordable price but, perhaps more importantly, to render them both meaningful and desirable. Gradually the new products began to be visually and symbolically aligned with the environments for which they were destined: kitchen-based items, restricted to use by the servant or housewife for example, usually retained a crude, mechanical appearance, whereas other objects, such as Hoover's 'Model O' electric suction sweeper which boasted an Art Nouveau pattern on its metal housing, were given a more sophisticated appearance, destined as they were to be seen throughout the house. Toasters intended for the breakfast table frequently had decoration applied to their surfaces. Thus were technological inventions transformed into meaningful objects of desire, their technical and utilitarian features having been joined by others which stressed their role as aesthetic and symbolic artefacts with a sociocultural function.[22]

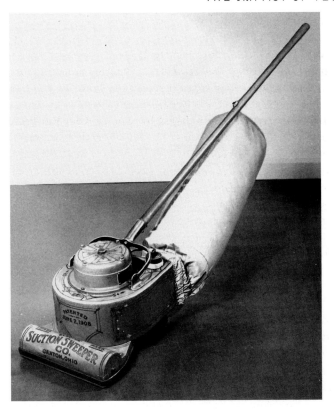

Figure 2.3   The Hoover company added Art Nouveau patterning to
the surface of the body of its Model 'O' suction sweeper of 1908 to
appeal to the housewife.

By the First World War the material landscapes in both the public and the
private spheres had been transformed by a wide range of new goods which were
the results of the technological inventiveness and manufacturing capability of the
era. Their presence engendered a strong belief in the power of science and
reason to transform the world for the better, a key ideological feature of early
twentieth-century modernity. This belief existed alongside the irrationality of
conspicuous consumption. Increasingly advertisers and marketing men had to
engage with rational arguments in order to be able to sell many of their goods –
especially those destined for the kitchen, but the appeal of what were seen as
accessible luxuries continued to play a strong role within the psychology of
consumption. Defined as a process within manufacturing, and as the seductive
tool of the advertiser whose task was to appeal to the eye and the heart as well
as to the head, design flourished in this new modern ambience.

Figure 2.4   By combining a description of its electric suction sweeper's functionality with an image of its fashionably dressed female user, the Hoover Company united rationality with luxury in this advertisement, which appeared in *Good Housekeeping* magazine in November 1918.

The materials of modernity

Base metals were transformed into marvels of Beauty, expressive of our own age.[23]

Throughout the twentieth century the discovery of new materials and innovations in production technologies constantly challenged designers to find forms and meanings for them. Ever keen to augment their profits, manufacturers increasingly sought less expensive ways of creating their goods and, wherever possible, substituted traditional materials which had been used for craft manufacture with new, cheaper ones suitable for mass production. This technological and economic drive forward was necessarily mediated by consumer acceptance, but aggressive sales techniques employing advertising and design were harnessed as a means of creating 'desire' and enhancing the modern appeal of the materials in question. Design acted as an important bridge between technology and culture, anticipating consumer demand and making new technologies and materials both available and desirable to the mass market.

The nineteenth and early twentieth centuries had seen iron and steel transform the environment, while plate glass had brought an unprecedented level of spectacle into the urban streets. In the hands of the lady interior decorators, chintz had moved from the country to become a *sine qua non* of the stylish interior, replacing the heavier velvets and brocades of the Victorian parlour. Abstract ideas about form, developed by fine artists conscious of the new visual nature of the environment they inhabited, had inspired change, and the democratisation of modernity had encouraged a new look for the materials of everyday life. Indeed it could be argued that new materials made everything feel and look different, thereby creating their own visual and tactile modernity.[24]

The desire to invent new materials played a significant part in the thrill of technological innovation. Indeed at no time was the urge to create new substances as strong as it was in the nineteenth century, and the materials of mid-twentieth-century modernity owed their existence to a number of key individuals who had been active in those years, as well as to a considerable amount of capital investment. Two key materials of inter-war modernity – plastics and aluminium – were discovered in the middle of the nineteenth century. Plastics were developed as a substitute for more expensive substances, such as amber, jet and jade, which were in short supply, but aluminium was a material that did not have an application at the time of its invention and was therefore dubbed 'a solution without a problem'. While the developments of these two materials were parallel in many ways, they also diverged significantly. By the 1930s, however, they had both come to be perceived by designers and consumers alike as modern materials *par excellence*, imbued equally with something which could not ultimately described but which was tacitly understood as representing modern life. The French cultural critic Roland Barthes came nearest to explaining why plastics had a charismatic presence for consumers of modern material culture when he wrote, some years later, that 'plastic ... is the stuff of alchemy'.[25]

Plastics and aluminium have both been considered by historians as important agents of cultural change. In his book *Pioneer Plastic: The Making and Selling of Celluloid*, Robert Friedel demonstrated the way in which this early, semi-synthetic material succeeded in establishing itself through its links with the early film industry, as well as through its application to products such as billiard balls and its ability to make novelty goods, such as hatpins and letter openers, available to a wide audience for the first time.[26]

Figure 2.5   The modern, streamlined appearance of the Fada baby radio of 1934 was made possible by the production process used to form this small cast phenolic artefact.

Plastics have received more attention than aluminium, partly because of their innumerable applications and partly because they are more immediately recognisable to the public at large, which has an understanding and appreciation, even if sometimes negative, of their impact. Throughout the history of their application plastics have been linked with certain products: celluloid, the first plastic, is known as the material of billiard balls and cinematic film, while Bakelite is the material of electrical fittings and 1930s radio cabinets. The most far-reaching account of plastic's history and its links with modernity has been provided by Jeffrey Meikle in his book, *American Plastic: A Cultural History*, which focused on the meaning of plastics to what the author described as 'a civilisation that seemed to be abandoning its ideals in pursuit of material goods'.[27] The acceptance of plastics, for Meikle, mirrored the growing materialism of modern society: they became a metaphor for it as well as a material manifestation of it. Bakelite, Meikle suggested, became synonymous with the modern streamlined style as the products it became linked with – radios for the most part – themselves became icons of modernity. Modern technology was made into a consumable form in the capable hands of far-sighted designers such as Peter Muller-Munk and Paul T. Frankl. Muller-Munk is quoted as saying that 'plastics became almost the hallmark of "modern design" ... the mysterious and attractive solution for almost any application requiring "eye appeal"', thereby anticipating Barthes' observations by some years.[28] Designers, Meikle suggested, were responsible for imbuing plastics with their identity. Referring to the aesthetic ideas of Walter Benjamin, he claimed, 'If there was in truth no uniform "Bakelite style" the stuff certainly projected a distinctive aura.'[29]

Plastics were the ideal materials for mass production, and their progress through the twentieth century was intrinsically linked to the idea of the democratised product to the extent that, after 1945, they lost their 'aura' by being held responsible for the appearance of cheap, 'tacky' objects fabricated in places such as Hong Kong. They had to be rescued and returned to the safe arena of high culture by a number of leading Italian designers in the 1950s and 60s. In the inter-war years, however, as the material which housed radios, television sets and domestic appliances, plastics were not competing with more traditional materials and did not, therefore, constitute a threat to consumers. Even plastic jewellery found a place alongside more precious objects, and mundane household artefacts, such as hairbrushes, powder containers and ashtrays, acquired a level of acceptance through their symbolic links with modernity. Objects such as these served to reinforce middle-class women's new-found freedom in being able to indulge in the luxury of self-beautification in the comfort of their own homes.

In their 'decorative' applications plastic objects for the most part emulated the forms of existing items, although the bright colours that could be achieved meant that the material inevitably brought its own 'look' to these cheap artefacts. Where new products, such as radios, were concerned, however, there was plenty of room for innovation. A number of designers rose to the challenge, creating many exciting new forms which quickly became icons of modernity and which are now considered to be 'classic' objects of modern design.[30] The aesthetically radical plastic radio cabinets designed by Serge Chermayeff and Wells Coates in Britain, for example, have become collectible items. The striking body-shells created by these modernist architect–designers performed the dual function of concealing the complex workings of the machines they encapsulated and, simultaneously, providing a powerful new visual imagery redolent of modernity. Given the strong cultural significance of the radio as part of the expanding interest in mass communications, and their dramatic impact on the lives of modern British citizens in the 1930s, the symbolism of these objects was far-reaching, and ensured plastics a high level of popular acceptance.

The example of the radio demonstrates the way in which – with the exception of precious materials such as gold, which has an intrinsic monetary value attached to it, and others such as worn stone, which carry memories within them – materials are impotent *per se* to convey meanings without the helping hand of the designer, who can imbue them with significant form and imagery.

Other 'classic' designs of the inter-war years included Raymond Loewy's famous reworking of the Gestetner duplicating machine of 1934, the scale of which, given the technical limitations of casting plastic objects in moulds at that time, was exceptional. Inevitably production technologies limited what designers could do: although casting, machining, laminating and rolling were all processes that could be applied to plastics, moulding was by far the most frequently used. In the 1930s the curves associated with the popular aesthetic known as 'streamlining' became widespread partly as a result of the fact that in the manufacture of plastic products sharp corners were hard to extract from moulds. In addition, crowned surfaces were used to compensate for the illusion that the surface of a plastic product was sinking inwards. It was the designer's role to provide a viable visual formulation for artefacts made from these materials, based on their knowledge of their physical properties. In addition to what have become iconic plastic products of the era, countless new objects emerged from the factories of plastics manufacturers in the USA and Europe in these years – from sewing machines and vacuum cleaners to items of office equipment – all of them owing their modern identities to developments in plastics technology and the designers who worked on them.

In its early applications aluminium was much less obviously a modern material for the public at large, in spite of the efforts made by many manufacturers to persuade consumers that it had the potential to be one. By the end of the 1930s, however, it had acquired a modern image through its application in aeroplane bodies, airships, tableware items, car bodies and avant-garde furniture.[31] Unlike plastics, however, even with the assistance of marketing and design, aluminium had to work hard to acquire an aura of modernity due to the fact that, in the form of cooking utensils, it stained in use and was thought to engender illness as a result. In an effort to refute the belief that it was a malevolent material a number of manufacturers, including the Aluminum Reduction Company of Pittsburgh, invested large sums of money to promote the material to housewives. In an effort to sell their products they organised department store demonstrations and advised on shop window displays.[32]

The most effective use of aluminium in these years was in early transport, especially aircraft, where its light weight was a huge advantage. Through its utilisation in objects associated with the modern age, the material gradually began to acquire a contemporary aura. In the inter-war years designers such as Marcel Breuer, and later the Dutchman Gerrit Rietveld, experimented with it in their furniture designs, using it to replace steel which was significantly heavier. Through its adoption by the American designer Russel Wright, it also entered the world of domesticity at this time. Aimed at the housewife, with her new image as a hostess Wright's stylish spun aluminium tableware became highly desirable, welcomed into the home and on to the dining table.

Figure 2.6 Russel Wright's design for this 'bun warmer', manufactured from spun aluminium in the early 1930s, reflected modernity through its form, its materiality and its role in modern living.

Following Wright's lead, and with the assistance of the designer Lurelle Guild, the American company Alcoa also moved into the production of household and small decorative items.

Ultimately, however, it was as a material for the new objects of transportation that aluminium gained its most potent modern identity. For example, it appeared as the shiny fuselages of aircraft, which could defy gravity. In turn aeroplanes became sources of inspiration for numerous other forms and objects created by designers who embraced the modern ethos. Other modern aluminium forms followed. For example, the classic aluminium chair the 'Landi', created by the Swiss designer Hans Coray for the Swiss National Exhibition held in Zurich in 1938, acquired a high level of iconic significance, not just because of its physical lightness but also, more significantly, as a result of its strong aesthetic relating to the idea of lightness, created by Coray's use of round holes punched repeatedly into the metal. In the bodies of BMW's racing cars from the 1940s, the symbolism and function of aluminium were combined and its light weight also gave the cars an advantage on the race-track. By 1945, through the intervention of design, the light, shiny metal had become one of the most symbolically potent of all the materials of modernity.

New materials played a crucial role in many of the modern designed forms that emerged from the USA in the 1930s, and the imagery designers created for them was often strikingly innovative. As Donald Dohner, the designer employed by the Westinghouse company, explained, 'Imitating other materials may be an interesting technical stunt for some engineers but it robs the new material of its birthright, destroys its identity and natural beauty, thereby degrading it.'[33] This strong commitment to the idea that new materials carried their own modern identity within them was echoed widely by many other designers who chose to work with them. Donald Deskey's interior work in Radio City Music Hall in New York has, for example, frequently been cited as an example of modern materials at their best. In his book, *Depression Modern: The Thirties Style in America,* the writer Martin Grief provided a long list of synthetic substances used in this era, which included Pyralin, Fiberloid, Nixonoid, Tenite, Ameroid, Durite Textolite, Makalot, Micarta and Insurok.[34] Increasingly consumers sought new materials in their everyday goods as a mark of their love affair with modernity.

The 1933 Century of Progress Exhibition, held in Chicago, at which an all-aluminium Pullman coach was on display, was a shrine to new materials. The central theme was described as 'the dramatization of the achievements of mankind, made possible through the application of science to industry', emphasising its exclusively modern focus.[35] The temporary buildings were made of plywood, light steel, asbestos and gypsum board, and the section of the exhibition entitled 'Homes and Industrial Arts' consisted of eight model houses, each one fabricated in a different material, among them steel, Masonite and glass.

Chromed steel also took on a modern significance in the inter-war years. This application of a shiny, reflective surface on to a base material appealed to the visually conscious consumers of modernity. Within modernism the notion of 'artifice', seen as the marker of a progressive, democratic and benevolent technology, came to be valued above 'nature', and the idea that technology could create its own objects, which in turn became the material manifestations of its own power and authority in the modern world, became widespread. At the same time, however, there was a limit to how far people would go to let technology enter into their homes, and chromed steel tube furniture only penetrated the most avant-garde of interiors, especially in Europe.

The new materials were driven by large-scale American corporations and were given forms by American designers who were happy to use their visual imaginations to this end. Progressive European architect–designers were also

Figure 2.7   Walter Dorwin Teague's gas range, designed for
the Floyd Wells Company in 1935, epitomises the 'magic'
appearance of an all-steel object made with a minimum
number of seams.

experimenting with the application of new materials, especially in the area of
furniture design. Through the efforts of Marcel Breuer and Mies van der
Rohe, Germany's achievements in tubular steel have been widely documented, as have those of the French architect Le Corbusier.[36] Steel tube, a
discovery of the nineteenth century and used, because of its combination of
low weight and strength, for the frames of bicycles, suggested itself as a structural material for furniture design. In the hands of Breuer, Mies, Le
Corbusier, and the Dutchman Mart Stam, among others, it facilitated a fundamental shift from the solid upholstered chair to a new skeletal structure that
exploited the aesthetic possibilities of space rather than mass.

In Finland the architect Alvar Aalto produced furniture designs made from
sheets of bent, laminated plywood which could be made to perform a similar
role to tubular steel in furniture design. Although not in itself a new material,
through the utilisation of new bending and bonding processes wood could be
made to work in new ways. Unlike their American equivalents these

experiments in new materials were led by designers and were less dependent, in the first instance, upon industrial manufacture. Quite quickly, however, the industrial significance of creating furniture with these materials was realised and large-scale production was undertaken. Examples included the mass-produced, tubular-steel chairs of the British company Pel. Aalto's furniture, manufactured by the Korhonen family firm in Finland, was imported into Britain in significant quantities in the 1930s by Finmar.[37]

New materials were not technology's only contribution to the forms and images of modern design, however. Production engineers also played a key role in making new forms possible. In steel manufacturing, for example, the challenge was to create ever larger pieces of steel which could form product casings with a minimum amount of seams. The modern look was one which had left nature far behind and which suggested that these new artefacts had fallen out of the sky. A seamless casing gave the impression of a kind of magic object, the product of science and technology seemingly untouched by human hand. Much effort went into the creation of an all-steel car body in this period. Early cars had been assemblages of components and materials put together with little regard for the visual effects of the end result. This gradually changed as steel bodies were developed and the aesthetic of streamlining began to unify the car's form. The all-steel, mass-manufactured automobile body eventually emerged in the USA in the 1910s, while the French company Citroën was the first to achieve the same result in Europe a little later. Efforts were also made to make the refrigerator appear as if it had been made from a single piece of steel, and developments took place in its manufacture to facilitate this. By the middle of the 1930s the body of the refrigerator (with the exception of the door) was made from a single piece of steel. The inability at that time to bend steel with small radii, however, meant that fridges were characterised by dramatic swollen forms which gave them pride of place in the kitchen and enhanced their role as primary status symbols, taking over from furniture which had performed that role since the mid-nineteenth century.

The inter-war years saw a huge expansion in the new industries that focused on new goods such as automobiles and domestic appliances. While the producers struggled to use new materials to ease their costs and benefit from the properties that they offered, designers were given the responsibility for making the necessary symbolic connections with consumers. The manufacturers of more traditional goods, such as ceramics and glass, also sought to modernise their production techniques in these years, even if the end products frequently maintained a traditional appearance. The home also underwent a number of technological transformations which helped nudge it into the modern arena. Innovations in this sphere included the use of linoleum in the bathroom, laminated plastics on kitchen surfaces, the introduction of

Figure 2.8   A 1948 advertisement for 'Balcora' velvets and rayons, emphasising the level of glamour and social status that could be achieved by wearing these fabrics.

mass-produced furniture into the living room, the addition of moulded glass and ceramic ornaments on the mantelpiece, aluminium pots and pans in the kitchen, and plastic-handled knives and forks on the dining table. They all

represented an entry into modernity through consumption, and an acknowl-
edgement of the impact of technology and design in everyday life. This was
especially apparent in the kitchen and the bathroom where new technologies
had an immediate impact.[38] The world of fashion was also dramatically transformed by the advent of rayon, the new 'artificial silk', and a little later by
that of nylon.[39]

The cultural impact of new materials, aided and abetted by design, was a
highly significant contribution to the modernisation of the lives of large
numbers of people in the inter-war years. Both the materiality of the new way
of life and the way in which these new 'seamless' products were catapulted
into everyday life, apparently untouched by human hand, provided consumers
with a new set of experiences which were determined by culture rather than
by nature, and which took humanity one step further away from the world it
had inhabited before industrialisation had changed things for ever.

Chapter 3

THE DESIGNER FOR INDUSTRY

Art and industry

The emergence of a new breed of visually trained, or at least visually aware, individuals who could provide the aesthetic options on the basis of which consumers could make their taste decisions was part of a developing picture in the years leading up to 1914. With the growth of the large-scale consumption of goods which brought the possibility of 'conspicuousness' to an expanded sector of society – and with the mass production industries having reorganised their operations such that their goods, images and services could meet the taste requirements of the mass marketplace – the need to clarify the nature of the design process and the work of the individuals involved in it became increasingly imperative.

Up until 1914, however, no single model for 'designing' presented itself, and the activity continued to evolve in an ad hoc pragmatic manner, dependent on the way things had happened in the decorative art industries in the past, the requirements of industrial production, and the vagaries of the marketplace. In short it remained the task of a wide range of diverse individuals – established fine artists, teams of lowly and anonymous art workers, architects, engineers, artisans, decorative artists, and a new breed of visualisers referred to as 'commercial artists' – to contribute in different ways to the creation of the visual face of the emerging modern material world. In addition, different areas of production – including traditional decorative arts, new consumer products, fashion items, two-dimensional designs of various kinds, and interior spaces and environments within the private and the public spheres – embraced design in different ways, developing models of practice which suited both their industries and their markets. In general terms, however, art and industry increasingly developed a strategic alliance with each other with the aim of creating products, images and spaces which would appeal to the expanded body of consumers, and which contained the complex sociocultural messages that were required of them.

Fine artists had been widely employed by the decorative arts industries, which had targeted elite markets. In the creation of the first mass-produced goods aimed at a larger scale audience, however, the 'art' content was frequently borrowed from elsewhere and transformed by the mechanical processes involved in industrial manufacturing. A number of design historical studies have focused on the changing nature of the design process in the shift from craft to industrial production, and on the new tasks developed for individuals engaged in the creation of the aesthetic component of goods such as textiles and ceramics. In particular they have studied the way in which the division of labour transformed traditional practices in these areas. In brief, from the eighteenth century up until the twentieth century different means of providing goods with their 'design' content co-existed in different industries. In the nineteenth-century British calico-printing industry, for example, as Hazel Clark explained, while freelance painters sometimes supplied prints to manufacturers, a range of in-house art-workers were responsible for them appearing on the calico.[1] In Manchester the local design school frequently supplied workers to local firms to undertake this task. In the early mass-production ceramics industry, as Adrian Forty demonstrated, another group of art workers emerged to make the manufacture of decorative wares for the mass market possible.[2] At the other end of the market for ceramic goods, Doulton for example continued to create its artefacts in its Lambeth Studio in a more traditional manner, employing fine artists to both model and decorate its wares. At the other end of its manufacturing spectrum, the same firm mass-produced stoneware drainpipes, the forms of which were also 'designed' but were not subject to the same treatment by fine artists. Without this more mundane area of production, however, the creation of the fine art ware would not have been financially viable.[3] Doulton highlighted the co-existence of two models of design practice which have remained in place until the present – that of the 'in-house', frequently anonymous art worker/designer, and of the external, consultant fine artist/designer, whose name was frequently used in the marketing of goods. Those designers who worked in a freelance capacity operated across a number of different industries while the staff designers were able to develop the levels of technical expertise required of them in the changing technological climate.

In the production of new goods dependent upon new technologies both for their existence and for their means of manufacture – such as items of transportation and new household machines – designing as an artistic practice was less in evidence in this period, and it was left to the engineer to play a key role in determining the appearance of these goods. In the case of early automobile design, for example, engineers were responsible for the creation of the chassis and of all the product's working parts. These were subsequently combined with the body, which was created by hand by traditional carriage-builders who simply transferred their skills to the new context. The extension into the new engineering industries of craft practices such as that of the carriage-builder affected not only the appearance but also the symbolic meanings of the products in question, and it is for this reason that early cars were frequently referred to as 'horseless carriages'. It was to be a little while before the car was considered an object of taste fulfilment. Later, in the 1920s, when differentiation between mass-production models became important to consumers, 'artistic' design entered the world of automotive manufacture, although it was referred to as 'styling' to differentiate it from the work of the engineering 'designer'.

Other mass-produced engineered goods also revealed the hand of the artisan, metalworkers in particular, their crude forms openly reflecting the manufacturing process. The application of the Art Nouveau scrollwork, painted in purple on a pink background, to the surface of Hoover's first electric suction sweeper, for example, was an attempt to transform this highly utilitarian artefact into an 'art' object for the female servant/housewife who used it. The addition of 'beauty' was crucial to any machine that was to play a role in domestic display and the consumption of which was more than likely the responsibility of the housewife. An American electric iron produced in 1912 was even named the 'American Beauty' in an attempt to bridge the gap between art and industry in the eyes of its potential consumer.[4] Aluminium pots and pans, however, remained primarily utilitarian artefacts in the early twentieth century, their appearance reflecting their process of manufacture and their functional requirements alone. The anonymity of their design origination and the lack of visual self-consciousness provided an important source of inspiration for the modernist architects and designers who, a little later, sought an aesthetic that was embedded in utility rather than in conspicuous display. Ironically the self-consciousness involved in the selection of utilitarian forms such as these inevitably transformed their designs into 'art' objects.

Gradually architects and decorative artists of repute began to add goods produced by the new manufacturing industries to their lists of achievements. The contribution of the English Arts and Crafts metal-worker W.A.S. Benson to lighting design is a case in point. His objects ranged from oil lamps designed in a simplified style, through bronze and copper candelabras, to electric light fittings. Benson had wanted to be an engineer, but turned to architecture instead. His work bridged the gap between the rarefied world of the artisan–maker and that of the metal-worker creating low-priced artefacts for the domestic sphere. As his obituary pointed out, 'he preferred to approach his subject as an engineer rather than as a hand-worker; to produce his beautiful forms by machinery on a commercial scale rather than single works of art'.[5] A number of other late nineteenth-century British decorative artists, many of them from architectural backgrounds, were also attracted by the more functional end of manufacture. Christopher Dresser, for example, who had trained as a botanist, worked across a spectrum of artefacts which embraced elite hand-made products at one end and, at the other, collaborations with metal manufacturers resulting in the creation of functional, mass-produced artefacts for the home.[6]

Although the second half of the nineteenth century saw the emergence of a new breed of artistically inclined individuals who wanted to engage with the creation of industrially manufactured goods, architects continued to rule the day. Not only did they create buildings and their interiors; they also began to venture into other arenas, among them the applied arts and industrial manufacture, believing them to be a natural extension of their territory. Right up until the late 1920s architects dominated the world of product design, seeing the creation of the forms and decoration of the banal goods that made up the everyday environment as part of their work in the built environment. Sometimes, in the cases of William Morris in England, Charles Rennie Mackintosh in Scotland, Henry van de Velde in Belgium, Frank Lloyd Wright in the USA and Eliel Saarinen in Finland, the extension of the architect's role into the decorative arts and design resulted from their desire to establish homes for themselves and their families and their inability to find adequate goods and furnishings for their own personal domestic environments. To remedy this they set about designing everything they needed themselves – from textiles to knives and forks – and finding ways of getting them made. This holistic attitude to designing, which derived from a belief in the idea of the *Gesamtkunstwerk* (the total work of art), dominated progressive design from the 1860s up to the 1930s, characterising the approach of architects to this new discipline. For example, the vast majority of designers discussed by Nikolaus Pevsner in his groundbreaking study *The Pioneers of Modern Design*, first written in 1936, were architects first and foremost. So powerful was this as a model for design practice that the philosophical and aesthetic ideals underpinning modern architecture were applied directly to furniture and other products created for use in interior spaces. Little thought was given, however, to the appropriateness or otherwise of this direct transference and, arguably, this 'colonisation' of design by architects had the effect of stifling the possibility of a theory of modern design for industry emerging on its own terms. The only other rationales available for creating goods and images in these years were those of commercial pragmatism or technological rationalism.

The German architect/designer Peter Behrens went further than most of his contemporaries in applying his creative skills to the products of the new industries. From a background in Art Nouveau poster design and the decorative arts

Figure 3.1 Three versions of an electric kettle designed by the early consultant designer Peter Behrens for the German AEG Company in 1909. They were one element of the corporate image Behrens created for AEG.

he went on to create an entire visual identity for the German AEG company, which was applied to its factories, its canteen cutlery and its publicity material, in addition to all its electrical products. Like William Morris and Henry van de Velde before him, Behrens had created his own family home and all its contents, and he adopted the same holistic approach to the design of the electrical company's corporate identity. The electrical products he worked on – fans and kettles in particular – combined a traditional decorative arts approach with more utilitarian ideas emanating from an engineering approach to design. The gendered ideology of the separate spheres determined the degree of decoration applied to these products. While the kettles, destined for domestic environments, boasted textured surfaces, the fans, intended for offices and factories, had a more overtly 'engineered' appearance.[7]

The requirements of mass consumption and mass production also generated new tasks and new workers in the world of two-dimensional design. By the turn of the century the development of the American advertising profession was fairly advanced, and agencies such as that of J. Walter Thompson were acting as intermediaries between manufacturers and artists. Often the latter were simply required to draw decorative borders around press advertisements. Craft skills continued to play a key role in this arena as wood engraving and lithography were the main means by which advertisements were created. The 'graphic designer', defined as 'someone who would receive instructions from a client, devise drawings and plans and then instruct technicians, typesetters and printers to realise the designs' emerged later than the 'commercial artist' who dominated the picture in the early years of the century.[8] Just as in factory production, this new industry saw the emergence of a new body of visually literate professionals whose task was to create a much-needed bridge between art and manufacturing.

Figure 3.2 The December 1902 cover of *Profitable Advertising*, one of the early graphic design periodicals to emerge in the USA which helped define the 'graphic designer' as a new professional.

Packaging design also expanded in these years, exploiting the skills of visually trained individuals. In the late nineteenth century in the USA packaging, branding and advertising began to be used together to turn unfamiliar commodities into popular products. The process of creating product packaging was a complex one involving visual artists, copywriters and packaging manufacturers. The identities created for goods were strongly dependent on a visual image or identity. but the decision to opt for a particular image was in this early period often arrived at in an ad hoc manner. The red and white on the now famous Campbell Soup can was, for example, suggested by someone who had just attended a football game where the Cornell University team had worn those colours.[10]

Making an impact with assemblages of packaged goods was the responsibility of the store designer or shop window display artist, who could be the retail proprietor or, in the case of department stores, visually trained individuals who applied their skills to this new, specialist area of 'design'. In his study of early shop display, William Leach provided a fascinating account of the professionalisation of this area of work.[11] Through the case study of L. Frank Baum he described how, alongside the level of spectacle created by coloured advertisements, electric sign advertising and mail order catalogues, the shop window became a key aspect of urban visual culture and modern display. Specialist magazines aimed at the store window artist appeared at this time, magazines were launched and national associations were formed (Baum formed the National Association of Window Trimmers in 1989) to help professionalise the activities of the skilled artists who worked in this expanding field.

The fashion couturier was another kind of designer to emerge in the years before 1914 and operate in an overtly commercial context. Although he was catering for an elite consumer, and his dresses were one-offs rather than serial productions, the Englishman Charles Worth initiated the idea of using live models on a catwalk, and was among the first to use his name as a 'brand' with which to sell his products. As a system that depended upon continual stylistic change, fashion provided a model for emulation by a number of industries which increasingly needed to inject a level of 'added value' into their products and images in order to make them appeal to the expanding market. Indeed, the application of art to many areas of commerce that would hitherto not have seen the necessity to involve it was a mark of manufacturers' growing awareness of the importance of 'eye appeal' in their goods. This was commensurate with the growing importance of the role of 'taste' in consumption choices, a concept which was becoming increasingly catered for by the presence of 'art' in mass-produced goods and images.

Many of the 'designers' who made an impact in these years were men. A few women were trained in the subject, but the application of their aesthetic

Figure 3.3 An evening dress of around 1896 created by the couturier Worth, who was amongst the first to use his name as a brand and sell his clothes by showing them on a catwalk.

skills was restricted, for the most part, to embroidery and to other delicate crafts such as jewellery-making and enamel work. In line with their special relationship with domesticity, women were considered as 'naturals' for the activity of interior decoration. Although a few women set themselves up as house decorators in Britain as early as the 1870s it was in the USA, in the first decade of the twentieth century, that they began to thrive in this field.[12] They emerged at a moment when increasing numbers of nouveau-riche clients, who didn't trust their own taste, sought to have their interiors decorated by a professional. Only a couple of decades earlier they would have used the services of architects who worked on the interiors of their own buildings, or those of an upmarket decorating and furnishing firm, such as the Herter

Brothers.[13] In 1897 Candace Wheeler advocated interior decoration as an appropriate profession for women as well as making a living from it herself.[14] Women's work on their own private spaces was, of course, unpaid. As a result the issue of professionalisation did not have the same urgency as it did for men. In addition it had become a truism that women's work was aesthetic in nature, and it was their duty to create the 'house beautiful'. In the early twentieth century the American actress Elsie de Wolfe became first an amateur and subsequently a professional, although untrained, interior deco-rator, and by 1914 a number of other women had joined her in the same activity.[15] In contrast to the European male architects who were also venturing into furniture and interior design and seeking, in the process, a new aesthetic that they felt to be appropriate to the modern, rational age in which they found themselves, the female decorators took a more traditional approach, advocating a return to historical style, albeit realised with a new modern sensibility. The clients of the professional interior decorators remained the wealthy; at all other levels of society interior decoration remained the responsibility of the 'amateur' housewife.[16]

If design was to be the harmonising force between a society which wanted to express itself through taste and a technology which aspired to ultimate rationality and efficiency, it needed to educate creative individuals who could understand both sides of the equation. In the years leading up to 1914 the level of provision of design education expanded significantly in a number of countries. For example, in Britain in the first half of the nineteenth century there had been much discussion at government level about 'taste' and the importance of the addition of 'art' to industrial production to improve the quality of British goods in the marketplace. The Victoria and Albert Museum, with its accompanying design educational institute, the Normal School, had been established to set about meeting this deficit. The latter was the first of a vast number of design schools which were set up around the country in key manufacturing areas, the graduates of which were employed by local indus-tries to inject a level of art into their otherwise banal products. In this context the word 'design' was used in the French sense – 'dessin', meaning 'drawing' – as students were encouraged to copy from models and to develop drafting skills which could be applied either to architectural or to product decoration. Other countries expanded their design education systems in the late nine-teenth century along the lines of the British model. In the USA, for example, the Cincinnati school was amongst the first to be created in that country, while in Germany the traditional Academies of Art were transformed in the early twentieth century by Herman Muthesius, the Superintendant of the Prus-sian Board of Trade for Schools of Arts and Crafts who, amongst his other stra-tegic decisions, appointed Peter Behrens to a position in Dusseldorf.[17]

Figure 3.4   The pioneer American interior decorator Elsie de Wolfe, photographed in the 1920s. De Wolfe was amongst the first aesthetic practitioners in the modern era to understand the close relationship between taste and social status.

Unlike architecture, which saw itself as being far removed from the marketplace and operating according to a set of elevated principles, product, fashion and advertising designers saw themselves as being increasingly defined by the market and its demands. The expanded taste requirements of the expanding market and the need for increased product differentiation, had, in essence, brought them into existence. Their task was to determine what was fashionable, to both reflect and form public taste, and to keep the public informed about the many products and services available to them.

By 1914 designing remained a very diverse and ill-defined activity. Indeed, it was not a single activity but consisted of a number of practices with different philosophies and professional/trade frameworks encompassing the work of humble factory workers, engineers, decorative artists, architects, couturiers and commercial artists. Only retrospectively can a single thread be seen to run across these varied practices, the practitioners of which, at the time, were unaware of each other's existence. There were signs, however, of an emerging conflict between those who saw themselves as operating within the commercial system and those (mostly architects) who had a more idealistic view of their involvement with the creation of material culture. The latter aimed to ignore the fads of the marketplace and sought more universal solutions. Both groups of practitioners, however, saw their roles as participating in the aesthetic elaboration of everyday goods and images. By the inter-war years the two approaches to the discipline were openly vying with each other, one sheltering under the banner of progressive architecture and the other openly embracing the commercial face of material culture.

The consultant designer

> The modern industrial designer has both a technical and a cultural background and a sense of the public into the bargain, and it is these three things which qualify him to perform his job of creating sales.[18]

In the years before 1914 the activity of 'designing' – even if it had not been named as such – had been firmly established in a range of manufacturing industries and commercial contexts as a fundamental aspect of the creation of goods, environments and images, as well as of more abstract activities, such as marketing and the creation of corporate identities. As an individual with a distinct job description, however, a broadly understood concept of the 'designer' had not existed. The responsibility for providing forms and meanings for the material and visual environment had been in the hands of fine artists, architects, engineers, inventors, artisans, interior decorators, couturiers, printers, a wide range of technicians, and many other kinds of art workers and creative thinkers – both trained and untrained. Their tasks had been many and varied and had differed according to the industry, the commercial context and the medium in question. Uniquely, however, they had shared the need to position themselves in the gap between producing and consuming, and had moved with ease between these two worlds which, in every other respect, were becoming increasingly separated from each other.

In the years between the two world wars the concept of the consultant designer for industry came of age, partly as a solution to economic challenges and partly as a means of bringing together the expanding numbers of tasks that were needed to link production and consumption in a way which was appropriate to the business needs of industry and the commercial sector and the consuming needs of the general public. The role required both a high level of specialist skills (in the area of visualising and conceptualising) but also a broad approach to enable the new professionals to be able to look across a wide range of industries and design fields.

The first consultant industrial designers to be named as such (with the exception of Peter Behrens in Germany in the early century) emerged at the end of the 1920s in the USA at a time when consumer practices were being dramatically transformed. The financial crisis that had led Henry Ford to close his River Rouge factory for a year in 1926, in the face of competition from the General Motors Company, marked an important moment in the emergence of the designer for industry. In response to changing consumer demands, General Motors rejected product standardisation in favour of a more flexible manufacturing system and, in 1926, as part of his strategic efforts to match consumer trends, Alfred P. Sloan, the Vice President of General Motors, hired the coach-builder Harley Earl to make his automobiles look more appealing.[19] The formation of the Styling Section at General Motors represented the first attempt, on the part of a serial manufacturer in this area, to introduce an aesthetic element into the mass-produced automobile. Although this had long been normal practice in the more overtly 'artistic' industries – fashion and the decorative arts among them – it was unprecedented in automobile production where the engineer had reigned supreme. As Sloan explained, Earl's contribution to the success of the Cadillac La Salle, his first project at General Motors, was very important to the company: 'The car made a sensational debut in March 1927, and proved itself a milestone in American automotive history by being the first stylist's car to achieve success in mass production'.[20]

The experience of the automobile industry was rapidly emulated by other manufacturers of new technological goods – refrigerators and other domestic appliances, office machines, telephones and radio sets. Affected adversely by the economic depression, they all decided to inject a level of artistic 'styling' into their products as a means of beating off their competitors. The phenomenon of American industrial design as it emerged in the late 1920s and 1930s has been documented extensively in a number of writings. Jeffrey Meikle's 1979 study, *Twentieth Century Limited: Industrial Design in America, 1925–1939,* sought to understand the impact of the emerging industrial design profession in the USA.[21] His analysis focused on the fact that 'technological innovation and mass production brought former luxury items to people at lower income levels' and on the intentions of industrial designers to provide a level of modern luxury in new goods, as well as aestheticising the commercial context – advertisements and retail outlets – which helped sell them.[22] Modern design, Meikle explained, represented accessible luxury for large numbers of new consumers. It was no coincidence that several of the leading industrial designers of the day had started their careers in graphic advertising and moved on to work with the department stores which, in emulation of French models, had embraced modern style as part of their commercial strategy. Raymond Loewy, for example, had worked for Saks of Fifth Avenue for a period of time, while Norman Bel Geddes had

Figure 3.5   A shop window display for the Franklyn Simon department store in New York created by Norman Bel Geddes in 1927. Bel Geddes went from designing theatre sets and shop windows to manufactured products.

created modernistic window displays for the Franklyn Simon store in New York. The move to refrigerators reflected a requirement to embed 'desire' in the industrial product itself.[23]

In his book *All Consuming Images: The Politics of Style in Contemporary Culture*, Stewart Ewen also approached the emergence of American industrial design from a cultural perspective.[24] He claimed that industrialisation had 'displaced the customary fabric of culture' and that the marriage between art and commerce, which had commenced with Walter Rathenau's employment of Peter Behrens at the German AEG company, was one of the means of offsetting that displacement by mending the schism between production and consumption. He described the work of one of the advertising pioneers of the early twentieth century, Earnest Elmo Calkins, as being focused on the effort 'to construct an unbroken, imagistic corridor between the product being sold and the consciousness (and unconsciousness) of the consumer' reinforced the close link between consumer culture and the American consultant design profession of the inter-war years.[25]

The best known industrial designers of the day – Norman Bel Geddes, Raymond Loewy, Walter Dorwin Teague and Henry Dreyfuss among them – also contributed their own personal accounts of their careers in which they reinforced their perceptions of themselves as idealistic modernists, linking themselves to the modern European architectural tradition as a means of disguising the commercial context which was, in fact, their *raison d'être*. In his 1940 text *Design This Day: The Technique of Order in the Machine Age*, Teague referred repeatedly to Le Corbusier, Walter Gropius and Ludwig Mies van der Rohe, suggesting perhaps that his name should be added to the list.[26] In his autobiography *Horizons*, published in 1932, Norman Bel Geddes also referred to European modernism, in this case the abstract work of the artists Pablo Picasso and Paul Cézanne, claiming them as his artistic predecessors.[27] Their need to justify their commercial work in this way suggests that they felt that they had to aspire to European artistic and architectural idealism in order to earn themselves a place in history and to distance themselves from the world of profit margins.

Although most accounts of the work of the American consultant designers of the 1930s have concentrated on the way in which they looked to the future in their advocacy of dramatic streamlined forms, most of their energies were, in fact, devoted to 'redesign' projects rather than to blue-sky thinking, and they worked for conservative markets as well as more adventurous ones. The modernist myth that has accompanied many accounts of their work has tended to play down their market-oriented pragmatism and present them as the celebrities they were treated as by the press of the day. *Time* and *Life* magazines both celebrated their work on several occasions, and reported on their daily lives as if they had been Hollywood stars. Undoubtedly this celebrity status was important to them as individuals but it was even more crucial for the manufacturers who employed them, as it granted their creations an instant aura of 'added value'. The designers became, in fact, branded entities, and their names were used as a form of product endorsement. The product, in this context, became its own advertisement, and the names of the 'celebrity' designers – represented as participants in modernity, pursuing modern lifestyles that were the envy of all – were used to reinforce the 'added value' of products.

The consultant designers were intrinsic components of the American commercial system that had engendered them, and an extension of the face of the commercial context in which goods were bought and sold. In an attempt to demonstrate that designers were themselves products of their environment, and should not be given too much credit for design change, the historian Adrian Forty undertook an analysis of Raymond Loewy's redesign of the Lucky Strike cigarette pack, in which he claimed that the designer's decision to change the colour of the pack from green to white was not an individual creative act but rather a reflection of the era's obsession with hygiene and cleanliness.[28] While this argument granted the cultural context rather more agency than was actually the case, it was, nonetheless, a useful exercise in offsetting the huge achievements these men claimed for themselves, and in understanding their role within the larger picture of things.

Two significant things can be learned from the American consultant design 'heroes' of the 1930s. Firstly, they demonstrated the way in which the commercial design process and profession was dependent on background skills that had been developed in the contexts of commerce and spectacle. The process of the aestheticisation of the marketplace, one of the defining characteristics of modernity, had begun before the emergence of the industrial designer. The countless 'artists' who had created shop window displays, exhibition stands and press and other kinds of advertising material, were the precursors of the modern industrial designer. Indeed, the most prominent individuals – Bel Geddes, Loewy, Teague and Dreyfuss – came to consultant design from backgrounds in advertising and store window display. Bel Geddes had had a first career in stage design, an appropriate training in dramatic effects which led logically on to his work for shop windows and in product design. Teague had created decorative borders for advertisements for the Calkins and Holden agency in the early years of the century. While the designers had claimed 'purist' European backgrounds for themselves, their actual experiences and backgrounds suggested that it was another tradition, that of commercial pragmatism and the irrational world of consumer desire, that provided them with the skills needed for their chosen careers.

Secondly, the American consultant designers represented the moment at which 'designer-culture' – the attribution of value, both cultural and economic, to an object, image or environment because it had a well-known designer's name attached to it, in emulation of the importance of attribution to the value of a work of art – came into being. Such was the power of the 'signature-designers' that the application of their names to the design of a railroad train or a biscuit immediately imbued those artefacts with a level of 'added value'. A number of sociocultural explanations have been provided for this phenomenon, but the most persuasive argument suggests that it represented the need for consumers to develop a level of identification, through consumption, with a commodity associated with an individual known to possess a high level of taste and, by implication, social standing. It also recalled the individualism of custom-made artefacts, which had guaranteed the upper classes their social status in the years before industrialisation and the rupture between production and consumption.

What the French social scientist Pierre Bourdieu has described as 'cultural capital' could be consumed, in the 1930s, through a material artefact, the visual appearance of which could be attributed to an industrial designer of note.[29] The cultural capital in question was enhanced by its links with 'the modern' seen, in the worlds of art and architecture, as being appreciated by only the most discerning. The association of a product with a designer's name also served to personalise anonymous products, thereby suggesting to consumers that their mass-produced, standardised object was directed at them personally. This was one means of restoring the individualism within mass production that Henry van de Velde had fought over with Muthesius back in 1914. As accessible standardised products became the norm, the need to preserve or re-inject a level of individualisation became paramount, both for consumers and for manufacturers. The consultant designers were acutely aware of the diversity of consumer tastes in the marketplace. Bel Geddes, for example, who acquired his knowledge of the market by undertaking extensive consumer questionnaires, proposed four different radio designs to the Philco Radio Company: the 'Highboy', the 'Lowboy', the 'Lazy-boy' and a radio–phonograph combination. Each was styled differently with a different market in mind, from the most conservative to the most progressive.[30]

The model of consultant design that emerged in the USA from the late 1920s onwards quickly established itself as a model for other countries to emulate as they also began to look for ways to integrate design with their emerging industries and to create enhanced levels of consumer desire. In the years after 1945 the dissemination of its design model constituted one of the USA's strategies of cultural imperialism. While the automotive industry preferred to keep its stylists in-house behind closed doors, maintaining their anonymity for the most part, the other new industries engaged in producing consumer machines, including domestic appliances and office machinery, benefited by bringing in generalist consultant designers who had an overview of the industry as a whole. Thus in Great Britain the Design Research Unit was formed in 1942 along American lines; in Sweden the industrial designer Sixten Sason offered his services to the Electrolux and Hasselblad companies among others; in Italy the graphic designer Marcello Nizzoli worked with the Olivetti company and the Necchi sewing machine manufacturer.[31] In their different ways these and many other designers and design groups extended the professional model of commercial consultant design that had been developed in the USA in the years between the wars.

The consultant designers focused most of their attention on the products of the new industries. At the same time the traditional decorative art industries also began to employ consultant designers in the inter-war years, many of them architects. By this time they tended to work either in a 'modern' style, influenced by the progressive work being undertaken in Germany in the 1920s under the name of the 'machine aesthetic', or in the 'moderne' style, influenced by many of the French decorative artists who had shown their work at the 1925 'Exhibition of Decorative Arts', held in Paris. The New Zealand architect Keith Murray, working in Great Britain, created some striking ceramic designs for Wedgwood and cut glass designs for Stevens and Williams, while Marcel Breuer, a graduate of the German Bauhaus school, came to Britain and collaborated with the furniture producer Isokon.[32] In Finland, Goran Hongell worked with the Karhula Glassworks, while in Sweden the graphic designer Wilhelm Kåge modernised the products of the ceramics company Gustavsberg. In Germany, Wilhelm Wagenfeld, a graduate of the Bauhaus metal workshop, worked with a number of glass and metal manufacturers, while Herman Gretsch collaborated with the Arzberg ceramic manufacturing company.

The professional graphic and fashion designers also crystallised their roles in these years. In Europe the modern graphic designer was rooted, like his product designer equivalent, in the British nineteenth-century reform movement. The poster movement of the same century had also been enormously influential. As Jeremy Aynsley explained in his book *A Century of Graphic*

Figure 3.6   The ceramicist Wilhelm Kåge, who worked for the Swedish company Gustavsberg and helped to develop the concept of 'Swedish Modern' design, which had a strong craft base. Kåge moved into ceramics in the early years of the twentieth century from a background in graphic design.

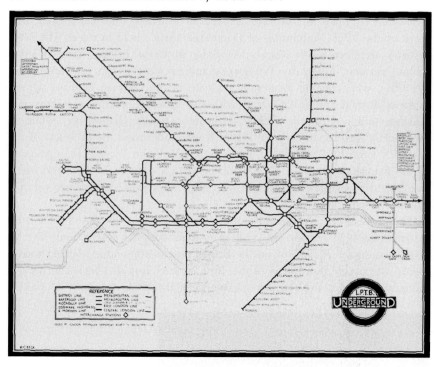

Figure 3.7   The graphic designer came of age in the inter-war years. Henry Beck's diagrammatic London Underground map of 1933, the first version of which is shown here, was one of the most striking graphic design successes of the era.

Design: Graphic Design Pioneers of the 20th Century, by 1914 'the book and poster arts were about to be subsumed into a greater whole: graphic design', a concept that was to emerge fully in the 1920s.[33] Fashion designers, or 'couturiers', had been in existence for many years, located in Paris for the most part and supplying a global wealthy clientele with custom-made hand-made clothing. With the advent of the sewing-machine and factory production, however, ready-to-wear clothing aimed at large markets made its impact in the first decades of the twentieth century, standing in opposition to its up-market equivalent, which was marketed on the basis of the name of the couturier in whose house it had been produced. Indeed, it was the branded individualism of the fashion designer that inspired general manufacturing industry to begin to sell its goods through designers' names. Ironically, given that the practice had been invented by the world of fashion, the mass-production industry was relatively slow to use the names of fashion designers. The couture trade remained very influential in the inter-war years, with names such as Chanel, Lanvin and Schiaparelli dominating world fashion from their

Figure 3.8   The Parisian couturiers continued to dominate the
world of fashion design in the inter-war years. Shown here is a
sketch for an evening dress, of 1930–35, produced by the house
of Coco Chanel – along with Schiaparelli and Lanvin one of the
period's leading couturiers.

Parisian base. The shift downmarket developed in these years in the USA,
where the first named fashion houses dealing with mass-produced clothing
were established.

There were increasing opportunities for women to become professional
designers in these years, but they were not spread evenly across all the design

areas. Aesthetic practice was still heavily gendered at this time: while male designers tended to work with the new technology-led industries, women could be commonly found working in the areas of ceramic and textile design.[34] Suzette Worden and Jill Seddon's survey of women who worked as designers in Britain in the inter-war years showed that many female designers had existed but that most of their names had been lost to history and, predictably, they had been most successful in the areas of craft, textiles and graphic design (especially illustration).[35] Most of the work undertaken on the subject of women designers in this period has either focused on the handful of successful modernists – Eileen Gray, Charlotte Perriand and Lilly Reich in particular; on the small number of women who achieved success working either in the private sphere or the decorative arts industries – Elsie de Wolfe, Ruby Ross Wood, Nancy McClelland and Syrie Maugham in interior decoration, Susie Cooper and Clarice Cliff in ceramics, and Marion Dorn in rug design; or on the anonymous women who worked either as 'art workers' in the art production industries, like the paintresses within ceramics manufacturing, or those who undertook 'design' work as amateurs in fields like home dressmaking. The 'hidden from history' approach, which has characterised so much work in the area of women's studies, continues to uncover forgotten names, but the broad picture is clear. Design in the new, technologically oriented industries was male-dominated, and the most aggressively 'modernist' end of the aesthetic spectrum was inhabited for the most part by men. In general terms women embraced a more conservative model of modernity and did not participate on a large scale in the world of professional design practice.[36]

By 1939 the professional designer for industry had clearly emerged, although still in a number of guises and not always named as such. Perhaps more significantly, however, designer-culture – the idea that designers encapsulated within their very beings the spirit of modernity and the added value that comes from being called an 'artist' – had also become widely visible for the first time. Arguably those designers whose names were used to promote goods were themselves also consumed in this process. Through their access to knowledge and power that was denied to others, they had become mythologised figures whose very names could add value to the products, images and spaces with which they were associated. Their artistic skills and their privileged position at the interface of the worlds of production and consumption granted them a cultural role that was considerably larger than their everyday tasks might suggest. At the same time they also performed a 'real' role within industry, bridging the worlds of production and consumption, enabling the products of industry to fulfil the needs and desires of consumers and, most importantly, ensuring that manufacturers were able to remain in business.

Chapter 4

MODERNISM AND DESIGN

Theory and design at the turn of the century

> We realised that the product made by machines could possess an 'aesthetic' properly derived from a confrontation between function and form.[1]

> ... the Bauhaus signalled a qualitative leap from a political economy of the product to a 'political economy of the sign'.[2]

The shift from the nineteenth to the twentieth century witnessed a number of simultaneous manifestations of a new approach towards the design of the material world. The growing dissatisfaction of an international body of progressive architects and designers with the expansion of conspicuous consumption, their increasing disillusion with decoration's ability to move beyond its association with social display, and the belief shared by many that the engineer's dependence on a quantifiable approach towards form and function provided a better basis on which to move forward than the commercial pragmatism of the marketplace, coalesced into a dramatic revision of the aesthetic and philosophical principles that had long underpinned the creation and role of the decorative arts. Divorced from the latter's historical relationship with the concept of 'decorum', which had governed social and cultural life in the west for several centuries, the idea of the 'decorative', now linked primarily with social display, was anathema to a new generation of designers who sought to renew the language of design in terms of the new challenges and imperatives of the day, be they technological, aesthetic, economic, political or cultural.

Much has been written about the development of early architectural and design modernism and the ideas that underpinned the process of aesthetic simplification and rationalisation which occurred within the world of industrially produced material culture and environments at the end of the nineteenth century and the early years of the twentieth century. Design-historical writing has tended to focus exclusively on the writings of practitioners and to highlight the work of those designers who were able to articulate their ideas and adopt a theoretical relationship with the modern world, usually architects.[3] In 1936 Pevsner pinpointed those architects and designers who, he believed, were the key protagonists in the formation of the theoretical framework which brought about the transformation from historicism to modernism. He charted a path of design ideas which moved from those of William Morris and his Arts and Crafts followers to those of Walter Gropius at the Bauhaus in Germany. Along the way he embraced the thoughts of, among others, A.W.N. Pugin, John Ruskin, Isambard Kingdom Brunel and the modern engineers, as well as French architects like Auguste Perret who used steel and concrete in their innovative architectural structures. The American architects Louis Sullivan and Frank Lloyd Wright were also included, as were the protagonists of rectilinear and curvilinear Art Nouveau and the early 'machine style' – Charles Rennie Mackintosh, Otto Wagner, Josef Hoffmann, Henry van de Velde, Hector Guimard and others. The members of the Deutscher

Figure 4.1 Hand-printing chintzes at Morris & Company's workshops at Merton Abbey in around 1910. Morris and the Arts and Crafts Movement signalled, for Nikolaus Pevsner, the first emergence of was later to become the fully fledged Modern Movement in design.

Werkbund – Peter Behrens, Richard Riemerschmid and others – were also marked out for attention. In describing the dominant design ideas of the years following the First World War, Pevsner focused on the work of the Russian, Dutch, French and German modernists who looked to contemporary innovations in fine art to help them make the shift from historicism to a new, simplified, geometric aesthetic, which took its lead from the modern machine.

In creating his famous lineage Pevsner established a 'stable' of pioneer modernists who have remained important historical figures to this day. In his seminal text of 1960, *Theory and Design in the First Machine Age*, Reyner Banham, a doctoral student of Pevsner, modified the list slightly. He added the work and ideas of a sequence of artists and architects from the Italian Futurists to the German Expressionists who, although undoubtedly 'modern' in outlook, had not been included in Pevsner's unrelentingly rationalist account of the progress of modernist thought.[4]

Banham's account built on Pevsner's and, like the latter, sought to penetrate the abstract forces that caused so many architects and designers to review the philosophical and aesthetic bases on which they practised. He focused on what he believed to be the three underlying causes of change – a growing sense of social responsibility (as epitomised by the work and ideas of the followers of William Morris and finding its full realisation in the activities of the Deutscher Werkbund); the structural approach to architecture (as in the case of Viollet-le-Duc); and the tradition of academic instruction, especially as undertaken in Paris.[5]

Banham's account emphasised the architect as the prime mover of environmental modernism but also acknowledged the role of the fine artist in bringing about change in this arena. He also established an important link between architecture and industrial design, demonstrating how the emergence of the concept of 'form' was to become crucial to functionalist design thinking later in the century.[6] The importance of designed artefacts as an inspiration for modernist architectural thinking at this time was referred to, by Banham, in a description of the ideas of the British architect W.R. Lethaby who, explained the author, 'frequently turns to objects like railway viaducts and bicycles whose value, for him, lay "in their nearness to need"'.[7] The growing association of architect–designers with the culture of industrial production was also seen as an agent of change. The work of Peter Behrens for the German company AEG from 1907 and the emergence of the Deutscher Werkbund created by Herman Muthesius were both highlighted by Banham, as they had been by Pevsner before him, as powerful influences upon the rational direction taken by architecture and design from that point onwards.

To date the accounts of early modernist theory and design provided by Pevsner and Banham have not been seriously challenged. They still provide a useful account of one face of architectural and design practice in the early twentieth century, a face that was rooted in modernist ideology and which determined the policies of many important twentieth-century design-related institutions, including educational establishments, museums and governmental bodies. Modernist beliefs have been reinforced over and over again and have had a dramatic influence upon the status quo in matters relating to design. They do not, however, provide a complete picture of design's cultural role and impact through the twentieth century, which, in reality, was much more diverse and influential across a broad sociocultural spectrum. Ideological modernism focused almost exclusively on the public sphere and the arena of high culture. It was politically driven and took little account of, and even despised, values emanating from the commercial arena and from the private sphere. As a result, neither Pevsner's nor Banham's accounts of early modernism represents the multiple stylistic or ideological variations that could be found underpinning the design of the full spectrum of visual and material culture in these years. They both stressed architecture as the unquestioned 'queen of the arts' and touched on interior design, furniture design and graphic design inasmuch as they were practised by pioneer modernists. They excluded most of the other areas of material culture from the period, among them fashion design, commercial graphic design, interior decoration, the design of luxury goods, product design, car styling and other specialist areas such as theatre set design and shop window display. Their accounts were heavily gendered and made no attempt to look beyond the metropolis or the western industrialised world to understand how different cultures were approaching the creation of their material worlds.[8]

In spite of these serious caveats, for an appreciation of the culture of modern design in its totality it is important to understand the theoretical basis on which modernism was formed: it became a hegemonic ideology underpinning the aspirations of countless cultural groups and nations throughout the twentieth century. Many developing countries felt the need, at one time or another, to embrace modernism as a sign that they had become part of the modern world. The world of commercial design practice also aspired to be 'modern' much of the time and sought to embrace many aspects of the rhetoric of modernism, whether consciously or otherwise. However, rooted as they were within the commercial system, which took a pragmatic approach to its activities and resisted the temptation to philosophise, most early 'designers for industry' were not prone to theorising. Architecture, on the other hand, was traditionally a creative art much more used to theorising its practice. It was not surprising, therefore, that it was architects who were responsible for developing the extended discourse about modern design in the early part of the twentieth century.

As both Pevsner and Banham acknowledged, the roots of modernist thinking, as it related specifically to design, lay within the reformist thinking which was first expressed in the writings of Pugin and Ruskin and which re-emerged in the thoughts of William Morris and others allied to the British Arts and Crafts Movement. Central to their ideas was a dissatisfaction with what they felt to be the overembellished, 'inauthentic' products of the factory which manifested, in their view, the loss of the control that had hitherto been held by the artisan. The way forward involved both a retrospective look at the medieval past and a sideways look at the natural world as an inspiration for 'right' decoration and form-giving.[9] For Ruskin, for example, ornament had to be 'visible, natural and thoughtful'.[10]

By the end of the nineteenth century a modernist vocabulary had begun to emerge which sought above all to move beyond aesthetics and 'inauthenticity'. It had been helped on its way by the writings of Gottfried Semper, a German resident in London in the 1850s, who had proposed a system of classification of objects based on function. In his attempt to find a classifying system that would sidestep the problem of what was, or was not, appropriate ornament, he had set out to link together objects that had common functions, such as 'pouring out' or 'containing'.[11] In the same spirit of rationalisation Owen Jones, and later Christopher Dresser, had also attempted to control arbitrary ornamentation.[12] It was to be some time, however, before the writings of nineteenth-century architects, fine artists, artisans and engineers on the subject of an embryonic 'machine aesthetic' would be applied by designers to consumer machines.

Another nineteenth-century phenomenon that fed into the theoretical underpinnings of design modernism was documented in 1970 by Herwin Schaefer. In defining what could be called the 'unselfconscious' or vernacular tradition, Schaefer usefully pointed out that, in addition to the over-decorated status objects produced for the middle-class population in the nineteenth century, another level of production had also existed which had stressed utilitarian rather than aesthetic values. It was to the 'honest', 'simple' qualities of these vernacular products that many reformers began to look.[13] Indeed, within early European modernist writings there was a strong sense of awe expressed in discussions relating to what were believed to be the 'simple' products of American mass production. Clocks, keys, bicycles, farm machinery and standardised bookcases were widely revered as unselfconscious products of the machine, and were seen as contrasting dramatically with the much-despised aestheticised products for mass consumption. This romantic idolatry was highly selective, however, and failed to take into account the full picture of American mass production, which David Hounshell has documented so thoroughly.[14] It was true that a number of goods reflected their means of

Figure 4.2 The crude, undisguised forms of this first patent model of Singer's sewing machine of 1851 were typical of those which inspired the early modernist designers who evolved the notion of the 'machine aesthetic'.

manufacture in their appearance, the joints between components often remained visible, and the absence of ornamentation bore witness to that fact. This was only a characteristic of a very early stage of serial production, however, and it was rapidly superceded by the manufacture of goods aimed at the mass of American society, which had learnt that goods brought status with them and that elaboration and stylishness were the *sine qua non* of manufactured goods in the sophisticated, urban society that the USA was rapidly becoming. The myth of utilitarianism – expressed in a number of modernist texts, including Siegfried Giedion's influential text of 1948, *Mechanisation Takes Command* – was based, in reality, on a short-lived moment during which a new body of consumers was coming to term with the world of goods and their complex meanings.[15] The modernists' shared nostalgic longing for this 'age of innocence' undoubtedly reflected their deeply felt anxieties about the growing commercial context of design and material culture.

The strong sense of rationalism that underpinned early functionalist theory was embedded in a number of areas of American life in the first years of the twentieth century. The influence of Taylorism on factory and office practice, for example, demonstrated the strength in the belief that the route to the future was through the application of logic, or scientific method, to everyday life. The extensive measuring and calculating that went into the recommendations made to managers as to how they should reorganise their work areas was part of a general belief in, and dependence on, the rules of science as the way forward for modern society. The infiltration of Taylorism into the domestic sphere reinforced its ideological dominance. The need for an economical use of space in the provision of kitchens in Pullman trains and ocean liners, for example, provided a lesson to architects in their use of space in kitchen designs for minimal dwellings, while Christine Frederick's writings of 1913 on the subject of 'step-saving' were to be enormously influential upon European modernist architecture in the 1920s and 30s.[16]

By the early twentieth century the theoretical base for design modernism as formulated by the design reformers had moved from Britain to the USA and to the Continent. It converged with parallel ideas emerging in the USA, exemplified by the writings of the sculptor Henry Greenough. In his short treatise *Form and Function*, written in the mid-nineteenth century, he praised the simple aesthetic engineers had achieved in their structures.[17] Like so many of his fellow proto-modernists he had evolved his ideas partly as a response to his anxieties about the superficiality of design as social display. 'Fashion', he proclaimed, 'has lived too long, and exercised an influence too potent for us either to deny or to escape it ... I regard Fashion as the instinctive effort of the stationary to pass itself off for progress.'[18] The famous words of the Chicago architect Louis Sullivan, 'form ever follows function, that is the law', reinforced the American search for a rational formula for architecture and design.

In mainland Europe similar thoughts were being expressed by members of the German and Austrian Werkbunds in the early century. One of the most powerful and influential texts in this context was the Austrian Adolf Loos' *Ornament and Crime*, which took the need to repudiate decoration to a new level of intensity and fervour. Loos' writings put forward the proposition that as mankind had rejected ornament it had become increasingly civilised. The most mature society, he maintained, was represented by the most simple of forms, and it was the responsibility of the modern architect-designer to adhere to this principle. 'The modern man who tattoos himself', he wrote, 'is either a criminal or a degenerate ... Ornament is wasted labour power and hence wasted health. It has always been so.'[19] His work has recently been the subject of a study by the feminist architectural historian Beatriz Colomina, who has shown that his interior spaces did not conform to his own dramatic rhetoric but were, in fact, more complex and more sensorial than one might expect from his writings.[20]

As the nineteenth century moved into the twentieth century there was a tendency on the part of architects and designers to leave the natural world and the focus on individualism behind and to search for a more objective formula which took what was perceived as the rationalism of machine production as a starting point. This opposition was reflected in the two faces of the Art Nouveau movement – its curvilinear and its rectilinear manifestations.[21] While the former looked directly at the sinuous shapes of nature in its raw state the latter took a more neo-Platonic, essentialist approach, combining what it felt to be the fundamental forms underpinning nature with the essence of, for example, 'chairness'. Although this way of thinking was not to reach its apogee until the Dutchman Gerrit Rietveld created his famous 'Red-Blue' chair in 1917, the work of Josef Hoffmann, Charles Rennie Mackintosh, Otto Wagner and others could seem to have been moving in this direction, while still retaining one foot in the decorative camp. Wagner was particularly articulate about his views and expressed a number of innovative ideas, among them that 'all modern forms must correspond to new materials and the requirements of our time if they are to fit modern mankind'.[22]

A collision of individualism with collectivism reached a high point in 1914 in the confrontation that took place between the Belgian architect-designer Henry van de Velde and the German diplomat Hermann Muthesius. Both men were members of the Deutscher Werkbund. Van de Velde had already articulated a number of ideas that were in tune with the proto-functionalist face of Art Nouveau – 'utility can generate beauty' he had proclaimed, while also maintaining that 'ornament should be structural and dynamographic' and that 'ornament and form should appear so intimate that the ornament seems to have determined the form'.[23] Moving beyond the idea of nature being a source of form, he had developed a theory of object symbolism which proposed that the object's own intrinsic structure should be expressed. A fine artist by training, Henry van de Velde left Belgium in 1900 to become the Head of the School of Decorative Arts in Weimar in Germany. When the Werkbund organised its exhibition in Cologne in 1914 he was asked to show his design for a theatre.

Muthesius was equally committed to an abstract aesthetic of the kind van de Velde had described but, unlike the Belgian architect, he believed in the idea of standardisation and of the sacrifice of the individual to the mass. His definition of design had no room in it for the individual 'artist' but sought instead a democratic availability of well-designed goods created by mass production. Van de Velde's reluctance to let go of what was still a craft ethic, and his refusal to let his aesthetic beliefs develop into a formula for the large-scale manufacture of goods, was perhaps typical of an architect who was not prepared to leave the safe world of the individual project and to leap into a world in which everyone could participate in the products of the designer's labour. The lively debate that occurred between the two men was a turning point for design modernism, as it pinpointed what was to remain a funda-mental dilemma for its adherents throughout its life-span – whether it repre-sented an attempt to develop a modern aesthetic using the idea of the machine as a key metaphor, or an ambition to design for machine production, thereby facilitating the widespread availability of goods created to bring the experi-ence of modernity to as wide an audience as possible.

By 1914 the seeds for both approaches had been sown and modernism's architecturally derived ideas were fully formed, and their implications for design – in the form of a theory based on the idea of 'form following function' and relating to a 'machine aesthetic' – quite clearly expressed. There was, however, a marked absence of an intellectual debate being articulated within the more commercial design arena. This is not to say that ideas were not being expressed in this context, simply that they were more fragmented, less visible outside their specialist arenas, and less rooted in traditional intellectual thought. In the area of interior decoration, for example, interesting ideas were being formulated about the relationship between the domestic interior and the development of personal identity, but they were being directed at the readers of women's magazines for the most part, and did not feed into main-stream thinking. Equally, early graphic designers were beginning to look for a scientific theory that would provide them with a set of rules with which to work, but their thoughts were only communicated within a closed community of practitioners. Fashion design remained untheorised for the most part but had a strong, intuitive sense of the way that consumption worked and how its practice related to it. Within the specialist areas of education, stage set design and store window display, for example, discrete discourses were also devel-oped that related to those specialisms alone. None of these ideas, however, was able to compete with the dominant design discourse that emanated from architectural modernism.

Figure 4.3   Lucien Bernhard's 1908 poster for Stiller showed that simplicity and rationality were entering the world of design for advertising in the early years of the twentieth century.

The hegemony of modernism

> Where the De Stijl movement was original as regards furniture design was in creating the first chair deliberately designed not for comfort, not for dignity, not for elegance, nor for rational assembly according to commonly accepted principles of woodwork, but simply 'designed'.[24]

The inter-war years witnessed an intensification of the debates and ideas that had begun to underpin the practices of modernist architecture and design in the early century. The 1920s, in particular, marked a moment when progressive architects, artisans and decorative artists in a number of centres discussed the relevance of their work in the context of an expanded picture of cultural modernity and technological change. Most of these debates took place in Europe, where ideas emanating from the avant-garde movements in painting and sculpture joined hands with rationalist ideas emanating from modern architectural theory. They fed into the theoretical basis of a movement that was to dominate design thinking, especially as it was expressed in the cultural and educational arenas, through the rest of the twentieth century and beyond. It was a movement which, in essence, took inspiration from the early material

manifestations of modernity – railway stations, bridges, aeroplanes and automobiles among them – as well as from the rationalism believed to underpin
the process of industrial production, and which was linked to the concepts of
objectivity, collectivity, universality and utility. It operated within the context
of the political, the social, the technological and the aesthetic. Its advocates
were vociferous in their rejection of the 'irrational', 'feminised', commercial
culture which represented the other face of material modernity.

What came to be called the Modern Movement, which gave rise to architectural and design 'modernism', has been widely documented. In his introduction to the book he edited, entitled *Modernism and Design*, Paul
Greenhalgh explained that, where its impact on design was concerned, the
Modern Movement had two main historical phases – 1914–29 and the
1930s. He went on to maintain that 'the first phase was essentially a set of
ideas, a vision of how the designed world could transform human consciousness and improve material conditions' while 'the second phase was less an
idea than a style'.[25] The 1930s can be seen as the period of the international
dissemination of the 'object' of the modern movement, the simple 'machine
aesthetic', which entered environments and interior spaces worldwide. It was
also the period when it was used by political regimes, including those of
Germany and Italy, to embrace ideologies completely opposed to the
democractic beliefs that had initially engendered it. Its clearly delineated rules
made it an effective tool of authoritarian control, whichever political ideology
underpinned it.

In the tradition of William Morris one face of modernist thought remained
closely linked with social and political idealism. From the early twentieth
century, material culture had been seen as playing an important part in the
left-wing political action that was spreading across Europe. In the years
following the Russian Marxist revolution of 1917, for example, graphic
designers participated in the propaganda campaign led by the Bolsheviks. In
the wake of the revolution, architecture, dress and products were seen as key
agents of change in the hands of committed artists and designers such as
Vladimir Tatlin, Alexander Rodchenko and Kasimir Malevich. Many avant-
garde artists, designers and architects saw within the world of material culture
an opportunity of injecting modernity into a previously backward-looking
society, and of defining design as a form of ideological activity that had the
power to change things. The propagandist role of graphic design was especially powerful in this context, and artists such as El Lissitzky were highly
articulate in expressing their ideas about its role in this revolutionary context.
Committed to industrial printing and the potency of typographical composition he developed a sophisticated approach that involved building up a page of
type with due attention to shape, size, proportion and composition. This

Figure 4.4   Alexander Rodchenko's design for the interior of the Workers' Club, shown at the Paris 1925 'Exhibition of Decorative Arts', showed the link in Russian design of that time between the modernist aesthetic and political idealism.

'constructivist' approach to building imagery and form from basic elements could as easily be applied to design and architecture as it could, metaphorically, to the idea of a new society.[26]

The link between social democracy and design remained a constant within the articulation of a set of modern design principles that emerged from, among other nations, Germany, France, Holland and Scandinavia in the inter-war years. Both explicitly and implicitly the two were considered as being interdependent. This belief that design was linked to the ideology of social democracy explains the hostility that was frequently expressed by modernist writers in connection with the bourgeois interior, and it made sense of the strong commitment manifested in all those countries to social housing; the concept of the minimum dwelling and its furnishings; and the role of standardisation in making cheap, functional goods available to all. Initiatives such as these were an intrinsic element of the modernist campaign for an egalitarian society with wide access to housing and goods.

The Dutch De Stijl movement – which embraced fine art, architecture and design and refused to accept hierarchical distinctions between them – was rooted in a desire for social improvement. It represented the shared ideas of a group of painters, architects and designers – Piet Mondrian, Theo Van Doesburg, Vilmos Huszar, Bart van der Leck, J.J.P. Oud, Robert van't Hoff and Gerrit Rietveld among them – who were united by the belief that the styles of the past were outmoded and that architecture and design had a social role to play. Importantly that role was performed, they believed, through the aesthetic function of images, artefacts and environments which, they maintained, had the power to transform lives. As Nancy Troy explained, ' … the De Stijl artists sought to preserve the primacy of aesthetic principles as agents of social reform in their own right'.[27] The cleansing process which underpinned the modernists' rejection of conspicuous consumption, and which resulted in the simplified geometry and minimal colours of De Stijl creations, was essentially a social process which, it was believed, brought about liberation from commodities. The glue holding the group together was provided by the magazine De Stijl, which ran from 1917 through to 1931, and which communicated the theoretical ideas that came to be associated with the Dutch movement. They can be summarised as a belief in a relationship between the individual and the universal (expressed in the idea of 'unity in plurality'), a faith in the role of technology, and a commitment to the agency of art, architecture and design to influence the future of social and cultural life.[28]

Although its outlook was international, De Stijl was born of specifically Dutch conditions. Holland adopted a position of neutrality in the First World War and the De Stijl protagonists were committed to the country becoming a modern social democracy. They expressed a strong desire for its citizens to lead prosperous lives and shared a strong belief in social justice. They were committed to eroding distinctions between classes and to providing environments that encouraged a lifestyle which could be shared across classes. Paul Overy has demonstrated, for example, the importance of the De Stijl domestic interior in this context, and shown how Gerrit Rietveld's interior for the Schroeder house was intended as a 'model for the future, a symbol of a new way of living which, it was hoped, would later be transferred to the public realm.'[29] Paralleling this high level of social idealism and commitment to materiality which characterised one face of modernism, a number of members of the De Stijl group, notably Mondrian and Van Doesburg, were interested in a more spiritually oriented approach to material culture, which drew them to Theosophy and the ideas of Rudolf Steiner. Their views reflected a more general interest in spirituality which was expressed by a number of inter-war modernists. For example, the work of Wassily Kandinsky and Johannes Itten, both teachers at the Bauhaus, has provided some of the raw material for revised readings of modernism, which now perceive the role of technology as inspiring as much 'irrational' thinking as it did rationally based ideas.

Swedish architects and designers also understood the potential links that existed between material culture, modern design and social democratic reform in the inter-war years. The roots of a modern movement in that country lay in its nineteenth-century craft traditions and ideas about social democracy. While the decorative arts industries took a little while to move away from their luxury backgrounds, the impact of the Deutscher Werkbund was such that, in the years following the First World War, the Swedish Society of Craft and Industrial Design (Svenska Sjlödföreningen) was ready to hold an exhibition in Stockholm on the subject of social housing. In 1919 its President, Gregor Paulsson, published an influential book entitled *More Beautiful Everyday Things*.[30] It wasn't until 1930, however, that the full blossoming of Swedish modernism was made visible to the rest of the world. The Stockholm exhibition of that year, conceived by a group of architects that included Paulsson as well as Gunnar Asplund, Eskil Sundahl, Sven Markelius and Uno Ahren, modelled itself upon the Stuttgart exhibition of three years earlier, with its emphasis upon social housing and its furnishings. The German functionalist aesthetic was also embraced and slogans such as 'The Functional is Beautiful' became the battle-cry for the Swedish architectural protagonists at the event.[31] The 1930s saw a battle take place between the 'Funkis' (the functionalists) and the 'Tradis' (traditionalists), the latter ultimately winning the day.

As well as being linked to social and political change, the twin qualities of rationalism and idealism that underpinned modernist thought were especially apparent in the education of designers. Nowhere was this more visible than at the German Bauhaus, where a new language of design was created through a highly systematic pedagogical model which provided an international basis for design education in the years following the Second World War. In *The New Architecture and the Bauhaus* Walter Gropius, the director of the school, explained that the dual principles of standardisation and rationalisation underpinned everything that went on within its walls. 'A breach has been made with the past', he proclaimed, 'which allows us to envisage a new aspect of architecture corresponding to the technical civilization of the age we live in.'[32] Like the De Stijl artists and designers before him, Gropius saw the development of type-forms as a fundamental prerequisite for an egalitarian society. Like that earlier movement he also promoted 'a fundamental unity underlying all branches of design' as a means of achieving a non-hierarchical society which valued all the arts equally.[33]

The painters Wassily Kandinsky and Paul Klee taught students basic principles during their first year. They worked on a *tabula rasa* basis, requiring that students brought nothing with them from the past, but rather built up their work through a series of creative strategies that enabled them to develop abstract images from the raw materials of line, colour and form.[34] This systematic cleansing process was used to enable students to find new solutions for new problems. As Gropius explained later 'The first task was to liberate the pupil's individuality from the dead weight of conventions and allow him to acquire that personal experience and self-taught knowledge which are the only means of realising the natural limitations of our creative powers'.[35] Students subsequently progressed to work in one of the craft workshops – focusing on stone, metal, wood, clay, glass and textiles – which were conceived as laboratories for mass production. There they applied the knowledge and skills they had acquired in the preliminary course and created designed artefacts, such as chairs, teapots, electric lights and woven wall hangings, which addressed the basic functional and structural elements of items. Inasmuch as all the objects were handmade a craft approach was adopted but, as they were built up from basic components and emphasised that fact in their simplified, undecorated aesthetic forms, the students' creations were metaphors for mass production as well as potential prototypes for it. A number of Bauhaus objects were put into mass production after its closure by the National Socialists in 1933.

The Bauhaus translated the aesthetic of functionalism into the production of objects. It was a theory which had been in existence within architectural circles for some time, but it had not yet been fed back into mass-produced goods themselves even though modern architects had been developing the idea of the 'machine aesthetic' for some time. Ironically, however, when attempts were made to apply functionalist principles self-consciously to the design of machines, it proved inadequate. Such was the complexity of industrially created mechanical goods that they could not replicate the craft-based ideas disseminated at the Bauhaus. As a set of constructional principles the machine aesthetic, and the theory of functionalism, were more easily and appropriately applied to a simple wooden chair or a silver teapot than to a vacuum cleaner or a radio, which ended up necessarily concealing, rather than revealing, their inner structural components. The body-shell principle of the car stylists and the commercial industrial designers, used to conceal inner workings and present a visual illusion of simplicity, proved much more appropriate in the end however much it negated functionalist principles.

In 1957 Edward Robert de Zurko published a book entitled *Origins of Functionalist Theory* in which he outlined the many diverse roots of this idealist aesthetic methodology. He showed that the attempt to relate the idea of utility to that of beauty had classical, medieval, renaissance, eighteenth-century and nineteenth-century foundations.[36] In his analysis of functionalism, expounded in his book *Changing Ideals in Modern Architecture*, Peter Collins showed that the theory had a number of analogies – biological, mechanical, gastronomic and linguistic.[37] Although in the inter-war years functionalism could still be used, very effectively, as a theory for architecture and for the manufacture of craft-based artefacts, its application to the world of industrial design proved more problematic. In the end it became a post hoc justification for the simple, undecorated style favoured by most modernist designers rather than a set of rules for practice. The concept of the 'machine aesthetic', equally, proved more useful as a metaphor than as a practical idea.

Within modernist ideas the engineer was a recurrent point of reference. The labelling of the engineer as a 'noble savage' by the French architect Le Corbusier was an encouragement for others to follow him. In Le Corbusier's words, 'The Engineer, inspired by the law of Economy and governed by mathematical calculation, puts us in accord with universal laws. He achieves harmony.'[38] If the modern European architects and designers saw themselves working in a continuum with contemporary avant-garde fine art in terms of their development of a minimal aesthetic which sought the 'essence' of material reality, they also saw in engineering a model both for their aesthetic theories and, more importantly, for their working process, which pursued the logical path of 'problem-solving'. This recourse to reason protected them from the illogicality of consumer capitalism and provided them with a system that could achieve a level of universalism. Le Corbusier developed his ideas about the engineer later in the same text claiming that engineering principles were essentially progressive, whereas those of the architect, who was dependent on past styles and upon taste, was moving backwards rather than forwards. The idea that taste should not enter into the equation was one more sign of the modernist fear that subjectivity and market values would undermine their belief in the power of rationality. At times it was almost a pathological fear, causing Le Corbusier to use strong language when describing what clearly represented his anxiety about conspicuous consumption – 'rooms too small, a conglomeration of useless and disparate objects, and a sickening spirit reigning over so many shams – Aubusson, Salon d'Automne, styles of all sorts and absurd bric-a-brac.'[39]

In its pure form modernism for the most part avoided the world of commerce. It remained within the gallery, the design school, the manifesto, the art journal and the craft workshop. When projects were realised they were usually for wealthy clients, such as Truus Schroeder for Gerrit Rietveld and Madame Savoie for Le Corbusier, who were happy to act as patrons to the artists, architects and designers who sought to express their ideas in material form.[40] Commissions such as these did not impose the kind of market constraints that were experienced by designers working with manufacturing industry. Inevitably, however, much designing went on in these years, some of it under the name of modernism, which would not have been accepted by the small coterie of purists who determined modernism's theoretical parameters.

Interior decoration, for example, lay completely outside the limits of modernism. Rooted in historicism and aimed at an elite and aspirational audience it betrayed most of modernism's rules and was looked upon with distaste by most modernists. The only impact of rationalism on the domestic interior came with the application of Christine Frederick's ideas about scientific management, and the influence of the tiny kitchens in railway trains, in the home in the area of kitchen design. This approach was visible in the small kitchens created by Grete Schutte-Lihotsky for the apartments in Ernst May's Frankfurt housing development of the 1920s. This urban rehousing project contained long thin 'galley' kitchens, which came complete with standardised storage units and items of equipment.[41] Such standardisation and efficiency was reserved for kitchens and bathrooms, however, and did not penetrate the living areas of the house.

The two areas of design which would seem less likely to have succumbed to the highly theorised world of rationalisation and idealisation underpinning modernist design – advertising graphics and fashion design – did show some signs of coming under its influence at their margins, however. Conscious that it worked on the emotions rather then the rational mind, the former sought to 'scientise' its activities by appealing to the laws of psychology. Ellen Mazur

Figure 4.5   The interior of Le Corbusier's pavilion of 'L'Esprit Nouveau', which was shown at the 1925 Paris exhibition. Le Corbusier's purism was rooted in ideas that derived from engineering.

Figure 4.6   Even dress, the least rational of the design areas, witnessed its own reform movement in the inter-war years, basing itself on ideas from the late nineteenth century when the concept of 'aesthetic dress' emerged. Pictured here is an example of folk-inspired aesthetic dress that appeared in *Le journal des modes* in 1881.

Thomson has documented a number of experiments that were undertaken from the 1890s onwards to measure the effects of advertisements.[42] Dress also had its own reform movement in these years, especially in the area of men's clothing. The Men's Dress Reform Party was founded in Britain in 1929. The emphasis was upon healthy dress and the development of a diversity of dress types for different needs. Physical comfort also played a key role, with open-necked shirts being favoured, while sandals were preferred to shoes. New materials, such as artificial silk, were promoted to remove the unnecessary weight from men's traditional clothing.[43]

The reform of material culture had its roots in the nineteenth century but it continued unabated through the first half of the twentieth. Modernism was one of its clearest manifestations. It sought not only to improve the quality of the material environment, but also to discover a new aesthetic that would both embody and express a new relationship between society and the material world. The strong moral imperative that underpinned the modernist campaign was, perhaps, its overriding characteristic. It was inherent in the concept of 'good design', which was undoubtedly its heritage, and which dominated debates about design in the years after the Second World War. A sense of morality and of 'truth' was believed to be present within the modernist aesthetic through the avoidance of decoration. The way an object was made, it was suggested, should be apparent through the visibility of its inner structure. In the words of Paul Greenhalgh, 'illusion or disguise of any kind ... was synonymous with a lie'.[44]

In spite of its heroic ideals, the modern movement had its limitations when applied to design. In spite of its determination to move beyond style, and its belief that it should penetrate society as a whole, it underestimated the fact

Fgiure 4.7   Walter Gropius' Bauhaus building in Dessau of 1925–6. In this building numerous modernist experiments took place, all of which attempted to move beyond the concept of style but ended up exhibiting a very recognisable 'Bauhaus' style.

that, in the end, it had a relatively small audience internationally and that, from the perspective of the marketplace, it was seen as just another style. In spite of Gropius' ambition to avoid this fate – expressed in his words 'A "Bauhaus Style" would have been a confession of failure and a return to that very stagnation and devitalizing that I had called it into being to combat' – the objects that emerged from the Bauhaus were all characterised by a strong, shared visual language which became synonymous with the term 'modern'.[45]

The limitations of modernism in design resided, ultimately, in its failure to achieve the level of universality to which it aspired. As I have explained in my study *As Long as It's Pink: The Sexual Politics of Taste*, inasmuch as it rooted its theory in the public sphere, emphasised the rational over the irrational, ignored the arena of consumption which was a strongly feminine site of activity, and minimised the role of the domestic interior, modernism was gender specific.[46]

> Architectural modernism implied an end to the rule of women's tastes in the domestic arena and a clean sweep of the slate such that their influence was eradicated once and for all. In their place it substituted the controlling hand of the professional (male) architect and designer, working in tune with modernity, defined in masculine terms, and with a renewed architectural language which aimed to minimise the possibility of a resurgence of feminine values in the formation of the material environment.[47]

The gendered bias of modernism was not its only limitation. In terms of other cultural categories, ethnicity and class among them, it was also myopic inasmuch as it related exclusively to white, middle-class values. In the 1930s the appeal of modernist architecture and design was limited to an audience of intelligentsia who appreciated its subtle message. In its incarnation in social housing it can be seen as a style which was imposed by one class upon another. In general terms it had a limited market appeal, especially in the context of domesticity.

In spite of the limited audience for modernist designs the impact of modernist ideology upon design theory and practice was, and remains, without equal. As a value system underpinning the role and purpose of modern material culture it penetrated the design education system and the cultural institutions dedicated to design to the extent that it became, and to a significant extent remains, the overriding philosophy of twentieth-century design. As such its influence was and is subtly pervasive and, although on one level its hegemony has been challenged by the advent of postmodernism, on another level it continues to dominate most discussions about design and value in the contemporary world.

Chapter 5

DESIGNING IDENTITIES

Representing the nation

A sophisticated understanding of the ways in which designed material culture could be manipulated and used by groups, institutions and countries to form identities and communicate them to large numbers of people was apparent by 1914. Interest groups of all sizes, concerned to persuade others of their status and authority, began to use designed artefacts and images as a means of expressing themselves and of attempting to persuade others of what they believed to be, or wanted to be, their economic, political, technological or cultural pre-eminence. Nowhere was this process more apparent in this period than in the way existing and emerging nations used design as a means of forming, expressing and promoting their individual identities and strengths both to their indigenous populations and to the world at large. The strategies employed to link material culture with national identity at this time were essentially twofold. They either involved looking back to craft traditions and readdressing them in the light of current preoccupations, or taking a leap of faith into the future and developing an 'art into industry' programme which proposed new forms and modern identities appropriate to the age of the machine. Inevitably the two strategies frequently overlapped, and the edges between them became increasingly blurred.

The consolidation of the strong nation-states and their empires, either reinforced or formed during the last decades of the nineteenth century, was one of the dominant themes in the history of the western industrialised world in the first years of the twentieth century. The desire to emphasise the nation as a political and economic unit above all others, the vying for hegemonic power that led to the crisis of 1914, and the strong sense of cultural identity that flowed from this preoccupation were, for the majority of their populations, both reflected and formed by the material culture surrounding them, with which they were encouraged to identify and, in many instances, consume. The story of design's alliance with national programmes of reform and international competition has been widely documented and flavours the most familiar accounts of twentieth-century design. Pevsner's *Pioneers of Modern Design* stressed the relationship between design and nationhood, and many other texts, including Fiona McCarthy's *A History of British Design 1830–1970*, have focused on the design achievements of a single nation.[1] The latter text documented the way in which design thinking and the concept of nationality developed hand-in-hand, such that the way in which national identity was expressed was inseparable from the material culture that accompanied it. McCarthy's text concentrated on British design, seeing it as a manifestation of ideology and a means of nationalist propaganda. The research underpinning her study derived for the most part from official records, and prioritised what might be called an 'official' account of design while ignoring its more commercial aspects.

John Heskett's *Design in Germany 1870–1918* focused similarly on the theme of national identity and the search for a national style and design ideology through which to express it. The unification of Germany in the late nineteenth century necessitated a highly strategic programme of design reform, which involved establishing museums and schools of applied art. Germany looked to other countries – London and Paris in particular – for examples: it held exhibitions (a German Art and Art Industry Exhibition, for example, was held in Munich in 1876); launched specialist magazines (*Innendekoration* was established in Darmstadt in 1891, two years before Britain's highly influential *Studio* magazine); and involved governmental agency in a number of different ways.[2] A Standing Exhibition Commission for German Industry was set up within the Ministry of the Interior.[3] In the form of domestic interiors created by Bruno Paul and Bernard Pankok, the country's presence at the huge Paris exhibition of 1900 was a mark of the German government's proactive support of a presence at this international event, where the imperial powers of England and France were also on public display. Interestingly the most intimate of designed spaces – the domestic interior – was used to express the German nation's wish to demonstrate that it had a private, as well as a public, face.

The ideological manipulation of material culture and of designed spaces characterised the numerous exhibitions that were held all over the industrialised world through the nineteenth century and into the twentieth century. Beginning with the first major international exhibition held in London's Hyde

Park in 1851, Britain, France, the USA and a host of other countries organised a series of events – universal exhibitions (the French term) and world's fairs (the American term) among them. Each had a different agenda to fulfil – including the improvement of taste in the home market; the enhancement of trade with competing nations; and the establishment of national, and in some cases imperial, identities that would serve to unify populations under a single banner or brand. In his book *Ephemeral Vistas: The Expositions Universelles, Great Exhibitions and World's Fairs, 1851–1939,* Paul Greenhalgh provided an over-view of many of these extraordinary events, showing how they all focused on a cluster of themes – among them new technologies, raw materials and manu-factured goods – which displayed the prowess of the nation in question.[4] Design played a key role, represented by the presence of decorative art objects, products of the new industries, and the achievement of the engineers in the areas of new technology.

Great Britain was among the first nations to exhibit the material achieve-ments of its industrial transformation. The Great Exhibition of 1851 has been widely documented and set a precedent that other nations felt obliged to follow: the USA in 1853, 1876 and 1893; Paris in 1867 and subsequently in 1889 and 1900; Vienna in 1973; and Italy in 1902, among many others. A show of material and technological achievements, the 1851 event set out to show the rest of the world how Britain led the way in the quality and the quantity of its manufacture. By the end of the century Britain had become associated in the minds of many other countries as the home of the Arts and Crafts Movement, and the various exhibitions held in the last years of the nineteenth century conveyed the strong commitment to design reform that characterised British design's message to the rest of the world.[5] Although the Arts and Crafts Movement was perceived as being synonymous with 'Britishness', it provided a model for a number of other countries which, in search of their own modern national identities through design, looked to their own indigenous craft roots for inspiration.[6]

Indeed, the lasting significance of the British Arts and Crafts Movement was ultimately less visible in Britain than on the Continent and in the USA, where it stimulated the emergence of a number of nationally conceived design movements. Ironically, in spite of the attempts to promote design through the interventions of Prince Albert in the mid-century – the establishment of the Victoria and Albert Museum, and the creation of a system of design schools throughout the country as part of the bid for economic and cultural superi-ority – Britain ultimately failed to achieve a strong modern design movement with which to promote itself as a nation. The Arts and Crafts Movement was successful in encouraging other countries to pick up the baton and take it forward: it played a role, for example, in the formation of the Deutscher

Werkbund, while Austria's Wiener Werkstätte was modelled directly on C.R. Ashbee's Guild of Handicraft. Founded by Josef Hoffmann and Koloman Moser in 1903, it openly acknowledged its debt to British achievements, as Hoffmann explained: 'We have founded our workshop ... it should become a centre of gravity surrounded by the happy noise of the handicraft production and welcomed by everybody who truly believes in RUSKIN and MORRIS'.[7]

The question of nationhood was extremely important to the countries associated with the Austro-Hungarian Empire. Walter Crane travelled extensively in Hungary and was embraced fully by that national culture when it came to evolve a national design identity for itself. The Gődollő Workshops, formed in Hungary in the last year of the nineteenth century, also set themselves up on the basis of Arts and Crafts idealism, although there the emphasis was upon reviving the craft of weaving to attain a national culture through continuity rather than discontinuity.[8] Hungary established a Museum of Applied Arts in 1872 and an Applied Arts Society in 1885, as part of its attempt to unite its traditional material culture with its modern national identity.[9] The new museum was opened by Franz Joseph, the Kaiser of Austro-Hungary. The Society focused on organising exhibitions and publishing professional journals. In essence the country pursued its own 'art in industry' programme, inspired by the British model.[10]

Czechoslovakia also responded to the need to represent its national identity through design. Three international exhibitions were staged in Prague – in 1891, 1895 and 1898 – and the country was clearly in a hurry to catch up with its neighbours in embracing design as part of its modern national identity. Like Hungary it looked back to its own folk traditions, but also projected itself forward, inspired by the urban modernity in its midst. In the area of glass manufacture, for example, leading artistic figures such as Jan Kótera created strikingly modern forms. Following the spirit of the *Gesamtkunstwerk* (the whole work of art), which was very much in the air in Europe at this time, Kótera worked on interior decoration as well on textiles, metalwork, lighting fixtures, wallpaper and linoleum. To demonstrate his commitment to the modern age he also even designed a saloon tram for Prague and a railway carriage for the Ringhoffer Company.[11]

The most influential and effective efforts to define national identity by applying art to industry were made in Germany in the early twentieth century. The work of the Deutscher Werkbund has been documented by a number of historians, notable among them Joan Campbell and Lucius Burckhardt.[12] Indeed it was recognised by Pevsner as a key catalyst in his teleological account of the birth of modern design. The main significance of the German Werkbund to an understanding of the evolution of twentieth-century design culture was the fact that it directed its efforts at industry rather than supporting the handicrafts as earlier organisations had done. Set up in Munich in 1907, its aim was simply to 'improve the design and quality of German goods'.[13] The larger aim, however, was to restore unity and national identity to German culture through the medium of improved industrial manufacture and to assert Germany's pre-eminence in the international marketplace. It was an ambition closely resembling that of Britain half a century earlier, but the difference in time meant that Germany could ally its programme to the context of turn-of-the-century modernity and seek a product aesthetic in tune with the progressivism of that era.

The Werkbund acted as a forum bringing together industrialists, artists, architects, artisans and any other individuals interested in the possible links between the artistic and economic aspects of mass production. It was highly supportive of the collaboration between the architect Peter Behrens and the AEG (Allgemeine Elektricitäts-Gesellschaft) company, which it held up as a model for others to follow. Frederick Schwartz's in-depth analysis of Behrens and his work for AEG demonstrated how innovative this work was at this time, and how far ahead it was of comparable companies in the USA and Britain, where engineering sang the tune and artists followed if it was felt to be appropriate.[14] During its early years the Werkbund supported a number of activities – lectures, exhibitions and publications for the most part. It also moved away from the applied arts and towards the products of modern industries – mechanical and electrical products and objects of transport. Its aim was to apply the rationalism of mass production to the design of the goods produced. A number of Werkbund-linked designers, Richard Riemerschmid among them, set out to apply the new principle of standardisation to the traditional craft area of furniture, developing the idea of the *Typenmöbel* (standard furniture items). It was, however, most at home within the public sphere where rationality and neo-Platonic ideas about form were deemed most appropriate. No attention was given to the problematic areas of fashion, or the notions of market demand and consumer desire. The concept of the 'minimal dwelling' was a primary concern, especially for the architects who made up a large sector of the membership, but it was at the more functional end of the built environment spectrum – railway stations and factories – where the Werkbund had its greatest successes. A travelling exhibition went to Newark in the USA in 1912. The culture of design thinking that it brought with it had an enormous impact in that country, which was struggling to integrate design into its national programme, dominated as it was by commercial preoccupations and competition in the internal marketplace.

In 1914, at the height of its influence, the Werkbund organised an enormous exhibition in Cologne. Inevitably the events of subsequent years overtook it and, although it continued its activities into the 1920s and beyond, the Werkbund never quite picked up the same momentum it had had in the early century. As a propaganda machine for modern design seen as an integral part of a national economy and culture, however, it had made its mark, and it was emulated by similar groups that were subsequently established in a number of other countries, among them the Österreicher Werkbund founded in 1910, the Schweizer Werkbund established three years later, and the Design and Industries Association (DIA) set up in Britain in 1915. Its unrelenting commitment to a highly rational model of design – with an accompanying aesthetic which took the metaphor of the machine as a starting point and which, it was claimed, operated outside the pressures of the marketplace – provided *the* model for a philosophy of modern design that was to dominate design education and design reform in the middle years of the twentieth century.

In the years leading up to 1914 the Nordic countries also moved towards a model of modern design culture with a craft basis. Accounts of events and strategies employed by these countries were articulated by David McFadden in his overview of twentieth-century design in Scandinavia. His publication provided an account of official intervention in the formation of the national identities of Sweden, Denmark and Finland, and their strong relationship with material culture as well as the tactics employed by the craft industries in those countries to transform their traditional production into one that embraced the concept of 'modern design'.[15] The Swedish Design Society (Svenska Sljödföreningen) had already been in existence for sixty years at the time of the Deutscher Werkbund's formation, but the Nordic body focused exclusively upon handicrafts rather than upon machine production. Knowledge of German design reform came to Sweden through a visit by Gregor Paulsson, soon to be the Society's director, to Berlin in 1912. He returned enthused by the ideas he had heard discussed there by Werkbund members. In 1909 the Society organised an Art and Industry Exhibition in Stockholm which emphasised, in the same spirit of social democracy that had been in evidence in Germany, the design of worker's and one-family housing. The exhibition stimulated a discussion about the Society's future role and it was reorganised, seven years later, along Werkbund lines.

The Swedish Society took on the role of a kind of employment agency, putting fine artists and manufacturers in touch with each other. As a direct result of this scheme the ceramics company Gustavsberg employed the artist Wilhelm Kåge in 1916, while the glass manufacturer Orrefors took on board the artists Simon Gate and Edward Hald a little later. Although trained as fine artists, all three men were quick to learn craft techniques and were soon working on mass-produced wares in close collaboration with other members of the production team. This was an important transitional moment for twentieth-century Swedish design. It represented the marriage of art and industry that was to become increasingly important to Sweden's identity on the world stage as the century progressed. Although Sweden's manufacturers were traditional applied-art industries, they pursued a programme of innovative practice where the aesthetics of their products were concerned. They rejected the relentless rationalism of Germany and developed in its place a softer, more humanistic, domestic, decorative modern style in the years following the First World War. The home market was amenable to the idea of modernity being expressed through material culture, and it is clear that the country's essentially middle-class population embraced a modern, democratic approach towards its material culture from a relatively early date.

At the turn of the century Denmark and Finland also developed heightened senses of their own national identities and the role that material culture could play within them. Jennifer Opie has explained that Finland reacted against Germanic classicism in the 1890s and embraced a more romantic ethos in its search for a national style.[16] Like many other countries, Finland created its own pavilion for the Paris 1900 Universal Exhibition, demonstrating its

Figure 5.1   The Gustavsberg factory in 1895. The decision to bring Wilhelm Kåge, a graphic designer, into the firm was part of an attempt to create a distinctly 'Swedish' design movement.

unique, highly national identity, which looked both backward and forward at the same time. Designed by Gesellius, Lindgren and Saarinen, it espoused a language of form that owed much to the Karelian traditions which infused Finland's national identity at that time. The team's commitment to creating an image for their homeland that hovered between its indigenous background and the need to relate to international modernity was recognised when in the following year they won the competition to build the National Museum, a monument to Finnish culture. Denmark allied itself more overtly with Germany and defined its national identity as being strongly linked to the neo-classical idiom. Like its Scandinavian neighbours it also looked to its own indigenous craft traditions and devoted its energies to the areas of furniture and ceramic manufacture in particular. The year 1888 saw the Nordic Industrial Exhibition held in Copenhagen, an attempt to rival events held in Paris and London. It was characterised by the awareness that a renewal of style with which to express Danish modernity in an international setting was needed. Like so many other countries, Denmark looked to the British Arts and Crafts for inspiration, and individuals such as the metalworker Georg Jenson owed much to this source.[17]

The Germanic countries set out on a programme of design reform linked to a search for national identity which was predicated upon the achievements of the mass production industries and which oriented itself towards the

Figure 5.2   The Pavilion of Electricity at the Paris Universal Exhibition of 1900. The event set out to show the rest of the world the level of France's achievements in the decorative arts.

population as a whole. France similarly sought a means of using its achievements within the area of material culture as a basis upon which to achieve a homogenous cultural image and identity that would make it a player on the international stage. However, it oriented its efforts less towards the concept of a modern democracy than towards the luxury end of production and consumption. The art historian Debora L. Silverman has provided an account of the ways in which the various craft organisation in turn-of-the-century France developed a programme of reform and activity that would allow them to move forward while not sacrificing their roots in the past.[18] The exhibitions of 1889 and 1900 were crucial showplaces for the French nation to show its wares to the rest of the world, as they were for so many other countries. More recently Lisa Tiersten has shown that, while the manufacture of decorative arts was an important aspect of French culture at this time, France was a heavily mercantile country and the developments in retailing of the late nineteenth century had created a strong consumer culture which heavily influenced the direction that a design culture, and indeed the country's national identity, was to take.[19] The Bon Marché store exhibited an interior at 1900 and it was clear that French culture was concerned to maintain links with its traditional luxury trades – fine-furniture making in particular – and to build a modern consumer culture on the basis of that established identity. France's was a much more evolutionary approach towards the development of a material culture that represented the model of modernity with which that country felt at home. Ironically, it was to have a greater impact upon mass taste than the democratised machine aesthetic promoted by Germany. Indeed, France was among the first countries to understand the way in which private and national identities needed to come together, and the importance of targetting female consumers in the attempt to instil a sense of 'modern nationhood' into its citizens.

The USA's national identity in these years was highly eclectic in nature, dependent as it was upon the many cultures it had absorbed through waves of immigration. Like its European counterparts, however, the USA had also exhibited designed wares in a number of large exhibitions in the second half of the nineteenth century. The 1853 New York exhibition had been its own version of the British event at the Crystal Palace, where the USA had shown its latest technologies, the Yale lock and the Colt revolver among them. The 1876 Centennial Exhibition, held in Philadelphia, had been a display of technological virtuosity for the most part. However, the Columbian Exhibition, held in Chicago in 1893, had shown that the USA was looking for a national style, and had found it in a form of classicism referred to as the Colonial Revival. Unlike Germany, the USA developed its national style from its past rather than from its present and its future. The presence of the Werkbund

Figure 5.3　The Columbian Exhibition held in Chicago in 1893 marked a moment in which the USA was seeking a national style for its own architecture and design. It found it in a form of neoclassicism referred to as 'The Colonial Revival'.

exhibition in Newark in 1912, however, stimulated a response from a handful of individuals who were keen to take the USA down the same route. A new 'American' identity was also emerging, in the late nineteenth and early twentieth centuries, which was linked with the idea of a modern, technology-enabled lifestyle free from the weight of European traditions. Specifically 'American' movements in material culture emerged, among them Mission furniture – a heavy wooden idiom that was linked, so it was claimed, with an indigenous vernacular style. These forays apart, in the years around the turn of the century the national identity of the USA was essentially that of a consumer society, defined by the wants and desires of the marketplace. All the material accoutrements of the culture of consumption from these years – the mass circulation magazines, the department stores, the shop windows, the advertisements among them – could be seen as part of the 'American way', helping to make its consumers 'Americans'.

By 1914 it was clear that designed material culture played a large part in forming and communicating a large number of national identities, especially the contested ones in Europe. It was an important means through which governments and corporations could define their citizens and their consumers, and, just as importantly, through which citizens and consumers could define themselves.

Corporate culture and the state

> National identification in this era acquired new means of expressing itself in modern, urbanised, high technology societies.[20]

In his account of nationalism between the two world wars the historian Eric Hobsbawm explained that two crucial factors had to be remembered in this period. Firstly, he explained, the rise of the modern mass media – the press, the cinema and the radio among them – had to be taken into account as they had the power to 'standardize, homogenize and transform popular ideologies as well as exploiting them for the purposes of deliberate propaganda by private interests and states'.[21] He omitted 'design' from his list. By these years, however, through the agency of industrial mass production and other forms of reproduction (photography and printing among them), designed objects and images had come to constitute an important component of the mass media, capable of performing the same roles as its accompanying forms. Arguably indeed, through its multiple manifestations – as representations, images, physical artefacts, spaces and environments – design was even more capable than other aspects of the mass media of communicating values and ideas in a persuasive way.

In the inter-war years modernist design became a powerful cultural force to reckon with in the arena of international high culture. This reached a peak at the 'International Style' exhibition held at New York's Museum of Modern Art in 1932.[22] Simultaneously, however, design developed a day-to-day relationship with the commercial context of the industries and consumers it served and, as a result, took on a rather different demeanour. Increasingly, nations chose to define and represent themselves through the commercial face of design, seeing it as a means of establishing cultural and trading identities for themselves, and of appealing to the popular audiences to which they addressed themselves. As a result, two distinct modern design styles emerged, which have been called 'modernist' and 'modernistic'.[23] While the former reflected a complete break with history the latter maintained a level of continuity with the past through the development of a language of decoration, which nonetheless took its inspiration from the contemporary world.

Figure 5.4   At its Exposition des Arts Décoratifs, held in Paris in 1925, France re-emphasised the importance of luxury and retail culture in its national design identity. Pictured here is Edgar Brandt's Porte d'Honneur.

The commercial face of European modern design was in evidence at the Paris Exhibition of Decorative Arts of 1925, where the leading department stores of the day (the Magasins du Louvre, the Galeries Lafayette, the Magasins de la Place Clichy, the Magasins du Printemps and the Magasins du Bon Marché) played a prominent role through the presence of the extravagant pavilions they created for the event. As it had already demonstrated in 1900, France's self-image was largely dependent upon its luxury manufactures and its strong retail culture.[24] Although the 1925 exhibition was international in scope and contained a number of modernist displays (the pavilions designed by the Russian architect Konstantin Melnikov, and Le Corbusier's Pavillon de L'Esprit Nouveau were the most prominent within this category and have been widely discussed), the event was dominated by the department stores' pavilions, which contained the work of France's leading decorators and artisans of the day – among them Süe et Mare, Jean Dunand, André Groult and Maurice Dufrène. The aesthetic with which these practitioners chose to work – with its emphasis on rare woods, animal skins and precious materials – reflected France's empire and its decorative artists' interest in exoticism. The exhibition as a whole reflected a national image of a country that was home both to design modernism in its most radical incarnation (in the work of Le Corbusier and others) as well as to a softer modern idiom. The latter proved the more popular, and by the 1930s had penetrated the mass environment on a significant scale, visible on shop fronts, factory and cinema façades and interiors, American skyscrapers and a wide range of mass-produced fashion accessories and decorative objects.

National identity and commerce went hand in glove at France's event. As Tag Gronberg explained, although the exhibition had the word 'industriels' in its title, 'it included none of the spectacular displays of industrial manufacture that had characterised other French exhibitions'.[25] Instead the nation, or at least the city – a microcosm of the nation – was presented as a 'shop window'. This strong emphasis on consumption was matched by the dominance of 'femininity': the city of Paris itself was characterised at the event as a centre for women's luxury shopping, the home of haute couture. It was this aspect of its material culture and modernity through which France chose to represent itself, rather than through its modernist achievements.

Design, the visible face of material culture, was used in 1925 to evoke a world in which luxury, interior décor, commerce, couture and the decorative co-existed. As Tag Gronberg pointed out, 'An indentification with *haute couture* was an important means of promoting Paris as the centre of modernity and consequently France as "in advance" of other nations'.[26] Moreover, the interiors displayed within the pavilions were aimed at offering a level of bourgeois distinction to the consuming public that visited them. Simon Dell argued that it was 'identity' itself, rather than 'objects', which was on display, and that 1925 marked the important moment when the basis for both individual and national identities moved its focus from production to consumption.[27] In spite of the high cultural dominance of international modernism in these years this powerful event chose to show it at the margins, and to focus instead on representing an alternative modernity which, in terms of the way people lived or aspired to live, was much more meaningful and relevant. Above all, it was linked to the all-important concept of 'nation'.

Although architectural modernism made an impact in the USA, its indigenous industrial design movement adopted a very different guise characterised less by a set of philosophical beliefs than by a pragmatic negotiation with the constraints it confronted in the marketplace.[28] Stylistically and ideologically, however, the achievements of the Europeans set a gold standard against which many projects were judged. Many American designers took off from a different starting point, preferring to let the 'right' solution arise from the problem at hand. A number of European émigrés – including Paul Frankl, Joseph Urban and Frederick Kiesler – came to the USA in the inter-war years, bringing with them ideas that had originated in the 'old world'. Quite quickly, however, their approaches were absorbed into the commercial setting in which they found themselves, and their work became integrated into the hybrid modern design movement which developed in the USA at that time. Design's origins – in the USA within advertising, marketing and the expansion of consumer culture – continued to determine its progress through the inter-war years. In 1925 it was one of the few countries that did not exhibit at the Paris exhibition, the reason given being that it was not yet ready to show itself to the rest of the world as its modern material culture lagged behind that of Europe.

The USA's relationship with marketing, however, was growing in strength. A number of individuals played a key role in this developing bond. For example, in the 1920s Edward Bernays, a nephew of Sigmund Freud, related his uncle's ideas about the irrational self to the world of business and, in so doing, developed a number of the fundamental strategies that have since underpinned mass marketing, and indeed mass propaganda. One of Bernays' marketing successes was to persuade women that smoking in public was an act of liberation.[29] The bridge he established between buying and personal desire was the focus of a study by the literary historian Rachel Bowlby, who showed that in the 1930s department store salesmen were trained to penetrate customers' subconscious minds and to utilise strategic selling techniques.[30] Another text from the period, Christine Frederick's *Selling Mrs Consumer* of 1929, explained the gendered role of consumption and showed how the appeal to the 'irrational mind' of women was a fundamental part of the process of consumption.[31] In 1932 Roy Sheldon and Egmont Arens wrote a book entitled *Consumer Engineering*, where they described a number of ways in which manufacturers could ascertain consumer needs and desires and fulfil them through their products. One chapter, entitled 'The Artist Comes in the Back Door', explained how art had come to be at the service of industry. In the authors' words, 'This unobtrusive artist was a realist of the machine. He simplified as he worked, discarding geegaws and flourishes. Convenience, fitness, cleanliness were uppermost in his mind. To these qualities he added beauty, good taste'.[32]

The 'artists' in question were collaborating with manufacturers who were operating in the economic context of Roosevelt's 'New Deal'. National identity and the future of the country were linked to the fortunes of manufacturing industry and to the large corporations that developed in these years. In turn they depended upon design. Nowhere was this more apparent than at the 1939 New York World's Fair, when the focus was upon the USA's large corporations – General Motors, Ford, Chrysler, Dupont, the National Cash Register Company, AT&T, Westinghouse, Lucky Strike Cigarettes, Firestone, the National Dairy Products Corporation and others. Collectively they *were* the nation, and in 1939 they used design and industrial design professionals to communicate their values to the visiting public.

Figure 5.5 A poster promoting the New York World's Fair
of 1939 at which the USA showed its national design identity
to be strongly linked to commerce and corporate culture.

The event has been well documented, with an emphasis upon the work of
the leading designers of the day – Norman Bel Geddes (who created the
General Motors 'Highway and Horizons' exhibit); Walter Dorwin Teague
(who masterminded the event, and designed the Ford Motor Company's
exhibit, the United States Steel exhibit and the State Reception Room of the
United States Government Building, among others); and Raymond Loewy
(who worked on Chrysler's contribution). The reason for asking the designers
to stage manage the event was provided with a telling statement, 'because the
industrial designers are supposed to understand public taste and be able to
speak in the popular tongue, and because as a profession they are bound to

disregard traditional forms and solutions and think in terms of today and tomorrow it was natural that the Board of Design should turn to them for the planning of the major exhibits in which the theme of the Fair is to be expressed.'[33]

The aesthetic idiom used in all the USA's exhibits was that of 'streamlining', a style that had its origins in automobile styling but which had rapidly been transposed into domestic and office machines, and finally into architecture. It evoked an image of futurity, of technological confidence and of control over the material world. Its seamless, undecorated forms were redolent of a progressive model of modernity which was materialised through a collaboration of art with industry. The very theme of the Fair –'Building the World of Tomorrow' – indicated the forward-looking thrust of the event, which set out to show the rest of the world that the USA was the most technologically, economically and socially advanced nation in the world. Above all, it sought to address its own consuming public as a unified, undifferentiated emotional mass. In the words of Warren I. Susman, the intention was both to educate and to dazzle, but most importantly 'to cut through divisions of class, ethnicity and ideological distinctions of left and right to form a basic sentiment on which a national culture might be founded'.[34] Modern design was used as a means not only of representing but also of helping to create what has subsequently been called 'the American way of life'.[35]

The striking sense of optimism in a future made possible by technology, which epitomised the USA's self-image as represented in 1939, was in sharp contrast to that of Great Britain, which presented itself at the same event through an exhibit featuring 'pageantry of the past'. Its display of heraldry marked a determination, on the part of Great Britain, to keep one foot firmly in the past and to present a conservative identity to the rest of the world. Britain hosted and participated in a number of exhibitions during the interwar years, at all of which the theme of its colonies dominated the picture. At the British Empire Exhibition of 1924, for example, which like so many other exhibitions of the same era placed a strong emphasis on trade, a variety of African arts and crafts were displayed.[36] It was suggested at the time that such artefacts might provide for modern designers an alternative inspiration to that of international modernism, the model embraced by the leading British design reform body of the day, the Design and Industries Association.[37] In general terms Britain took an ambivalent approach to modernism and only a relatively few private residences and social housing schemes embraced the radical style that was emerging on the Continent.[38] Instead, when it represented itself as a nation through exhibitions, Britain called much more frequently on its indigenous traditions, mythical and otherwise. In her study of the Daily Mail Ideal Home Exhibitions, Deborah S. Ryan has shown that progressive ideas about efficiency in housework co-existed alongside the display of Georgian- and Tudor-style housing.[39] The influences of the French Art Deco style and of American streamlining were also in evidence in these displays, which were aimed at an audience of female consumers.

Such was the power of consumer culture in the inter-war years that no nation which saw itself as advanced, and which wanted to present itself to its own population as such, could avoid presenting an identity of itself through its commodities. In the creation of those identities, therefore, material culture, and its richly nuanced meanings, played an unprecedented role. The Ideal Home Exhibition had both educational and commercial intentions and promoted a model of domestic 'Englishness' that hovered between the modern and the nostalgically traditional. The 'conservative modernity' thus represented paralleled that which characterised the 'middle-brow' fiction of Daphne du Maurier, Agatha Christie and others described by Alison Light in her book *Forever England*.[40]

Figure 5.6   An early version of Ferdinand Porsche's design for the Volkswagen, or 'People's Car' of 1936–37. Adolf Hitler commissioned the car as a small inexpensive vehicle, suitable for the autobahns he had created as part of his modernisation programme for Germany.

Figure 5.7   Giovanni's Palazzo dell'Arte, built in Milan in 1933 in the neoclassical style known as 'Novecento'. This style of architecture was embraced by Mussolini as an appropriate idiom for his fascist rule, which valued both the past and the future.

Two countries that used design effectively in exhibitions to represent themselves as nations in the 1930s were the fascist states of Germany and Italy. Like Britain, both countries embraced a mixture of the international modern and the traditional with which to create their respective national identities. While Germany combined the *volk* ethos with modern manufacturing and imagery in the production of cars, ceramics and metalware, Italy looked to its craft traditions, its neoclassical past and international modernism simultaneously to convey the idea of nation with both a strong past and a progressive approach towards the future.

Many other nations became increasingly sophisticated in their use of designed material culture, and exhibition displays as means of presenting themselves both to their own populations and to the rest of the world in these years. Inasmuch as no industrialised nation could afford to appear insular, the internationalist message of modernism played a key role, but a careful balancing act was needed if countries were also to remain as distinctive. Countries such as the newly formed Czechoslovakia – created in 1919 as a democratic state created from Bohemia, Moravia, Slovakia and Ruthenia – embraced modernism as part of its bid to enter the international arena, and to create a modern national identity for itself and its people. In order to make that identity distinctive it flavoured the international style with some local inflections. 'The aspirations of the young republic', David Elliott explained, 'were reflected in a desire for new styles of art, architecture and design which were accessible to the people and which drew inspiration from the vernacular language of the village and the city street.'[41] Although it drew on a wide range of contemporary European avant-garde tendencies – from Futurism to Dada, to Constructivism to Surrealism – it also developed its own modern design movement. 'Devetsil', as the Czech movement called itself, embraced the cubist ceramics of Josef Havlicek and Antonin Heythum and the typographic experiments of Karel Teige. Although Devetsil did not enter the world of mass production its potency lay in its attempt to bring Czechoslovakia into the modern world through the creation of a progressive material culture that could represent modernity. Inevitably another face of the country was represented by folk production, and cut glass continued to be shown at international exhibits, expressing quite a different identity for this new republic. When the country succumbed to Stalinist rule in 1948 the modernist experiment came to an abrupt end.

By 1939 the USA had moved the furthest in integrating design into its private corporations, rather than, as in more centrally controlled countries and totalitarian states, maintaining it as a tool of ideological control. However, there were also signs in other countries that corporate design was becoming very powerful. In Britain, for example, the Shell Company used poster design to promote its services very effectively, while in Italy the Olivetti Typewriter Company understood, as AEG had before it, the way to use designers to create a forceful, high-quality company image. Although Italy had a regime of autarchy in the 1930s, Camillo Olivetti operated in an international arena. He had visited the USA and met Henry Ford, and had implemented American manufacturing techniques in his typewriter and office-machine factory in Ivrea. In 1933 he produced fifteen million office machines and nine thousand portable typewriters.[42] Design was soon added to his successful commercial formula. The initiative to implement a design strategy – in the form of modernist buildings, graphics and product design – was taken by Camillo's son Adriano, who employed a number of Bauhaus graduates, including Xanti Schawinsky, as well as a leading architect of the day, Eduardo

Persico. Finally, he brought the graphic designer Marcello Nizzoli into the group to work on product design. The result was a totally modern corporate identity.

By the end of the 1930s design had become a tool available for use both by private enterprises and nations to persuade others either to consume their goods or to recognise their authority. As a medium for propaganda, both economic and political, it had enormous potency. It was capable of transmitting values that fulfilled consumer desire and of stimulating a level of aspiration that encouraged consumers to buy goods and images as a form of identity-formation. The same powers of persuasion and offers of identity could be used by political regimes to encourage national loyalty. Unlike the radio and the other forms of the mass media, design could function in a multi-layered way such that the meanings of commodities and images, already coded by designers, could be presented by other designers within the doubly coded context of an exhibition, a shop window, a printed page, or an advertising campaign. By the inter-war years many nations and corporations had come to depend on design for their various commercial and/or ideological ends, and were fully aware of its potential both to persuade and to fulfil needs and desires.

PART TWO

Design and postmodernity, 1940 to the present

Chapter 6

CONSUMING POSTMODERNITY

The dream of modernity

> The conditions were present for the arrival in Britain of that complex and pervasive phenomenon to which J.B. Priestley, returning on 1954 from a visit to the USA, affixed, by a happy stroke, the name of 'Admass'.[1]

In the years following 1945 the concept of design became linked with that of 'modernity' in the eyes and minds of ever-increasing numbers of people. Inevitably the war years themselves had seen a temporary reduction in mass consumption and more emphasis upon 'making do and mending'. In the late 1940s and 50s, however, Great Britain and Europe experienced conditions similar to those that had determined the economic, social and cultural progress of the USA in the years before the advent of the Second World War, with many of the developments that had occurred in that former country being mirrored almost exactly across the Atlantic. This was especially the case in the arena of mass consumption, and post-war Europe saw many more people, from a wider spectrum of classes, beginning to see consumption as their main form of self- and group identification.

The result was a further democratisation of the expression of taste in the marketplace manifested in a flurry of purchasing material goods – especially homes, furnishings, consumer gadgets, clothing and cars – on a scale that had not been seen before. Made possible by new levels of earning, it was motivated by people's desire to improve their material conditions and their social positions. In turn these new levels of expectation were part of the drive, on the part of many of the countries in Europe, to establish new national identities for themselves. Nuclear families were targeted as the main unit of consumption and, although the new lifestyles on offer in the marketplace were expressed through individual consumption, they also helped to define the new nations as modern, liberal democracies.

A number of studies of Britain and Europe have described the new phenomenon that hit their shores in the 1940s and 50s as 'Americanisation'.[2] Inevitably this brought with it a model of consumption, but it was not the only model that operated in Europe as conditions varied from place to place. Although the American model of consumer modernity was emulated to a greater or lesser degree in most modernised and modernising countries it was inevitably affected by, in the words of Victoria de Grazia, 'very different relationships between state and market, varying modalities of class stratification and different notions of the rights and duties and citizens'.[3] Thus, for countries such as the USSR and those in the Eastern bloc, for example, consumption had a strong 'needs' component within it and the variety of goods on offer was severely restricted. Nonetheless the American model was highly influential and even in the German Democratic Republic (GDR), as Ina Merkel has demonstrated, American-style consumer culture eventually took a hold. Merkel described the conflict that took place in East Germany as ideas from the West gradually infiltrated that country: 'One the one hand, in the East, the idea of socialist equality with its holy trinity of work, bread and housing was paramount ... On the other hand, social and cultural differentiation in the West had developed and deepened deriving from experiences of upward mobility and postwar economic successes'.[4]

In the more affluent, capitalistic European countries of the 1950s – Britain, Germany and Italy among them – consumerism (as well as the material goods and images consumed) played a large part in everyday life. Countries with a strong tradition of social democracy behind them – the Scandinavian countries for example – and others that had a cultural antipathy to the 'American Way' – France in particular – attempted to resist the impact of USA-style, conspicuous consumption, but were only partially successful. To a significant degree, the model of consumer modernity that had begun to make an impact on 'ordinary' American citizens before the Second World War was felt as a wave which engulfed Europe in the years after 1945.

Americanisation was accompanied by new levels of materialism and, for increasing numbers of people, by the place of consumption at the heart of everyday life.[5] The economist J.K. Galbraith, in his 1958 study The Affluent Society, described the new consumerism as it affected the USA, while more recently historians, such as Erica Carter in her account of 1950s German consumerism, have looked at its influence on European countries.[6] The impact of mass consumerism was heavily criticised by a number of writers who set out to describe the new cultural forms of the highly Americanised society of which they found themselves a part. In Britain, for example, Raymond Williams wrote in *Culture and Society* (1958) of the dangers inherent in emulating the American experience.[7] In so doing he was, in many ways, echoing the pre-war anxieties of the members of the Frankfurt School who had expressed serious doubts about the benefits of the advent of mass culture.[8]

Along with Richard Hoggart, Williams was one of the founders of what became, in Britain, the academic discipline known as Cultural Studies. He was fearful of a wholesale embrace by society of the mass media, including the products of the mass production industries, concerned that it would mean a loss of traditional culture and an erosion of standards. 'Isn't the real threat of mass culture', he wrote, 'of things like television rather than things like football, or the circus – that it reduces us to an endlessly mixed, undiscriminating, fundamentally bored reaction?'[9] He highlighted advertising as playing a very special role within the mass media that brought about this transformation. 'In a sense', he explained, 'the product has become irrelevant: the advertiser is working directly on image and dreams ... all ordinary values are temporarily overridden by a kind of bastard art, not clarifying experience but deliberately confusing it.[10]

The mass media – film, television, magazines, advertising and mass manufactured products and images themselves – were instrumental in communicating a number of 'lifestyle models' that could be appropriated through consumption.[11] While those models had different impacts in different places, many of them encouraged aspirations that had implications for consumption patterns and, importantly, for design. The ideal of the 'modern', or as it was referred to at this time the 'contemporary' home, was widely disseminated through the mass media and, to a considerable extent, it displaced the concept of the 'traditional home' as an aspiration, especially for new homemakers who had not previously had the opportunity to own their home and consume on such a scale. Indeed, for a large sector of the population, inhabiting a home furnished in the 'contemporary style' represented an important material sign of the arrival of modernity into their lives.

The American version of the 'contemporary home' was disseminated through numerous popular television programmes, among them *I Love Lucy*, which was also broadcast in Europe. In Britain the 'contemporary' style featured in the sets developed for several British TV programmes.[12] Above all, homes decorated in this style filled the pages of popular women's magazines on both sides of the Atlantic. Elizabeth Wilson has described the way in which Mary Grieve, the editor of *Woman* magazine, understood the close link between consumption and women's entrance into modern life, and geared her magazine to exploit that association.[13] For new consumers, buying a house for the first time, often located in suburbia, and equipping it with contemporary furniture, a kitchen filled with new gadgets, a large refrigerator (in a range of new colours with exotic names) and a new car in the driveway, represented their primary material means of proclaimimg their membership of the affluent post-war world. It also helped them define themselves as individuals. However, as the American writer David Riesman explained in his influential text *The Lonely Crowd,* first published in 1950, as mass society expanded so individuals became increasingly isolated.[14] Inevitably the mass media, and mass-produced visual and material culture, played a role in this process.

The do-it-yourself movement was imported to Britain from the USA in these years, offering people the opportunity to modernise their own interiors economically. The consumer-oriented *Do-It-Yourself* magazine succeeded the much more technically oriented *Practical Mechanics* of the pre-war era, its front covers showing couples working together to build cupboards and strip walls. More often than not the wife was pictured holding her husband's ladder while he precariously drilled holes in the wall. The myth of 'togetherness' was widely disseminated, helping to confirm the importance of the close-knit, post-war nuclear family. On another level it served to consolidate the isolation of such units and the loss of a traditional sense of community. Increasingly, self-identification was formed through consumption and participation in the fashion cycle. It was also a means of both establishing and confirming consumers' social status. In Britain the importance of design to this process, and its strategic role within the nation's desire to build a new post-war society and identity, was explicit in the words of a government report on the subject of education written by John Newson. He explained that:

> Our standards of design, and therefore, our very continuance as a great commercial nation, will depend on our education of the consumer to the point where she rejects the functionally futile and aesthetically inept and demands what is fitting and beautiful ... Woman as purchaser holds the future standard of living of this country in her hands ... If she buys in ignorance then our national standards will degenerate.[15]

It was clear that consumption, rather than production, was seen as a key to Britain's future, and that it needed to operate within a context of educated taste which, at that time, meant a preference for the 'modern'. The main responsibility for consumption fell unequivocally to women. Believing that if the home market for 'good modern design' expanded, then production would increase to meet the new demand and trade with other nations would improve, the work of the British Council of Industrial Design, formed by the Board of Trade of the Coalition Government in 1944, focused on the

Figure 6.1 This advertisement for Kenwood's 'Steam-o-Matic' iron from the 1950s depicted a smiling housewife, thereby clearly suggesting that the promotion was aimed directly at women as the key consumers of domestic electrical products.

education of consumer taste. Although women were clearly highlighted as the nation's main shoppers, there was evidence that men were also becoming consumers. In his study of the consumption of menswear in Britain in these years, Frank Mort outlined the way in which a particular image of modern masculinity manifested itself in dress, lifestyle accessories and a commitment to popular culture. The work undertaken on the emergence of the concept of the 'teenager' in these years has also demonstrated that the consumption of certain key items provided entry to a range of youthful male subcultural groups – those of Teddy Boys and later Mods and Rockers in particular – which were manifested in their possession of specific material goods, especially their items of clothing.[16] Older men undoubtedly consumed as well, although rather more silently.

The consumption of modern material culture became the primary means of identity formation and a manifestation of social aspiration and achievement for the majority of people in the western industrialised world in the 1950s and 60s. Most importantly, for the new consumers in particular, the emphasis was upon the consumption of *modern* goods and images, and it was generally acknowledged that designers had the necessary visualising skills with which to represent the image, or images, of modernity. Several texts, notable among them Thomas Hine's *Populuxe*, have provided detailed accounts of the exuberance of contemporary American material culture in these years.[17] It was undoubtedly an era that pushed imaginations to the limit in the search for ever new and evocative forms with which to entice consumers – especially in the areas of domestic goods and automobiles which accounted for the vast majority of private consumption choices. In the USA forms reached their zenith by the end of the 1950s, and a similar delight in colour, modern forms and decorative surfaces was visible in Europe as well.

While at the level of high culture the visual and ideological language of modernism remained in place, such was the expansion of the market for designed goods and images that a multiplicity of modern forms of material culture began to appear in the marketplace. A concept of 'popular modernism' emerged that sat alongside other contemporary manifestations of 'popular culture', including Hollywood films, advertisements, pulp novels and popular music. The disparity between what was sometimes called 'highbrow' and 'lowbrow' cultures was widely discussed by cultural critics, and what Adorno and Horkheimer described as 'safe standardised products geared to the large demands of the capitalist economy' were seen, by many, as regrettable manifestations of modern society.[18] For others, among them the members of the Independent Group which met at the Institute of Contemporary Arts in London through the early 1950s, the emergence of popular culture, which included designed artefacts and images, represented a new energy and aesthetic exuberance that pointed the way forward, beyond design modernism into a new 'postmodern' sensibility which would openly embrace the desires of the marketplace.[19]

Not all the accounts of 1950s consumption and design have suggested that the impact of modernity upon people's lives was always accompanied by optimism. In her case study 'Inside Pramtown: A Study of Harlow House Interiors, 1951–1961', the design historian Judy Attfield took a cooler look at the way in which the vision of modernity that consumers were expected to embrace and live with had a downside as well. Attfield described the fact that the working-class women who were housed in Harlow suffered a severe loss of community and found that because their kitchens were located at the front of their houses, they were consequently permanently overlooked and therefore intolerable to spend time in.[20] While this case study focused on social housing, an area in which the level of consumer choice was severely restricted, other studies have looked at the consumption of clothing items where more choice was exercised and where the possibilities of pleasure being experienced were, potentially at least, greater. Such was the case in the consumption of stiletto-heeled shoes, as the design historian Lee Wright has claimed. They could, she suggested, be seen as an example of a means through which many women entered the world of modernity for the first time. 'Expressions of femaleness', she maintained, 'can signify power'.[21] Although feminist writings of the 1970s were critical of what they saw as women's passivity in the marketplace, Wright looked back at the 1950s with a more sympathetic approach to women's consumption, and argued that women's acceptance of overtly modern items of material culture, such as stiletto-heeled shoes, could have helped them form their own model of modernity and become empowered as a result. The debate between the approach of the first generation of feminists and Wright's 'post-feminism' hinged upon the different ways in which designed artefacts were believed to carry meaning. Were they simply non-negotiable symbols of the ideological status quo, or could they act as bearers of potential power, giving meaning to women's lives, selected on the basis of free choice and experienced in different ways by different individuals? While 1970s feminsim reflected a neo-Marxist view of historical change and agency, attributing to objects a single ideological position as 'commodified', the latter view was more in sympathy with a pluralistic, non-deterministic, non-ideological approach to the way in which material culture has the potential to relate to society and culture.

A similar argument about designed artefacts' ability to act, in semiotic terms, as 'floating signifiers', and to change their meaning according to their context, was presented by the cultural theorist Dick Hebdige. In his article on the Vespa motor scooter, the cultural critic described the way in which this small object of transport had undergone a transformation from a mainstream cultural artefact, developed to replace the bicycle in Italy in the 1940s and 50s, to become, in the 1960s, a customised, cult object that played a key iconic role within the visual identity of a British subcultural group known as the 'Mods'.[22] The identities that were formed by the consumption of material goods in the early post-war years were highly gendered. Following women's experiences of 'gender liberation' during the Second World War, when they had had to take on a number of roles which were almost indistinguishable from those of their male counterparts, the post-war period saw a rapid re-gendering of women and men and a reversion to the ideology of the 'separate

Figure 6.2   The Italian 'Vespa' motor scooter, manufactured by Piaggio from 1946 to the 1980s, began life as an alternative to the automobile in Italy but became transformed, in the 1960s, into a lifestyle accessory of the subcultural youth group known as the 'Mods'.

spheres'. In Britain the overriding motivations underpinning this volte-face were linked to the need to rebuild the population, and to construct a nation-state made up of settled, committed citizens. On another level it was a means of facilitating the expansion of individual consumption, which was part of a larger strategy aimed to improve the status of British trading in the rest of the world.

In the idealised imagery of advertisements and films the 1950s were frequently depicted as a highly 'feminised' decade in which housewives looked like glamorous hostesses and products took on a range of colours that emphasised their role as aestheticised lifestyle signs rather than functional tools. Design contributed significantly to this effect. In the area of women's dress, for example, the 'New Look', presented at the Paris fashion show of 1948 and created by the couturier Christian Dior, was widely disseminated by emulation and by representation in the mass media. This overtly feminine, full-skirted, longer length, extravagant image of the ideal female, complete with pinched waist, was highly 'feminine' and was offered to female consumers in an era when they were encouraged to return to the home to become wives and mothers. This was also the era in which the home-based selling of cosmetics and food containers became highly popular. The strategy of getting women to combine their social activities with economic exchange was a subtle one. It served to overcome the isolation of suburban life and to link the idea of consumption, in women's minds, with the concepts of plea-sure, personal beauty and housewifely efficiency.[23] The appearance of many new consumer goods in this period contributed to the image of exaggerated femininity. The overtly feminised pastel colours of items of plastic kitchen equipment – for example, washing-up bowls and drinking beakers – played a part in a new visual landscape encouraging women's sense of 'belonging' in the domestic sphere.

The strong emphasis upon gendered and youth identities in these years did not escape the marketing man, nor the designer, and was to a considerable extent a result of their joint activities. The need to reach ever larger audiences for their products led manufacturers to increase the size of their marketing and design departments to assist them in their decisions about the nature and appearance of their products. Men, women and young people were frequently targeted separately: in the area of radio manufacture, for example, large, table-bound models were offered to men, while lighter, portable models were created for women who needed to carry them to and from the kitchen as they undertook their domestic duties. By the end of the 1950s the minia-ture transistor radio, which teenagers could secrete under their bedclothes, also came into being. Styling decisions were based upon assumptions about gendered consumption patterns, although of course they played a significant role in determining them as well. The 'Detroit' aesthetic of American auto-mobiles, for example, featuring chromed features and complex instrument panels that denoted high performance, was echoed in a range of products aimed at men – from hi-fi equipment to razors. Increasingly designers responded to what they saw as the cultural needs of the marketplace and differentiated their products and images to suit them.

Many developments took place in the field of retailing in these years as well: for example the department store experienced yet another incarnation in the post-war years. While it continued to meet the needs of middle-class consumers, less well-off customers were also welcomed and were encouraged to use credit facilities with which to buy goods. In Britain many retailers put more effort into demonstrating the modern character of their goods, often in collaboration with bodies such as the Council of Industrial Design. Consumers were increasingly introduced to the concept not merely of modern design, but more particularly of 'good design', the visual and material equivalent of what they were encouraged to use when shopping – in other words, 'good taste'. On one level this spirit of design reform, at its strongest since the mid-nineteenth century, can be seen as a response to the rapidly expanded picture of consumption which involved hitherto 'uneducated' sectors of the population. The fear of being overrun by the 'kitsch' or 'bad design', associated with an uncontrolled marketplace that threatened an ordered society, was experienced internationally. In the USA the Museum of Modern Art in New York ran a series of exhibitions entitled 'Good Design', intended to help educate the consumer to be able to make discriminating choices. In Great Britain the Council of Industrial Design involved itself with the mass media in order to promote its message, while in Denmark Den Permanente, that country's design reform body, added a retail outlet to its activities in an effort to educate the public into an understanding of the craft-based 'good design' that had come to signify that country's passage into modernity.[24]

Advertising took on a new face in this context of expanded consumption, with American techniques of persuasion moving rapidly across the Atlantic. American agencies, such as that of J. Walter Thompson, became active in Britain, and several British graphic designers – such as Alan Fletcher, a founder member of the Pentagram design group – spent time in the USA, learning the 'American Way', before setting up their businesses back on British soil. The American industrial designer Raymond Loewy, who maintained one foot in graphic design, set up an offshoot of his company (based in New York) in Paris, thereby introducing his commercially led approach to design into Europe.

The 1960s saw a dramatic shift in the cultural picture of consumption and design that had dominated its evolution in the USA and Europe since 1945. In essence design's strongly gendered nature, and its determination to maintain a link with high culture through modernism, was challenged even more strongly by the growing force of popular, or mass, culture. The result was a widespread crisis of modernist values. In addition, youth took over from gender as the dominant cultural category defined by consumption. With these shifts came the first fundamental revision of modernism and a growing awareness that design's relationship with the culture of consumption and the world of commerce had become its dominant face. As a consequence, many mainstream cultural institutions finally had to come to terms with the implications of this fact, and review the values that underpinned their activities.

Figure 6.3   In her 1960s dress designs – shown here are the 'mini', the 'smock' and 'hot pants' – Mary Quant made women look like pre-pubescent girls, helping to emphasise the link between design and youth that characterised that decade.

Consumer culture and postmodernity

The crisis in modernist design values that occurred in the 1960s initiated a new phase in the relationship between design and culture. Indeed, culture itself was redefined as it was encouraged to embrace different social and cultural group-ings and give them all an equal voice. Within this new definition of culture, design was forced to break with its earlier idealistic links with modernism and embrace a more pragmatic, market-oriented, popular approach. What came to be called 'postmodernism' was predicated upon an inclusive attitude.[25] In the words of the architect Robert Venturi, one of its earliest advocates, 'I prefer "both–and" to "either–or", black and white, and sometimes gray, to black or white.'[26] This was manifested, culturally, in a tendency to ignore the line that had hitherto separated high culture from its popular equivalent; to begin to find ways of bringing 'marginal' voices – those defined by gender, sexuality and race, among other categories – to the centre, and to avoid value judgements based on the criteria of the 'old order'. For some there was a perceived danger that in embracing this all-inclusive definition of culture, all values had been overthrown and that 'anything went'.[27] Indeed many of the theorists of postmodernism saw it as the dominance of fantasy over reality.[28]

By the 1970s it began to look as if the idealistic, politically motivated, univalent, production-oriented concept of design, as it had been defined within modernism, had been replaced by a new emphasis on the concept's long-established role within consumption, in particular within advertising, marketing, branding and identity creation. This was manifested culturally in a number of ways, including the move on the part of a number of radical Italian architectural groups to conceptually oriented work without a material outcome; sub-cultural dress taking its inspiration from the street rather than from the Parisian fashion houses; and the widespread expansion of a popular interest in the past, manifested in the emergence of stylistic revivals and the growth of the heritage industry. The emergence of the 'Craft Revival' – a movement characterised by groups of 'makers' in Europe and the USA who chose to work outside the confines of mass-production industry – also made a significant cultural impact in these years. Where the style or 'language' of popular material culture was concerned, the use of 'vernacular' pinewood replaced the chromed steel, sci-fi-inspired spaces of the 1960s ideal home, and the spiral of stylistic revivals – from Art Nouveau, to Art Deco, to 1950s popular styling – replaced the earlier preoccupation with styles representing the future. The idea of purchasing and collecting objects from the past with a high nostalgia content also acquired a popular following at this time.

This aesthetic response to the growing sense of a popular lack of faith in the future was especially apparent in consumer choices of visual and material artefacts and images. The shift away from the modernist paradigm towards one in which consumers saw modernism as just one of the stylistic options in the marketplace did not mean an end to design, however. Chameleon-like, it was able to transform itself by strengthening its links with consumer culture and by making a virtue of so doing. Because its roots were embedded within the emergence of modern consumer culture it was able to adapt to its changing requirements. Indeed, from one perspective modernism can be seen as an interlude in the history of modern design, a cul-de-sac that interrupted its primary mission to democratise taste and luxury, and to disseminate the concept of modernity to the widest possible audience. By the 1970s, however, that single vision of modernity had been replaced by a notion of 'postmodernity', which was multivalent and complex, in a state of continual flux, and represented by a diverse and pluralistic material culture.

In the shift from modernity to postmodernity the enhanced role of the media inevitably played a key part by dramatically accelerating levels of information dissemination for increasingly large numbers of consumers. While on the one hand increased interaction with the media resulted in a breakdown of traditional modes of social communication, on the other it provided access to a wider range of possible lifestyles to which consumers could aspire in their search for renewed social and individual identities. More than ever before design and designers aligned themselves with the mass media and played a central role within the construction of the numerous lifestyles that were on offer. This new way of communicating with consumers meant that, on one level of the market, design became very closely allied to the processes of marketing and brand creation as the visual appearance of goods, images and spaces increasingly depended on communicating an instant message in which there was a seamless unity between 'look' and 'brand identity'. At the same time the democratisation of design helped create multiple, fragmented markets for designed goods. They included a niche market for goods with 'added value', which depended heavily on the identity of the designer for their distinctiveness. Such was the power of brand selling, however, that designers themselves were increasingly transformed into brands as well and were used to sell goods that required a level of individualisation to make them distinctive. Thus by the 1980s and 90s 'designer jeans' – with the names of Gloria Vanderbilt, Armani, Versace, Calvin Klein and Donna Karan attached to them – had become hybrid garments: standardised and mass-produced, but simultaneously individualised and distinguished from the 'herd' by their designerly associations. This kind of ambiguous message become a commonplace in a world dominated by emotions and instant responses. The German critic of postmodern culture W.F. Haug, among others, was anxious about this phenomenon, about what he described as 'the domination over people that is effected through their fascination with technically produced artificial appearances'.[29] In his view, this represented just one more strategy used by advanced capitalism to exploit people for financial gain.

Through the 1980s and 90s the culture of consumption, with design at its centre, became a dominant cultural, economic and political force affecting many areas of everyday life, from shopping to tourism, embracing a wide range of leisure activities from visiting heritage sites, museums and theme parks to buying branded fashion items. As town centres emulated theme parks, and shopping malls resembled seaside resorts, it became increasingly difficult to separate the 'real' from the 'fantasy' or 'constructed' experience. Within the postmodern experience of the shopping mall, for example, design played a key role determining the spatial shell and all its contents, from the general interior and directional signage to the individual shop interiors and the

Figure 6.4   The Bluewater shopping mall in Kent, designed by Eric Juhne and Associates. In the shopping mall of the 1980s and 90s the designer was responsible for everything, from the architectural frame to the products on sale.

objects, packaging and brands displayed within them.[30] The realisation of the omnipresence and enormous power of the role played by designed material culture inspired much writing within the arena of cultural studies in these years, among them the texts of Jean Baudrillard and Umberto Eco, both writers who sought to understand the nature of the consumer culture which, they felt, increasingly sought to define contemporary society.[31] The significance of consumption within postmodernity was also recognised by many scholars, among them Jean Baudrillard, Pierre Bourdieu, Mike Featherstone and Fredric Jamieson. While not all of them openly acknowledged the existence of the concept of design, their ideas were largely stimulated by its effects.

Through the 1970s, 80s and 90s, the activity of shopping came to the fore as a core postmodern experience. It inspired a body of literature that was forced to acknowledge the important role played by visual and material culture in everyday life. A body of writings relating to the department stores of the late nineteenth and early twentieth centuries was the first to emerge, emphasising shopping as a primarily feminine activity. However, in the 1990s the pendulum began to swing back and a series of books on the subject of masculinity began to appear which acted as a balance to the picture provided by feminist writings. A picture of male consumption also began to emerge.

Frank Mort's study of 1996, for example, focused on the way in which men created their identities through consumption in 1980s Britain. Mort directly addressed the agency of designers in his account, positioning the work of the graphic designer Neville Brody and the fashion stylist Ray Petri alongside that of the journalists Julie Burchill and Robert Elms and of advertisers and marketing professionals. For Mort they all played key roles as creators of identities that were available in the marketplace for young men.[32] This close alignment of design with other cultural and commercial activities served to demonstrate the way in which the gap between them was being continually eroded in the context of consumption, whether mass or niche.

A number of other studies of consumption in this period also discussed design's important role within identity formation. Joanne Entwhistle's essay '"Power dressing" and the construction of the career woman', for example, focused on the work of the fashion designers Ralph Lauren and Donna Karan, showing that it was the mediation of their clothes, and of clothes like them, in television programmes such as *Dallas*, as well as the advice given in books such as John T. Molloy's *Women: Dress for Success*, rather than the clothes per se that rendered them capable of identity creation.[33] Although the physical details of the clothes themselves – their heavily padded shoulders, for example, which gave their wearers a masculine appearance – provided them with a set of potential meanings, it was only in the context of mediation that those meanings became both specific and capable of conferring an unambiguous identity on their wearers. To use a linguistic analogy, words have to be contained in sentences before they acquired fixed meanings. Studies such as these built on the work of Dick Hebdige, written a decade earlier, which had shown that artefacts could be made to contain multiple levels of meaning.

By the 1980s and 90s design had come to be understood as part of a larger process that included the work of advertising and marketing, as well as the role of the mass media (magazines, television, films and so on) more than ever before. In conjunction with them it was able to create specific identities that could be consumed along with designed goods and images. This was not a static process, but one which was perpetually in flux as consumers sought to continually redefine themselves. Once one set of unsatisfied desires was met, they were simply replaced by others. The process built on the socio-economic system that had been described by Thorstein Veblen back at the end of the nineteenth century, but the simple idea of 'trickle down' emulation was now rendered more complicated by the ever-increasingly complex shape of society, the multiplicity of markets, and the multifarious pulls and pushes of influence that characterised the postmodern era.

Social psychologists also began to address the issue of commodity culture and the formation of personal identity in the early 1990s.[34] The assumption

Figure 6.5   With the advent of Sony's little portable tape-cassette, the 'Walkman', the link between the concept of 'design' and that of 'brand' became stronger than ever, and it was difficult to separate them.

made by Peter K. Lunt and Sonia M. Livingstone followed in the wake of those of the anthropologists Mary Douglas and Baron Isherwood, that people needed goods 'for making visible and stable the categories of culture'.[35] It led them to undertake fieldwork in order to discover the particular ways in which people constructed their sociocultural identities through their consumed goods; their findings reinforced the idea that consumption, and the goods and images consumed, played an important role.

Through the 1990s analysts of contemporary culture sought to understand design in the context of other related commercial practices. On one level, as it merged into the umbrella arena of the mass mediation and representation of images and identities, the concept of design itself could be seen to be disappearing as a distinct subject of study. Paul du Gay's work on the Sony Walkman, and Celia Lurie's on Nike trainers, among other studies, positioned the concept of design as a component of branding and defined the material commodity as a manifestation of the process, but only at the margins.[36] Another perspective on the relationship between consumption and design was articulated in the writings of Zygmunt Bauman, who claimed that the expertise acquired by consumers through the art of shopping acted as a compensation for the fact that they had no understanding of the frequently complex technologies that were contained within everyday commodities. 'What is being sold', he explained, 'is not just the direct use value of the product itself, but its symbolic significance as a building-block of a particular cohesive lifestyle – as its indispensable ingredient.'[37] Inasmuch as they created the language of style and desirability that attracted the consumer in the first instance, and provided the basis on which consumption decisions were made, designers, his argument suggested, provided a key interface between the commodity and the consumer.

The concept of the brand took on a new significance in the 1980s and 90s. Although it had been in existence for nearly a century, with early American examples such as those of Kelloggs cornflakes and the Hoover vacuum cleaner, having had long and successful lives, the 1980s saw a revitalisation of the concept on a global scale.[38] It was especially apparent in the areas of clothing and fashion accessories where the logos of manufacturers such as Nike, Reebok, Benetton and Swatch came to stand for the items themselves and the lifestyles they denoted. The idea of the brand had long played an important role in the area of designer fashion and, following the model of Coco Chanel in the 1920s, Giorgio Armani, Ralph Lauren, Calvin Klein, Issey Miyake and others now gave their names to the perfumes and other lifestyle accessories that reinforced their marketing identities. As Naomi Klein explained in her best-selling book of 2001 on the subject of global branding, describing the operations of a new kind of corporation – Microsoft, Tommy Hilfiger and Intel among them – 'What these companies produced primarily were not things ... but *images* of their brands. Their real work lay not in manufacturing but in marketing.'[39]

One of the most successful design-related branding exercises of the late twentieth century was that undertaken by the household electronic goods designer and manufacturer James Dyson. His work was heavily dependent upon the 1930s idea of the cultural potency of product design to suggest advanced and efficient technology, and to create its own, unique selling point and product brand.[40] Dyson took that idea several stages further, however, combining visually desirable material culture artefacts with a very strong

Figure 6.6   Horticulture at Disneyland® Resort, Paris – Sleeping Beauty Castle in Disneyland® Park. The Disneyland phenomenon brought the concept of consumption ever closer to those of leisure and the brand, so that even a day out could be seen as a form of branded consumption.

brand which was synonymous with the notion of 'product design'. Perhaps the most sophisticated of all the branding exercises of the 1990s, however, was that undertaken by the Japanese company Muji, which adopted a 'no name' policy as its mark of distinction and 'good taste'. The strategy involved creating an extra layer of desirability for its products through the creation of the illusion of having removed itself from the commercialism of the marketplace and of turning to the purity of neomodern universalism. It was a sophisticated strategy that cleverly acknowledged the popular anxiety, expressed at its fullest in the 1990s, about conspicuous consumption. Many other manufacturers responded similarly to the widespread fears of 'ecodisaster' and marketed their products under the 'green' label. This covered a multitude of possibilities – those of materials, or product, recycling or of artefacts being made from materials that would not create an imbalance in the world's ecosystem. While much serious and important research went into these areas in the 1990s, and there were signs that design would play an important role in helping governments and manufacturers address these key issues, one immediate result was a new marketing opportunity for companies that allied themselves with current consumer sensibilities as a means of selling their goods.

While perfume, clothing, foodstuffs and products were all branded so were places, especially leisure sites, that were offered for 'consumption' by tourists. This became an increasingly widespread phenomenon in the 1980s and 90s but it had been pioneered by Disneyland, the American theme-park, many decades earlier. The use of Disney's name, applied to what was in effect an elaborate fairground, immediately evoked in the minds of consumers a particular kind of experience, familiar to watchers of Disney cartoons and characterised by charm, magic, humour, fun, childish innocence and pleasure. The brand image was carefully maintained through the realisation, in real space, of the imagined, two-dimensional world. It was both a branding and a design exercise of huge proportions and exerted an enormous influence on design for leisure experiences worldwide.

The Disneyland phenomenon represented the possibility of recreating the 'real' out of the 'imaginary', the material from the merely visual. As such it reversed the usual process of culture formation, which was to create fantasy out of reality. This inversion of what had happened in the past, of the traditional practice of stage sets emulating real spaces and settings, was a key characteristic of postmodernity. It featured in the construction of numerous leisure environments of the late twentieth and early twenty-first centuries, from the casinos of Las Vegas to reconstructions of English country house interiors and the regenerated areas of many cities. Moving as many of these constructed spaces did from the imagined to the real, they were at home in a global setting and did not depend on the specificity of location, except when weather conditions were a precondition of the experience. The advent of the world wide web built on this new, geographical flexibility of experience and enabled huge numbers of people to access a wide range of simulated experiences either in two dimensions or, with the help of multimedia technologies, in 'virtual space'. The opportunities offered to designers to create those experiences were enormous.

Some of the most strikingly designed, and eagerly consumed, experiences of the last three decades of the twentieth century were created by the heritage industry. Both museums and other sites, on both sides of the Atlantic, provided a means of experiencing the past on an unprecedented scale. Like Disneyland, the roots of this phenomenon lay in the mass media, not this time in the child's cartoon but rather in the adult television and film costume drama. The heritage industry was the subject of studies by Robert Hewison, by Patrick Wright, in *On Living in an Old Country*, and more recently by Raphael Samuel, in his first volume of *Theatres of Memory*.[41] All three texts focused on the strong tendency – exhibited especially strongly in Britain, but also in the USA, Europe and the Far East – towards a nostalgic invocation of the past. It was for the most part a romanticised vision, as conveyed for example in the televised version of Evelyn Waugh's *Brideshead Revisited* or, more recently, of John Galsworthy's *The Forsyte Saga*, set in suburban west London. Spurred by the public's delight in such nostalgic offerings, and the need to create a new image of nation as the old industrial infrastructure went into decline, Britain put much effort into recreating the past for the pleasure of a leisure audience. From the refurbishment of the stately home – which had begun in the 1950s through the work of the interior decorator John Fowler, working with the National Trust – to the recreation of industrial centres for the 'tourist gaze', Britain underwent a reconstruction of selected aspects of its past.[42] From the Jorvik Viking Centre in York, opened in 1984, to the Ironbridge Gorge Museum, the refurbishment of Liverpool's Albert Dock and the National Trust's reconstruction of Paul McCartney's and John Lennon's Liverpool childhood homes, Britain set out on a path of memory evocation. This was a long way from the modernist vision of design but it had no less significance for the material culture at the heart of this new experience. Both Hewison and Wright saw this phenomenon as a mark of a nation in decline, and the latter pointed to what he called 'the cultural manipulation [which] pervades British society'.[43] For architects and display designers, however, it represented a new challenge, one that could be realised as a reconstruction of neoclassical housing – as in Quinlan Terry's scheme for Richmond-upon-Thames, which came complete with landscaping and public areas – or as an extension of nature itself, as in the recreation of the terraces above Lake Rotomahana in New Zealand.[44]

The need for designers and architects to utilise their imaginative skills in the creation of 'theatres of memory' such as these represented an important aspect of their cultural role in the last decades of the twentieth century. Exhibition designers, including the firm of Casson/Mann in London, which created new display areas in both the Science Museum and the Victoria and Albert Museum, were in hot demand. The Millennium celebrations also brought work to vast numbers of designers worldwide. The emphasis upon design for experience had come to overshadow many of designers' other roles, thereby linking the design process firmly to the experience of postmodernity. Ultimately the emphasis upon design for experience served to bring about a cultural shift and it quickly became increasingly hard to differentiate between the 'real' and the 'artificial'. The landscapes of Disneyland and Las Vegas permeated the environments of shopping malls and city centres worldwide to the extent that it became impossible for consumers to know whether they were going shopping or out for a leisure trip. The film set and television set entered the everyday environment to the extent that experiences derived from the media became part of everyday life. Umberto Eco's concept of 'hyper-reality' became, for many, the *sine qua non* of everyday life in the postmodern world, and design played a complicit role within it.[45]

Rooted as it was within the early years of mass consumption and moving professionally, as it had done, from advertising and shop window display to the physical manipulation of the product itself and the creation of real and virtual experiences, design was easily assimilated within the consumer culture of postmodernity. Indeed, one could argue that it was the wellspring of postmodernity. Its strategies were intrinsically aligned to its ends and its

Figure 6.7 The Millenium Dome, designed by Richard Rogers and constructed in Greenwich, London, housed a range of designed experiences that, in their creation, encouraged designers to take a different approach from that which was required when working directly with manufacturing industry.

processes were fundamental to it. Whereas within modernism the product had been generated by architecture (Le Corbusier designed his chairs to fit within the spaces of his houses), within postmodernism that process was utterly transformed. Products emanated, as indeed did buildings, from the desires and identity requirements of consumers, or rather from the whims of architects. In Disneyland and the shopping mall, for example, meaning was generated less by the individual components of the environment, which, like the elements of a stage set, lacked individual significance, but rather by the promise of the stimulation of desire or the fulfilment of pleasure.[46] Arguably this could be seen as a reworking of the *Gesamtkunstwerk* that, ironically, had inspired the early modernists to envisage their complete environments.

Within the context of postmodernity the aim of design was to provide a backcloth for experiences, and many of the designers who came to the fore in these years were skilled in the art of display, image-making, spatial design and online interaction. The product and furniture designers – the heroes of modernism – were displaced to a certain extent, surviving only as the creators of high cultural icons with 'added value', which acted as the inheritors of modernism. Only within this elevated level of culture could modernism survive. Through the pages of upmarket lifestyle magazines such as *Wallpaper** and Sunday newspaper supplements it continued to provide the idealistic, aspirational face of the visual and material culture available in the marketplace.

Manufacturers continued to direct their marketing towards niche groups, but increasingly these came to be defined less by geographical identity, class, gender or age, than by taste cultures, lifestyle values and personality types. As brands and experiences took over from individual products, so design became part of everyday experience, from tourism to shopping. Increasingly this became a global phenomenon crossing geographical boundaries. By the end of the twentieth century, as the creators of the visual, material, spatial and experiential environments through which the mass of the population worldwide formulated both their group and individual identities, designers had found a role for themselves that was unassailable.

Chapter 7

TECHNOLOGY AND DESIGN
A new alliance

The materials of abundance

In the years after the Second World War consumer demand continued to set the pace for a new attitude towards material culture, and it was the speed of technological change that made it possible. This was apparent on a number of levels. On the one hand new production technologies, emanating for the most part from the USA, dramatically influenced the way in which industry organised its manufacturing almost on a worldwide basis. Mass production, modified to the tastes and desires of the marketplace, became the common means of ensuring that consumers had large numbers of goods available to them at prices that made them accessible. On the other hand technology joined with design in a hungry pursuit of new materials with which to meet consumers' desire for novelty and industry's demands for ever cheaper means of producing more and more goods. It continued to be the designer's task to ensure that these new materials aquired forms and meanings that were appropriate and desirable.

The period after 1945 saw the beginning of a new phase of industrial expansion in the western world, and a significant move in the direction of the corporate globalism that was to become such a strong feature of late twentieth-century culture. This phase was characterised by the consolidation and expansion of the large-scale American corporations formed in the early century – General Motors, DuPont and General Electric among many others – and their increasing presence in Europe and beyond. The developments that took place in the USA were largely in response to consumer demand and were facilitated by technological breakthroughs, many of which had occurred

Figure 7.1   The Fiat Mirafiori automobile plant in Turin in the 1940s with Fiat 500s and 1100s coming off the production line. Fiat modelled its production methods directly on those of the River Rouge Ford factory in the USA.

during the war years. As an in-house publication explained, the changes made at Dupont, for example, clearly reflected this:

> post-war America had new needs and made new demands. It was to satisfy these that the company now turned its attention. The program included modernizing plants and adding manufacturing facilities to fill expanded markets for pre-war product lines. Also it encompassed facilities to develop new processes and products which had been delayed by the war.[1]

Dupont moved into the development and manufacture of a range of new synthetic fabrics – among them Orlon and Dacron, in addition to the already familiar Nylon, which had been launched back in 1941. Its experience was replicated by many other 'producer-goods' industries including the automobile producers – General Motors, Ford, and Chrysler – as well as the large-scale manufacturers of household goods, among them the Tupperware Corporation and General Electric. Although they were all committed to standardised mass production, their growing orientation towards the consumer was such that they became increasingly design-led in their product decisions and offered the market a huge variety of goods to allow for the greatest possible degree of consumer choice. In 1957 one American furniture manufacturer, for example, offered 'twenty different styles of standard sofas ... eighteen styles of love seats and thirty-nine upholstered chairs'.[2] Inevitably these ranged from traditional to modern, with various shades in between. The fact that several of the companies directing their goods at the open market-place – General Electric, Westinghouse and Chrysler among them – were also contracted to the military gave them a level of economic stability.[3]

The same period saw increasing numbers of American companies establish European subsidiaries, large-scale pre-war European companies flourish, and the emergence of new large-scale manufacturers in Europe. The period from 1945 to 1950 saw a period of energetic industrial reconstruction in those countries that had been worst hit by the war, Germany, Italy and Great Britain among them. Much of the limited production that had been going on during the war years had been focused on the war effort, and the skills of designers had been utilised to military ends. Britain, for example, had employed many of its creative individuals in its Ministry of Information, utilising their graphic and narrative skills within their propaganda campaigns. This put the country in a position of strength with a number of designers ready to apply their newly honed skills in the context of peace.

The industrial reconstruction of Europe in the post-war years was largely made possible by the injection of American funding as part of the Marshall Plan.[4] Conceived less as charity than as a means of creating a trading partner and a defence against the Communist bloc, the Plan poured huge sums of money into Europe to assist in the work needed to restore its ailing industrial infrastructure. Inevitably this financial imperialism had practical and ideological implications. The model of American corporatism dominated the picture leading to the creation of large, mass-production centres that utilised the manufacturing principles established by Henry Ford, and modified by Alfred J. Sloan, earlier in the century. Thus in Italy, for example, companies such as Fiat and Olivetti modelled their factories on American lines, while the American giant corporations in the areas of electrical goods – General Electric and Westinghouse among them – continued to enlarge their European subsidiaries to make local manufacture possible. In Holland the Phillips company emerged, while in Germany the AEG company continued to develop and new corporations, such as Bosch, also went from strength to strength.

The importation of American industrial and corporate models into Europe inevitably affected the way in which design was integrated into manufacturing and the type and nature of the goods that were directed at the expanding market. In the areas of domestic machines and automobiles new production technologies, such as innovative methods of steel pressing, were shared. The result was that the aesthetic of streamlining was transferred to Europe along with the technology that could create it. National cultural variants modified the stylistic imperialism of the USA, however. In Italy, for example, the exuberance of American pressed metal goods embellished with chromed surface detailing was tempered by a softer, less elaborate, more sculptural approach to product design. Battista Pininfarina's car designs for Ferrari, and Marcello Nizzoli's design for a sewing machine – the 'Mirella' – manufactured by the Necchi company, epitomised Italy's sophisticated version of streamform, which had more in common with contemporary sculpture than with bulbous automobiles.[5]

While on one level Europe embraced American funds, support, technology and corporate culture, on another it continued to develop its indigenous, craft-based, small-scale industries in the post-war years. This was especially apparent in Italy, where the manufacture of textiles, furniture, ceramics, glass and metalwork was underpinned by historical, craft roots. During the 1950s and 60s numerous small companies were able to modernise their production while still remaining small-scale, and to introduce design in such as a way as to be able to create 'high cultural' modern goods aimed at an international, niche market that demanded goods with a high 'art' content. This particular kind of cultural production, which combined crafts skills with high technology manufacturing and which put a strong emphasis upon design defined as an extension of 'art', was emulated by many other countries at a later date, Spain and Japan among them. Like Italy they were confronted by the challenge to link one level of their manufacturing industry with design as a means of creating ranges of goods with 'added value' for their most discerning customers.[6] In the 1950s much of Europe's manufacturing was aimed at an American market. This was the case both for French and Italian haute couture and for much of Italy's production of decorative goods – ceramics in partic-ular. An Italian exhibition of 1951, entitled 'Italy at Work', toured a number of American museums in an effort to attract consumers for Italian goods, while a large exhibition of Scandinavian design, motivated by a similar agenda, toured the USA between 1954 and 1957.[7] The European 'art' and 'design' industries filled a gap in the American marketplace, the rest of which was filled with cheap, mass-produced, indigenous ware. Italy's sophisticated 'lux-ury' cars of the 1950s also found an enthusiastic, albeit niche, audience in the USA. For nearly a decade North America remained a key market for these elite goods, thereby enabling Europe – Italy and the Scandinavian countries in particular – to develop high-cultural, high-quality design movements that depended upon manufacturing which was craft-based but which embraced sophisticated production technologies as well. French couture, the most luxurious of all Europe's production, found an outlet in Canada.[8] As a fashion expert, Dora Miller, explained, it was 'as important to the economy of the nation [i.e. France] ... as the automobile industry [was] to the United States'.[9] By the late 1950s Europe had realised the economic potential of its modern decorative and luxury goods in the USA and had organised one level of its production, and the design and distribution associated with it, accordingly. The following decade saw the emergence of a European home market for the same goods, and the need to export to the USA became less urgent. The result was the emergence of a strong modern European design movement with strong centres in Italy (Milan in particular), Sweden, Denmark, Finland and Germany.

While one face of the relationship between technology and design in the years after 1945 related to the exportation of American 'know-how' to Europe in order to facilitate the latter continent's move into lucrative mass production along American lines, and to the development of a North American market for European luxury goods that were manufactured along more traditional, craft-based lines, another related to the continual challenge presented by the emergence of new materials. The war years had seen many advances in this area, especially in the fields of plastics, metals, wood technology and in the bonding together of these of materials. The last two areas – wood technology and bonding – both fed into post-war design in a striking way. In the USA the work of the architect–designer Charles Eames was dependent on both for the new ranges of furniture he created with the Finnish designer Eero Saarinen in the 1940s. During the war years, while working on a commission from the US Navy to produce a series of leg splints, Eames had experimented with moulding laminated wood. With Evans Products of Detroit he went on to create a moulded plywood stretcher. In his book *The American Design Adventure*, Arthur J. Pulos discussed the way in which plywood moved into the area of temporary housing at this time of great need.[10] Eames developed his own experiments, at first with the assistance of Evans Products and subsequently with that of Herman Miller, which reached a peak with the manufacture in 1946 of his laminated wood chair, which had 'shaped veneer laminates attached to a base of welded steel rods by means of rubber shock mounts'.[11] With Saarinen, Eames developed a highly innovative, modern furniture aesthetic that was widely emulated over the next decade in Scandinavia, Britain and Italy.[12] Through the use of the moulding technique furniture could be mass-produced, and the 'new look' furniture quickly moved into the public arena, filling school rooms, halls and lecture theatres.

Plastics also went through a transformation during the war and immediately afterwards. Polythene, PVC and polystyrene, amongst countless other manifestations of this synthetic substance, were added to the already lengthy list of

PLASTICS IN THE HOME

Figure 7.2   Plastics brought about dramatic changes in everyday life. This image – a frontispiece to a book of 1947 entitled *Plastics in the Home* – showed the countless ways in which the new plastics had penetrated the household.

synthetics to have entered everyday life. Diverse cultural responses to these new possibilities were expressed. In Britain, for example, as Claire Catterall explained, there was significant establishment unease about the new material world, which was seen as being 'slick, streamlined and shiny'.[13] In Italy there was more enthusiasm for the design potential offered by these new synthetics, and the late 1950s and early 1960s saw experiments undertaken by leading architect–designers of the day – Vico Magistretti, Marco Zanuso and Joe Colombo among them – with plastic chairs. They exploited the 'non-natural' properties of materials such as ABS by utilising a range of vibrant colours, including bright red, black and white. So strong was Italy's relationship with plastics, seen as materials with a capacity for high-cultural design statements, that several of the designers linked with the 'anti-design' movement of the late 1960s chose to employ a range of 'soft' plastics, polyurethane foam among them, for their artistic statements about the need to move beyond modernism and to incorporate ideas about flexibility and mutability in the designed artefacts that constituted the contemporary material environment.[14]

A number of design historical studies have focused on the effects of new materials and their cultural impact in the post-war years emphasising the role that they played in the construction of a picture of modernity aimed at a large audience. Judy Attfield's 1994 study of the emergence of the tufted carpet in Britain, for example, focused on the way in which an object can be seen as 'a material manifestation of cultural forces' – in this instance, of the reluctance of a conservative industry to embrace change and novelty.[15] Her work highlighted the slow take-up, by the carpet trade, of synthetic tufted carpets in Britain in comparison with the USA, and the continued dependence on carpets made from woven wool, which were considered to be superior products.

Figure 7.3   In the 1960s a number of Italian designers set out to restore the image of plastic products to one which could be aligned with the concept of high culture. The sophisticated products they created included the 'Stadio 80' table and chair shown here, designed by Vico Magistretti and manufactured by Artemide in 1968.

A similar picture of British caution was described by Samantha Pile in her account of the response to latex foam in furniture design. Although, as she explained, it did not 'herald an immediate design revolution' in Great Britain, it was received more enthusiastically in Scandinavia and Italy, which were quick, after the war, to understand the way in which this new form of rubber could create a new aesthetic depicting modern comfort for an audience seeking a new look in its domestic interiors. As Pile pointed out, the ability of latex foam to reduce volume and weight was highly appealing to the Italian designers and manufacturers, who sought a new furniture aesthetic inspired by contemporary abstract sculpture, while the Scandinavians favoured a softer version of domestic modernity.[16]

The complexity of the way in which materials, design, society and culture worked with each other in these years was documented in Alison Clarke's 1999 account of the development of the American polyethylene food containers manufactured by the Tupperware Corporation. The author described the way in which the iconic meaning of this product could not be understood by its design alone, but rather by the way in which its advertising, marketing and distribution helped to construct a place for it within a feminine model of domestic modernity.[17] Thus, in Clarke's words, Tupperware was 'an example of the historical specificity of material culture and the mediation of related social relations and cultural beliefs'.[18] As such its material novelty was only a part of the sociocultural context in which it was made to play a meaningful role. Arguably, inasmuch as it denoted modernity and efficiency, polyethylene's 'newness' was an important component of Tupperware's success, but, as Clarke showed, it was highly dependent on the manufacturer ensuring that although the objects were transformed from rational products to emotional gifts their material meaning was consistent through the whole process from production through to consumption. The aesthetic of the Tupperware container was neutral enough for it to be able to act as an empty vessel, capable of containing all the dreams and aspirations of 1950s American society, especially those of its female, suburban consumers. The same could be said of nylon stockings, which were almost invisible as objects with very few overt aesthetic features. They carried within them, nevertheless, a high level of utopianism. Susannah Handley's *Nylon: The Manmade Fashion Revolution* of 1999, focused on DuPont's successful foray into the manufacture of nylon in the post-war years. Stockings made of this new material brought with them a vision of modernity, defined less, by this date, by rational production than by glamour, to a mass audience of female consumers which had been deprived of this level of self-expression during the Second World War.[19]

The meanings of new materials were highly charged in the post-war years, although their acceptance varied according to the area of material culture

Figure 7.4   The synthetic material nylon had a dramatic impact on the world of clothes. In June/July 1946 the cover of Dupont's house magazine depicted a bride in a nylon dress looking every bit as glamorous as if it had been made of silk.

within which they were utilised. At the mass market level they were most successful when they could be made, through intensive marketing and inventive distribution systems, to appear synonymous with consumer desire and aspiration. Thus nylons, Tupperware food containers and a plethora of other small household goods were embraced by female consumers as messengers of a modernity which was defined by its link with an image of the glamorous and efficient housewife/hostess. Their new forms, defined by mass production

techniques and bright colours, quickly became part of the everyday environment. As they entered into everyday life, however, they became vulnerable to
the gaze of the design reformers and were added to the marginalised world of
material culture defined as 'kitsch'.

On the level of 'good design' new materials had to wait until they could have a
new, modern aesthetic attributed to them by designers. In addition to the Italian
chairs described above, the Kartell company (also Italian) worked with the
designer Gino Colombini to create striking-looking plastic buckets and lemon
squeezers which, by virtue of the way that they were presented as isolated objects
on plinths in stylish magazines such as *Stile Industria*, came to be seen more as art
objects than as banal items of household equipment. This elevation of mundane
goods to a new level of significance was a mark of the impact of designer-culture
in a world in which the relatively low cost of new materials – plastics in particular
– meant that, potentially at least, most people could participate in modernity
through the consumption of modern material culture. Through aesthetic manipulation, the cheapest of goods could be transformed into new modern luxuries,
and the most democratised of materials could become elite.[20]

In Scandinavia stainless steel become the new silver. The Danish architect–
designer Arne Jacobsen used this highly practical modern material for the
items he created as part of his stylish 'Cylinda Line' manufactured by the
Stelton company. Other materials, such as glass, that had traditional craft
roots were also transformed by technology in these years. For example, oven-
to-tableware glass – created in the USA under the brand name of 'Pyrex',
manufactured by Corning and first sold in 1921 – became widespread internationally in the 1950s. Like Tupperware and nylon stockings, Pyrex eventually
found a mass market through its appeal to women but only after a long period
of time, during which the manufacturer had sought endless ways of making it
desirable. Its appearance was given much consideration, and designers were
brought in at several different stages in attempts to make it more appealing to
housewives. However, according to the historian Regina Lee Blaszczyk it
owed its success in the end to a female home economist, Lucy M. Maltby,
who set up an experimental kitchen and managed to persuade housewives of
Pyrex's superior qualities in the kitchen. As a result of her experiments she
redesigned several of the Pyrex products, although she was aiming for
improved performance rather than aesthetic appeal.[21] In her study of the
batch-produced ceramic- and glass-ware created in the USA in the mid-twentieth century and sold to female consumers, Blaszczyk argued that, at this
level of the market, products proved successful less as the result of the intervention of male industrial designers than by the input of a number of significant women who, 'empowered as consumers and linked to producers by
fashion intermediaries … shaped the design of household accessories'.[22]

By 1970 many more new materials and manufacturing techniques had transformed the face of the everyday world, making it a very different one from that of thirty years earlier. They spoke a language of modernist utopianism to an audience that still trusted the power of technology to provide it with a better world, to improve the quality of everyday life, and to empower them as consumers. Inevitably the cultural response to change varied according to the level of investment that different people and classes had in the past. Those with the least invested in it had less to lose. Design played an important role in ensuring that technology, as expressed through material culture, communicated appropriate messages. At different levels of the market, as we have seen, design interfaced differently with technology. Where the mass market was concerned it co-existed alongside all the other activities that were part of the context of production. As the democratisation of material culture developed, however, design, wearing its high-cultural or 'high-brow' hat, sought to put in place a neomodern form of 'added value' into goods made from new materials, formulating a so-called 'authentic' aesthetic for them which removed them from the category of 'kitsch'. By 1970, however, that second wave of modernism, which sought to reinstate a level of 'taste' into the materials of mass production, was also coming under attack, and its alliance with certain new materials – hard plastics and metals in particular – was put under scrutiny.

Technology and lifestyles

The emphasis through the 1970s, 80s and 90s on consumption and consumerism tended to eclipse the important relationship that design continued to have with the worlds of production and technological innovation. The concentration on the concept of 'lifestyle' and on the significance of consumers' relationships with the material and immaterial world of designed goods, brands, leisure environments and other experiences meant that 'meaning' became exclusively linked with the concept of consumption in its broadest sense. Nevertheless, in the years after 1970, advanced technology continued to play a crucial part in the ways in which goods, images and spaces themselves were made or constructed, as well as in their cultural significance.

The 1970s witnessed an enhanced impact of high-technology Japanese consumer goods on western markets. The manufacture of the sophisticated and highly complex electronic products – hi-fi equipment and cameras among them – that emerged from forward-looking companies such as Sony, Sharp, Canon, Toshiba and Hitachi depended upon automated production systems. Not surprisingly, the appearance of these products reflected the 'high-tech' environment in which they had been created. In spite of the fact that they were destined for the living-room their complex control panels and multiple knobs and switches, redolent of the interiors of space shuttles, suggested high performance levels. The degree of technological utopianism represented by these overtly masculine artefacts, coloured black and silver to reflect that stereotypical gendering, was expressed not only by their looks, but also by their multiple and newly defined functionalities. No longer was a watch simply a timepiece: it was also a stopwatch and an alarm clock.

The faith in the power of technology to transform leisure time was expressed in an aesthetic language born of technology itself, seemingly unmodified by a third party but, of course, in reality constructed by industrial designers. It became known as a 'high-tech' aesthetic, which moved beyond the workplace to transform leisure environments and the private sphere. The modish 'high-tech', neomodern aesthetic of the 1970s and 80s, immortalised in a book of the same name penned by the New York-based design writers Joan Kron and Susanne Slesin, characterised not only Japanese electronic consumer goods but also many of the leading architectural constructions of the era, from Renzo Piano's and Richard Roger's Beaubourg Centre to Norman Foster's Hong Kong and Shanghai Bank.[23] It became a self-conscious aesthetic language characterised by the visibility of the structural components and services of the building in question. The London-based furniture designer Ron Arad adopted the same language in a number of his creations from this period, including a design for a shelving system made out of scaffolding clamps. The transference of a language deriving from the workplace and the public sphere into the domestic arena brought technology closer to many people's lives and suggested a reincarnation of the modernist idealism of the mid-twentieth century.

However, this widespread faith in technology's ability to carry society through the politically and economically bleak years of the 1970s and on into the boom period of the 1980s represented, at one level at least, an extension of the early modernists' belief that rationalism and self-determination could function as antidotes to cultural confusion and revisionism. By the 1980s it was evident that the technological 'look' was not a rationally based alternative to conspicuous consumption, but simply another manifestation of it. The complex 'machine aesthetic' of what came to be called 'late modernism' had – in contrast to its simpler, early century equivalent – become just another stylistic option in the aesthetic free-for-all that was postmodernity.

Japan's deep commitment to technology was expressed not only through a visual language of complexity representing the fact that technical knowledge had moved beyond the ability of society to keep up with it, but also through the creation of the new behavioural patterns that it made possible. Nowhere was this more apparent than in the behaviour-transforming effects of Sony's little 'Walkman' – a portable cassette tape player launched on the market in 1982.[24] In use its small components – a tape holder and linked earphones in essence – became technological extensions of the body. The object's miniature size and portability allowed the user a freedom of movement that was not feasible with a room-bound piece of equipment. Such was the impact on the nature of everyday life of this radical piece of technology and design that the activities of music-listening, of walking down an urban street and of sitting on a subway train were transformed beyond recognition.

The combination of advanced technology with advanced consumer culture provided a strong challenge to the designer whose role was to package it in

Figure 7.5   More than any other single high technology object, with the exception perhaps of Sony's 'Walkman', the mobile phone transformed people's behaviour worldwide in a dramatic manner. Its portability was, without doubt, its most radical feature.

such a way that the technology/culture interface was appropriately envisaged. From the 1980s onwards this challenge was presented many times over by a number of new technological 'gadgets' that transformed conventional behaviour patterns in both the private and the public arenas. From the Walkman to the laptop computer, the digital camera, the mobile phone and the portable minidisc player, the worlds of work and leisure were both utterly transformed by people's increasing ability to perform what had been hitherto room-bound activities in the street and in other new environments. With this transformation came a profound shift in the conventional boundaries between work and leisure, as well as between those of the private and the public spheres. What had hitherto been spaces dedicated to certain activities – the domestic hallway for the telephone, the study or office for the typewriter, the living room or bedroom for the hi-hi system – became redundant as they were replaced by a host of alternative possible venues.

Although design played a key role in this process by ensuring that the forms in which technology reached users were both visually and symbolically appropriate and usable, technology undoubtedly called the tune and designers followed, creating attractive boxes for the complex electronics that went in to them. In *Technopoly: The Surrender of Culture to Technology*, published in 1993, Neil Postman expressed his anxiety about the supremacy of technology.[25] Referring back to C.P. Snow's famous lecture of 1959, 'The Two Cultures and the Scientific Revolution', he claimed that, rather than existing in two different spheres, the two cultures that Snow had referred to – the humanities and the sciences – were, rather, fighting for supremacy. 'Once a technology is admitted,' explained Postman, 'it plays out its hand: it does what it is designed to do. Our task is to understand what that design is – that is to say, when we admit a new technology to the culture, we must do so with our eyes wide open.'[26]

In the years after 1970 the warning provided by Postman proved highly relevant given the changing nature of the relationship between technology and design. It sounded a note of caution to a culture which, in its continuous search for novelty, needed to understand the consequences of that search. The challenge to the designer, presented by Postman's fears, was to act as an important bridge between technology and culture, a means, that is, of 'acculturising' the former, such that society could attempt to keep up with its progress and ensure that the 'humanities' were adequately represented. This took a number of forms in the years after 1970. On the simplest level it was manifested in the work undertaken by industrial designers to make machines, such as computers, look desirable and blend into the environments in which they were used. Apple Computer Inc., based in California's Silicon Valley, went the furthest in realising this aim, hiring first the German design consultancy frogdesign, and later the British designer Jonathan Ives, to style their

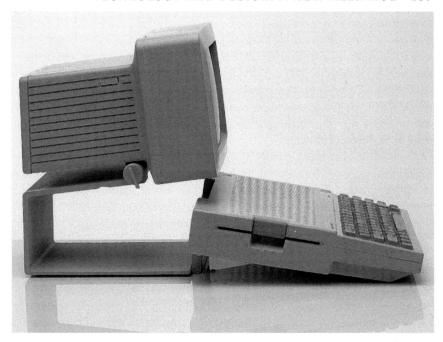

Figure 7.6   Apple Computer Inc.'s 'Snow White' IIc computer designed by frogdesign inc., was launched in 1984. It represented the first attempt to make a computer appear friendly and not like an alien piece of high-tech office machinery.

machines in such a way as to minimise their uncompromising boxiness, and give them an appearance which would appeal to users and which was not overly technology-led. Frogdesign's 'Snow White' IIc model of 1984 was the first attempt to create a small, neat, visually pleasing machine that had a user-friendly appearance.

Given the severe constraints that came with the design brief to create a box to house a computer terminal's inner workings, attention was paid to the points at which a designer could make a contribution: to the radii of curves and to the lines and colour of the body shell. Apple also paid attention to the user-friendly needs of the computer programmes themselves, conscious that the 'feel' of both the object and its performance were of equal importance in helping consumers reach a purchasing decision. The implementation of these principles served to counter the strong technological pull of the machines in question. Later, in the 1990s, Apple pursued this line even further through its collaboration with Ives, which resulted in a series of designs for computers which transformed them into lifestyle objects rather than mere boxes shrouding the technological components of these advanced technological machines.[27] The ability of designers to create easily usable onscreen systems became increasingly important as the computer took away many of the roles hitherto performed by the graphic designer, and CAD (computer-aided design) systems transformed the ways in which many designers – architects and product designers in particular – went about their daily work. Technology also transformed the nature of the images, consumer goods and services that it brought within the reach of the consumers. Designers had to respond to the challenges this offered and redefine their roles and practices in the light of them.

In addition to transforming the design process itself, new methods of manufacturing were introduced in the last decades of the twentieth century, making a greater diversity of goods available in the marketplace. The shift away from Fordist mass production to what David Hounshell called 'flexible mass production', in turn, reinforced the importance of design in ensuring product diversity and the niche marketing that flows from it.[28] As a result of sociocultural change, the democratisation of consumption and the move of manufacturers to large-scale batch production, the concept of the global niche market became increasingly dominant. In order to appeal to their intended consumers, designers ensured that goods had distinctive identities and manufacturers increasingly modified their production systems to be able to produce enough goods with a sufficient level of diversity. Nowhere was this strategy more apparent than in the example of the Swatch Company's watches, which were produced in large numbers, at low prices, but with a huge stylistic variety that was constantly being updated. The Swiss company's new approach was predicated upon technological innovation and virtuosity – Swatches were slimmer than watches had ever been – but also upon a sociocultural transformation in which the watch ceased to be an expensive object bought to last but became, instead, a cheap fashion accessory to be discarded when its style became outdated.

From the 1980s onwards Japan – followed quickly afterwards by Taiwan, Singapore, Indonesia and China – recognised the varied needs of world markets and set out to cater for local and national variations in taste. Where television sets were concerned, for example, discovering that Germany favoured black cabinets while Italy preferred white boxes and Britain wood-effect plastic casings, the Japanese electronics manufacturer Sharp designed and marketed appropriate products for each country. Many Japanese manufacturers automated their production lines and utilised numerically controlled machines to make the necessary variants, which it described as 'many versions in small lots'.[29] At the other end of the market variation was achieved by the continued presence of the system of small-scale flexible manufacturing that could be found in Italy, where traditional craft workshops brought in advanced electronic equipment to help them produce batches of high-quality goods. Describing the nature of what was referred to as 'the Third Italy', the economic historian Charles F. Sabel pinpointed the presence of what he called a 'high technology cottage industry' in that country explaining that, 'Most of the shops and factories ... employ from 5 to 50 workers ... the tools [are] the most advanced numerically controlled equipment of its type; the products, designed in the shop, sophisticated and distinctive enough to capture monopolies in world markets.'[30] In the second half of the twentieth century both Japan and Italy contributed, in different ways, to developments in manufacturing techniques that reinforced the role of design in meeting the needs of niche markets through the creation of distinctive and diverse products.

While technological advances affected the way in which the design profession redefined itself and the methods of manufacture that suited changing global consumption patterns, they also had cultural ramifications which influenced the way in which design was perceived by society at large. In her book *Feminism Confronts Technology* the sociologist Judy Wajcsman argued that 'the traditional conception of technology is heavily weighted against women ... the very definition of technology has a male bias'.[31] One of the effects of the enhanced relationship between technology and design was the increased masculinisation of both the material and the immaterial cultures that accompanied the world of high technology and made it accessible to consumers. This was reinforced by the traditionally small number of women working in the computer and software industries, and by the masculine bias of that culture.

That same gendered picture defined one area of product design that had always had a strong technological orientation, namely automobile styling. Although women were frequently pinpointed as the consumers of cars, through the twentieth century the design and meaning of automobiles was over-ridingly masculine. In the words of Virginia Scharff, 'American popular culture has treated the automobile as a phallic prosthesis, penetrating time and space with a speed and force surpassed only by the prophylactic image of the he-man test pilots pushing the inside of the Envelope'.[32] The traditional exclusion of feminine values from this arena has only recently begun to be addressed, as female designers – such as Anne Asensio, working for Renault and subsequently with General Motors – have begun to adopt a different design approach to automobiles, which is based less of the exterior form of the artefact than on the comfort and functionality of the interior space. It was Asensio, for example, who introduced drinks holders for the back-seat passengers of the Renault Scenic. The gendering of goods with a high-technology content as masculine derives, not surprisingly, from the culture of the workplace. In *Boys and their Toys*, a number of authors examined

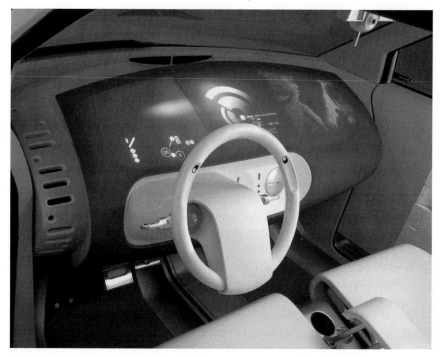

Figure 7.7 The interior of Ford's 24.7 Concept 22 automobile. This little car displayed its association with advanced technologies through its used of modern materials and its inclusion of an internet facility on its dashboard.

the labour situation in different parts of the automotive industry and discovered the existence of an over-riding masculine culture.[33]

While technological innovation led to the manufacture of a host of new goods that infiltrated everyday life in the years after 1970 and brought a particular value system to dominate the culture of everyday life, it also resulted in advances in the development of new materials which, in turn, affected the cultural milieu in which goods were consumed and used. The advances in materials technology that took place in these years were less the result of new discoveries, as they had been early in the twentieth century, but rather the result of the development of new combinations of known materials. So complex were the possibilities of combination, especially in the area of plastics, that by the end of the twentieth century there was an enormous gap between the knowledge and understanding of, on the one hand, materials scientists and, on the other, of the consumers of products made of the new materials. There was little possibility, for example, of users knowing the names of the multiple synthetic materials that made up their running shoes or the ball-point pens that they used on a daily basis. Their understanding of the fabrics used to create their clothing was likely to be just as minimal. By the 1990s the idea of 'smart materials' – which could respond electronically to stimuli from the body – was also being widely discussed in the context of monitoring health and working with the disabled. The gap in knowledge and understanding between makers and users provided yet another opportunity for designers – with their unique bridging, communicating and creative skills – to come to the rescue.

In his influential book of 1986, *The Material of Invention*, Ezio Manzini outlined the way in which the innate flexibility of plastics had led to their becoming highly complex and unknowable. 'The word plastic', he explained, 'covers such a range of options that it tends to lose it meaning.'[34] He demonstrated his point through a caption to an image of a shoe which, he pointed out, combined 'modified polybutylene terephthalate (PBT) with a strip of ethylene-propylene rubber'.[35] The cultural implications of this new level of complexity in the world of materials, much of it being led by research in the arenas of aerospace and the military with spin-offs for the consumer, included a new relationship between object and user such that the latter had to develop an understanding of the former which excluded knowledge of its fabrication process. Inevitably this extended the rupture between production and consumption discussed earlier. While the rift between man and making, which William Morris had so regretted back in the nineteenth century, was not new, it reached a new level of intensity in the late twentieth century. For designers it offered the renewed challenge of providing objects with meanings deriving neither from their production process nor from the materials from which they were fabricated, but relating, rather, to the object in the context of consumption. As the new materials of the early twentieth century – concrete, steel and glass among them – had still been comprehensible, in production terms, to their audience of consumers, and the creed of functionalism had required designers to find visual expressions for the materials with which they were working, this gave designers a level of aesthetic freedom that had been unavailable within modernism. The combination of the loss of this possibility of comprehension; the use of automated production systems; and the emergence of ever-complex electronic, digitalised products, meant that the golden rule of modernism – form follows function – had finally lost all relevance, even metaphorically, and could no longer be implemented meaningfully by designers. In its place was a new opportunity for designers to create objects, services and systems that offered consumers new identities and new meanings which were linked to these identities and which depended more heavily upon the cultural, rather than the technological, context in which they found themselves. It also provided a space for designers to think of new functions for designed artefacts, particularly in the area of physical and social needs.

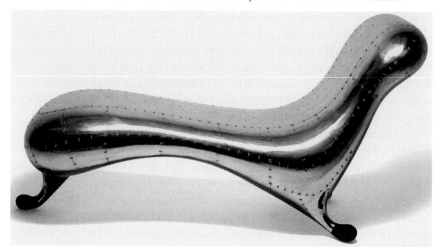

Figure 7.8   Marc Newson's 'Lockheed Lounge' of 1985, which, covered with its riveted sheets of aluminium, recalled an aircraft's fuselage. It succeeds in looking simultaneously both nostalgic and of its time.

By the end of the twentieth century the known modern materials from the early century had become part of history, capable of engendering a level of nostalgia for a period when consumers had a reasonably close relationship with the materials of everyday life. Aluminium, for example, enjoyed a new popularity among designers in the 1990s, its shiny surfaces representing a simple modernity that had been lost. A number of innovative designers turned to this light metal for cultural solutions to the problem of identity loss. Marc Newson's 'Lockheed Lounge', a chair made of riveted pieces of aluminium which recalled the fabrication and aesthetic of early airplanes, was one example of this search for a new simplicity, while Audi's use of aluminium in its TT automobile, launched in 1999, recalled racing models of the 1930s.

While one aspect of materials research focused on the functionalities of new innovations – the need for lightness in sports equipment, of strength and resilience in materials for the automotive industry and of recyclability as part of the sustainability agenda – designers also set out to exploit their aesthetic and symbolic potential. An exhibition held at New York's Museum of Modern Art in the late 1990s entitled 'Mutant Materials' set out to show the results of designers' interactions with the range of new possibilities. It emphasised the importance of the process of providing an interface between users and the world of materials. Writing about the way in which designers were needed to perform that task, and to make culture out of technology, Paolo Antonelli claimed that:

The best contemporary objects are those whose presence expresses history and contemporaneity; those that exude humors of the material culture that generated them, while at the same time speaking a global language; those that carry a memory and an intelligence of the future; those that are like great movies in that they speak a sense of belonging – in the world, in these times of cultural and technical possibilities – while they also manage to transport us to places we have never visited.[36]

In the early twenty-first century the pace of technological innovation and change continues unabated, and both culture and design are running to keep up with it. It involves a constant process of imagining and translating such that the untamed and unarticulated developments of material scientists are transformed into meaningful messages for consumers.

Chapter 8

DESIGNER CULTURE

International designers

As economic, social and technological forces combined to ensure that more and more people were able to define themselves through the consumption of visual and material culture, so the need to provide levels of differentiation within that culture became increasingly imperative. Design was one of the ways in which that differentiation could be ensured, and in the years after 1945 it increasingly sought to separate out two modern worlds – that of modern mass culture and that of a new elite, luxury, 'high' culture defined by its links with the notion of 'good taste'. While the mass market could afford to consume the former it nonetheless increasingly desired, and aspired towards, the latter. The Veblenesque model of 'upward aspiration' did not, however, characterise all of society's relationship with material culture as a variety of different 'taste cultures' emerged, some committed to traditional values and others influenced by the tastes of subcultural groups that had developed their own internal aesthetic codes.

While all manufactured goods, services, images and spaces were designed, only some were understood by consumers as being the direct result of a designer's hand and as possessing the 'added value' that came from that intervention. Through the 1950s the gap between the former and the latter grew as designers' achievements were promoted through advertisements, magazines, exhibitions, television programmes and the work of a growing number of institutions that were briefed to encourage 'good design'. A comparison of two texts, both written by Lesley Jackson, which focused on design in the 1950s and 60s respectively, with another study of material culture from the same period, Thomas Hine's *Populuxe: The Look and Life of America in the '50s and '60s, from Tailfins and TV Dinners to Barbie Dolls and Fallout Shelters*, reinforces the difference between the two levels of designed goods and environments that co-existed at that time.[1] Jackson's books focused on what in an earlier period would have been called the 'decorative arts' – ceramics, fashion, furniture, glass, lighting, metalwork, textiles and wallpaper – and the frequently named designers who were responsible for creating the most innovative forms in an international setting. She stressed the influence of fine art on this level of design, highlighting, for example, sculpture by Henry Moore as source of visual inspiration for designers. The art-historical slant of the books reinforced their emphasis upon the high-cultural achievements of 'designer culture' and its dependence upon fine art as a means of making it distinct from popular culture. Most of the designers selected for discussion by Jackson – from Arne Jacobsen to Tapio Wirkkala to Robin Day – were male European architects and artisans who had moved across to product design. In sharp contrast, Hine's text focused on that anonymous level of American material culture that accompanied everyday life in the same post-war decades. Fewer designers' names were mentioned and he placed his emphasis less upon the decorative arts than on popular interiors, automobiles, domestic machines and public spaces. While equally 'modern' as the one described by Jackson, this latter world did not depend on the names of designers, nor on references to fine art, to validate it. Its meanings were confirmed, rather, in the contexts of consumption and use.

The need for a high-cultural face of design in the post-war years related to the desire on the part of a middle-class sector of society to distinguish itself, through the exercise of educated 'taste' in the act of consumption, from the consumers of mass culture. The consumers of the material culture documented by Hine, however, were more concerned to align themselves with particular lifestyles than with the concept of 'good taste' *per se*. Inevitably, however, as the dynamic created by aspiration and emulation, both upwards and in other directions, moved onwards, the desire for 'designer goods' became increasingly widespread, and the taste-conscious classes had to find another way of developing a body of knowledge with which to distinguish themselves.

In the 1950s designer culture was still finding its international voice. While the well-known American product stylists of the inter-war years – Loewy, Teague and Dreyfuss among them – had become household names through their visibility in the media, this was not yet such a familiar phenomenon in Europe, where product design was still in the hands of architects and artisans for the most part. When designer culture finally found a footing across the Atlantic in the years after 1945, it tended to locate itself at the more traditional, decorative arts end of the design spectrum, rather than with the products of the new industries which had inspired the Americans. However, a new generation of European designers who transformed the look of the home, office and street quickly became increasingly visible as the decade progressed, their faces and names frequently featuring in both specialised and popular household and women's magazines. These were years of great idealism and optimism where design was concerned and designers, with their modernist heritage behind them, were seen as possessing the power to improve the quality of everyday life.

In Italy the specialist magazines, *Domus* and *Stile Industria* in particular, promoted the work of a new generation of architect–designers who turned their attention away from building and towards furniture items and domestic products; in Sweden *Form* magazine performed a similar role within that country's design community, while in Great Britain *Design* magazine, the mouthpiece of the newly formed Council of Industrial Design, brought the names of a new generation of designers to the notice of interested parties in that country. Even the weekly British magazine *Woman* dedicated an article to the home of the married couple Robin and Lucienne Day. The two designers were also the subject of an article published in the *Daily Mail*'s *Ideal Home Yearbook* of 1952–53, written by the Days themselves, in which the couple, photographed in modern domestic bliss, explained how they had created a modern paradise for themselves.[2] One picture showed the office in which the couple worked with drawings carefully positioned on a table and Day's own furniture designs filling the space. It recalled the reconstruction of Raymond Loewy's office, which had been exhibited at the Metropolitan Museum of Modern Art in New York back in 1932, echoing the way in which fine artists were frequently depicted in their studios – a similar attempt was being made to depict designers as creative individuals, surrounded by their own creations in their own working environments. The *Ideal Home Yearbook* was also careful to promote designers as authoritative, high-cultural individuals. Ernest Race's international credibility, for example, was confirmed by a reference to the fact that 'His work has been exhibited in many countries and he was awarded an honourable mention in the International Competition for Low Cost Furniture by the Museum of Modern Art, New York'.[3]

The enhanced level of journalistic and popular interest in design and designers was partly a response to manufacturers' public relations exercises promoting their stables of designers. In Italy and Scandinavia, in particular, small-scale manufacturers named their collaborating designers and marketed their achievements as if they were art objects. As the design writer Ulf Hard af Segerstad explained in his 1961 account of Scandinavian design, 'we must always keep in mind that it is first and foremost the individual designer who

Punch, December 7 1955

When not actively engaged in designing highly individualistic furniture and textiles, ROBIN and LUCIENNE DAY are apt to be entertaining visitors from Europe or America. For this purpose they both agree that SMIRNOFF VODKA, either on its own, well iced, or as a base for long or short drinks, is an offering which is invariably accepted with alacrity.

In two strengths 65.5° and 80° proof, 34/- and 40/- a bottle.

Figure 8.1   The British designers Robin and Lucienne Day, featured together in the 1950s in a strikingly modern interior. Their image as a well-known 'designer couple' was reinforced by their frequent appearance in the media.

created and continues to create the good Scandinavian applied arts'.[4] The text of his book highlighted the work of many designers, including the Danish ceramists Lisa Larsen for Gustavsberg and Axel Salto for the Royal Copenhagen Porcelain Factory; the Finnish glass designer Goran Hongell for Karhula-Iittala; the Swedish glass designer Eric Hoglund for Boda; and the Danish furniture designer Hans Wegner for Johannes Hansen. A list at the back attributed designers' names to manufacturers, showing how some firms employed a number of individuals, while others, such as the Danish furniture manufacturer E. Kold Christensen, worked exclusively with a single designer, in this instance Poul Kjaerholm.

The picture was similar in Italy, where furniture and product manufacturers promoted their designs through the names of a group or a single designer. In the 1950s the furniture manufacturer Cassina abandoned its production of mass-produced, standardised furniture for the Italian navy and moved into the arena of 'designer furniture', firstly through a collaboration with Franco Albini and subsequently with Gio Ponti and Vico Magistretti. This development coincided with a shift from their production of traditional to that of modern furniture, and the realisation that the way forward for many modestly sized Italian furniture firms was the batch-production of high-quality, designer-led, modern furnishings for an international, taste-conscious, elite market. The link with the designer worked in two ways: it insured innovative, modern work but it also allowed the product in question to be sold in the name of 'art'. This was reinforced by developments in the infrastructure of design, which included, in Italy, the continuation of the Triennale exhibitions in Milan (the 1954 exhibition was subtitled 'The Production of Art'); the instigation by the Rinascente department store of an annual design prize – the Compasso d'Oro (the Golden Compass); and the formation in 1956 of the ADI (Association of Industrial Designers).[5] The 1950s saw many important manufacturer/consultant designer partnerships – among them those of Achille Castiglioni with Flos and Brionvega, and of Marco Zanuso with Arflex and Kartell – develop in Italy. The same model was adhered to by the large-scale manufacturer Olivetti. Working extensively with Ettore Sottsass on a consultancy basis, the company understood the benefits of working with an external designer in addition to its in-house employees. While the former provided a high level of innovation and 'cultural capital' for its goods, the latter ensured that the designs could be realised.

A number of American manufacturing companies with a traditional, decorative-arts orientation also developed high cultural design strategies in these years. The Grand Rapids-based Herman Miller furniture firm, which had employed Gilbert Rhode and subsequently George Nelson to advise on its design policy, had been working in this way since the 1930s. Through Nelson a link was established between Herman Miller and the architect Charles Eames. Together they went on to create one of the most well-known of all post-war manufacturer/consultant designer relationships. By the 1950s Eames had established himself as a leading international figure. Like Robin and Lucienne Day a little later in Britain, Charles and his wife Ray represented a modern couple who created for themselves, and lived, a highly desirable modern lifestyle. They even made a film about their house in Santa Monica, which was filled with their own designs and objects they had collected on their travels. The idea of the 'beautiful' couple living in a modern idyll, created by themselves for themselves, provided a role model for others. By

Figure 8.2   The addition of the graphic designer Marcello Nizzoli, whose Lexicon 80 type-writer of 1959 is depicted here, to the Olivetti team mirrored the way in which the American consultant designer of the inter-war years had moved from the world of graphic, to that of product, design.

implication it was an idyll which was accessible to other people through the purchase of an Eames-designed Herman Miller chair.

Pat Kirkham described the way in which Eames was very aware of the power that this reputation afforded him, and suggested that he was reluctant to share it with his wife.[6] Her biographical account of the couple set out to redress that imbalance and to show that, in reality, Ray Eames made a signifi-cant contribution to the couple's achievements. The author pointed out that Charles (who preferred to be called an architect rather than a designer, presumably because there was more tradition behind it and more status attached to it) and Ray Eames were very conscious of their sociocultural role and the significance of the way in which they lived their lives, to the extent that they paid enormous attention to their appearance, preferring to retain a level of artistic bohemianism in their dress, for instance, rather than wearing more conventional clothes. 'They bought or had specially made high-quality clothing,' Kirkham explained, 'chosen … for reasons of utility as well as beauty and never ostentation. In clothes, as in other areas of design, the Eames's were sticklers for detail and quality.'[7] Like Le Corbusier before them – who was always photographed wearing his signature circular glasses – the

Eames understood that the culture of design was greater than the creation of a new chair. It was part of a much bigger sociocultural process of 'adding value', both culturally and commercially, through an injection of creative individualism which distinguished 'designer goods' from the world of mass production.

Eames first exhibited his chairs in New York's Museum of Modern Art (MoMA) in 1940 and again in 1946. In the post-war years, under the curatorship of Edgar Kauffmann Jr, the museum took on a role as an important arbiter of taste, and its seal of high cultural approval became internationally recognised. The British Furniture company Hille, for example, first encountered the work of its long-term collaborator Robin Day at the prestigious New York museum, and many other manufacturers looked to it for guidance. MoMA set out its stall as an authoritative arbiter on the subject of 'good design', which it equated with the concept of 'modern design'. Kaufmann's rhetorical description of the tenets of good design stressed the qualities of 'integrity, clarity and harmony', overtly echoing Le Corbusier's neoclassical approach towards form.[8] Significantly the examples of good design he cited were all chairs, created by early modernists – Marcel Breuer and Le Corbusier among them – as well as by a number of later adherents of the same school of design, including the Scandinavian designers Finn Juhl and Bruno Mathsson and the Americans Charles and George Nelson. Just as Pevsner had created a stable of pioneer modernists back in the mid-1930s, so Kaufmann's work at MoMA established an elite group of second-generation inno- vative designers who would become important internationally. The agenda of MoMA was clear: modernism was alive and well in post-war Scandinavia and the USA, epitomised by the work of individual chair designers. Above all, in the resounding words of Kaufmann, 'Streamlining is not good design'.[9] The USA clearly sought to define its post-war, high-cultural design strategy by emulating Europe, rather than through acknowledging its indigenous, modern industrial design movement, which it considered vulgar by comparison. The spectre of the superiority of European taste still lingered on even at this late date.

As the concept and role of designer culture became increasingly reinforced in both Europe and the USA in the post-war years, so the professional framework for design practice, and the educational system that supported it, became strengthened. The professional status of different designers remained uneven, however, dependent on their backgrounds, the disciplines within which they worked, and the national design strategies which supported them. In Italy, for example, most designers working in the 1950s and 60s had been trained as architects in the rationalist tradition of the 1930s. As a result of the lack of architectural projects and the enthusiasm of the transformed furniture and product manufacturers to work with them in the post-war years, they redefined themselves as designers but, like the American consultants before them, they

Figure 8.3   The Finn Tapio Wirkkala, whose 'Kantarelli' vase of
1946 for Iittala is shown here, represented a Scandinavian designer
whose basis in craft production determined the nature of his output
to a significant extent.

retained the ability to work across a wide range of goods, from chairs to
vacuum cleaners to ashtrays. While the flexibility of the Americans was rooted
in their broad backgrounds in commercial design the breadth of the Italian
designers derived from their training as modernist architects in the inter-war
years, committed to the idea of the *Gesamtkunstwerk*.

Many Scandinavian designers had craft skills which were applied to an
industrial context. As a consequence, many of them maintained a level of
specialisation and restricted themselves to working with a limited number of
materials, whether clay, glass or metal. The American model of consultant
designer also penetrated those countries: the Swede Sixten Sason, for
example, had a background in graphic design and was responsible for, among
other designs, a car for Saab, a vacuum cleaner for Electrolux and a camera
for Hasselblad.[10] In Britain a handful of American-style consultant designers
also emerged in the inter-war years. Douglas Scott worked in Raymond

Loewy's office in the 1930s before he was engaged by London Transport in the 1950s to work on its buses, for instance, while Kenneth Grange, trained in fine art in the early post-war years, was given his first product challenge by Kodak to work on a camera.[11] It was to be some time before the work of either designer was to be openly acknowledged, as the companies presented their products in the marketplace without a designer's name attached to them. On the whole European designers who worked for mass production industries were less visible in these years than their American counterparts.

Interior design, graphic design, fashion design and automotive design all expanded as specialised areas of professional design practice in the post-war years. Rooted within the ideology of modernism, the newly defined interior design profession broke away from the older, pre-modern, discipline of interior decoration, which had been tainted by its links with amateurism, femininity and domesticity, and linked itself more strongly with architecture and the language of modernity. An international community of interior designers – including figures such as Richard Neutra in the USA, Jean Royère in France, Edgar Horstmann in Hamburg, Alfred Altherr in Switzerland and Jaap Penraat in Holland – created a new language of modern interior décor defined by features such as open bookcases, low buffets, suspended lamps, splayed-leg chairs, exposed staircases and textured walls. It appealed to taste-conscious clients who could afford their services.[12] By that period most interior designers were trained first as architects and, in the spirit of the modernist idea of the *Gesamtkunstwerk*, saw the interior as a natural extension of their work.

The idea of using a designer's name to sell a product had originated in the world of high fashion. In the early post-war years the elite fashion design profession, which had based its reputation upon the names of a handful of well-known individuals, was still centred around the couture houses of France and, increasingly, of Italy. Figures such as Christian Dior, Pierre Balmain, Jean Patou and Pierre Lanvin continued to dominate the picture at this end of the market. The inter-war years had also seen the formation of a designer-led sports clothes phenomenon in the USA and, by the late 1950s, the Italian fashion industry had begun to move into a similar arena with companies such as MaxMara targeting a new level of the market. Middle- and mass-market clothing resisted naming its designers, however, and was recognised instead by the name of its manufacturing company. The link between designer culture and luxury goods was thereby maintained.

The maturation of the graphic designer as a specialised professional also occurred in these years. Between the wars the term 'commercial artist' had still been widely used to describe the mostly fine-art-trained individuals who had applied their skills to commerce in a number of ways. After the Second World War, with the expansion of mass travel, new communication technologies, advances in paperback publishing and the growth of corporate identity programmes, the opportunities for work increased exponentially and the term 'graphic designer' came to replace that of the 'commercial artist'. In time this was to give way to yet another term, that of 'visual communicator'. As the new profession defined itself it also adopted a more proactive role in certain contexts, attempting to push rather than simply being pulled by the industries it served, and implementing the lessons learnt through its engagement with the modernist experiment.[13] This was reinforced by the expansion of graphic design education, especially in Germany.

One area of professional design practice concealed the name of its protagonists in favour of those of manufacturing companies until very late in the twentieth century. It even avoided the word 'design'. Automotive 'styling', as it was called to differentiate it from automotive engineering, epitomised that aspect of design practice which, almost exclusively in the USA and to a significant extent in Europe as well, catered increasingly for the mass market in these years. As a result the elite products of carriage-builders, which had commonly traded on the names of their creators, were joined by a vast range of cars which were only known by their branded identities – the combination

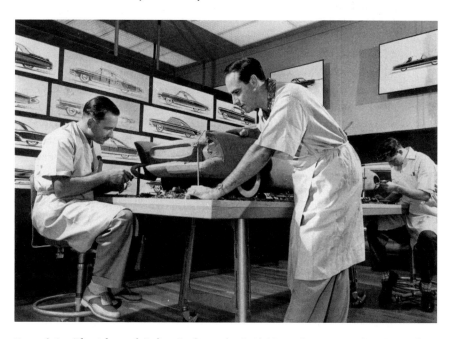

Figure 8.4 The Advanced Styling Studio at the Ford Motor Company in the 1950s. These inhouse 'stylists' worked anonymously on their clay models, hidden under the brand names of their creations.

of evocative, invented labels added to the name of the manufacturer which produced them – the Ford Thunderbird, for example. In this particular industry designers continued to be highly specialised, in-house individuals who worked anonymously as part of a team in emulation of the engineering profession which had made this industry its own.

Alongside the emergence of 'designer culture' as a key international marketing strategy, designers were being redefined professionally and acquiring a wide range of professional identities for themselves. Education played an important role in helping designers define themselves in preparation for their professional lives ahead. For the most part post-war design education – whether at London's Royal College of Art, Germany's Hochschule fur Gestaltung in Ulm, or the USA's Institute of Design in Chicago or Cranbrook Institute, all of which took adopted different models of design pedagogy – rooted itself within the ideology of modernism and encouraged potential designers to see their role as cultural as well as economic. Through the 1950s and 60s designers increasingly positioned themselves as cultural professionals through the organisation of their own associations and events, among them the celebrated Aspen conferences in the USA which provided designers across a range of specialisms with a forum at which they could air their opinions and exchange ideas.[14]

The bubble of designer culture began to burst in the 1950s, however, when Vance Packard and others began to criticise American designers for their role in the process of product obsolescence.[15] However, it wasn't until the late 1960s that, along with dominant political and economic systems, designers became the target of criticism in Europe. Seen as the handmaidens of capitalism and the creators of conspicuous consumption, some designers and architects, particularly in Italy where design debates were at their hottest, were able to divert the attacks by becoming their own critics and by seeking a cultural role outside the commercial system. Teamed up in groups with anonymous names such as 'Gruppo Strum' and 'Gruppo NNNN', they attacked the 'superstar' designers whose primary task had been to create high levels of consumer desire, sell the products of industrial manufacture, and thereby perpetuate the capitalist system.[16] For a while the designer faded into the wings, only to re-emerge in the 1980s.

The new designers

> ... in our consumerist world the designer again rules. Yet this new designer is
> very different from the old[17]

The early post-war years had witnessed the emergence of a second generation of modernist designers whose names entered the public arena, serving to mark out the goods with which they were associated as having a layer of 'added value'. The presence in the mass media of the overtly commercially oriented American industrial designers of the inter-war years had been extended to embrace a new generation of creative individuals whose goals were more clearly high cultural in nature and whose roots lay less within advertising than in architecture, furniture and product design. Thus, in the 1940s and 50s companies such as Herman Miller, Knoll Associates and IBM in the USA; Hille in Britain; Braun in Germany; and Artemide, Kartell, Cassina and a host of others in Italy had promoted their 'upmarket' products through the names of the designers who had worked on them. Design criticism and scholarship followed their lead, documenting the work of the named designers and thereby, in the way that critics and historians of painting and sculpture had done for centuries, reinforcing the value of attributing names to designed goods. The result was to align design more closely with art practice and to give those manufacturers who worked in this way a leading cultural edge. The proliferating design journals of these years focused on the work of the relatively small community of designers whose work was recognised internationally, thereby extending their reputations and those of the companies for which they worked. The cultural recognition of certain designers' work also had an effect commercially. The result of what was essentially a marketing strategy was the creation of a 'taste divide' between those goods which had a designer's name attached to them and those that did not.

In the years from 1970 onwards, in which the values of popular culture showed themselves to be as important in the marketplace as those emanating from a concept of high culture deriving from early century modernism, and following the attacks of Vance Packard and others 'designer culture' had to redefine itself in order to sustain its potency. Most importantly it did not go away, but simply adjusted to the new context in which it found itself. New named designers emerged who embraced postmodernism and championed it in the same way in which an earlier generation had the modernist ideal. The 'cult of personality' remained firmly in place and, indeed, became increasingly powerful as a form of identity formation and cultural communication. Now, however, it functioned with the mass market, the designer taking a place beside film stars and football players. Within the media-dominated, final decades of the twentieth century the 'celebrity' came to the fore as a dominant mass cultural force, extending the potency of the Hollywood 'star system' of the inter-war and immediate post-war years, and the 'pop idol' concept of the 1960s into a new phenomenon which embraced the 'designer'.[18] Inevitably this system was totally dependent upon the media both to form and reinforce it.

As had been the case since the nineteenth century, fashion design led the way. From the 1960s onwards the increased democratisation of fashion, combined with the effects of the Pop revolution that had overturned the dominance of the high-cultural elite group of creators who had previously held sway in the fashion worlds of France and Italy, a growing number of young designers and retailers looked to 'the street' for inspiration and appropriated the subversive styles and idioms they found there. They rapidly transformed them into fashion garments and modified conventional production and dissemination systems to combine catwalk shows with a new structure of retailing and promotion which aligned itself to youth culture. Catherine McDermott's study of 1987 focused on a group of young British design professionals who functioned within this new hybrid context which hovered somewhere between youth culture and the traditional world of the designer.[19] Within this new setting the British fashion designers Vivienne Westward and Katherine Hamnett and the graphic designers Malcolm Garrett and Neville Brody, among others, created a new identity for the designer which was half pop-star, half 'style guru'. Most significantly perhaps they represented a new definition of the designers as media-conscious messengers whose role was to instigate and represent changing cultural codes and, in the process, sell products and services.

In the 1980s this new role for designers as named cultural catalysts visible in the media, and above all conscious of their role within contemporary culture, underpinned the work of the group of designers who worked loosely together under the umbrella of the Memphis experiment, which was led in Italy by Ettore Sottsass from his Milanese base. Perpetuating the tradition of the 1960s radical groups, the Memphis designers used the power of the media to communicate a message about the inadequacy of modernism to continue to meet the cultural needs of contemporary society. A series of small exhibitions in Milan was organised for which the designers in question – some based in Milan and others spread across the globe – created a number of prototype furniture items which, because of the visual shock tactics they employed, they knew would attract a significant amount of attention from the press. The strategy was likened to a fine art performance, although Memphis' message was communicated, not only through reproductions in the mass media, but also through mass replication and emulation as the striking surface patterns developed by its designers were reproduced on a plethora of everyday items, from carrier bags to magazines to advertising brochures. Within this process the concept of the 'designer–star' was exploited, and Ettore Sottsass became the subject of numerous articles and interviews within the specialised and the general press.[20] Sottsass, who had had a long career as a radical designer as well as working for Olivetti, was skilled at 'using' the media to his own ends, in other words as a means of disseminating his radical ideas to the widest possible audience. The model developed by Sottsass and the young designers around him – one which involved acting first and foremost as agents of cultural change through their visibility in the mass media, and secondly as accessories within the commercial exchange of goods to an aspiring market only – became widespread through the 1980s and 90s. It was a model that had first operated within the world of avant-garde fine art practice in the early years of the twentieth century, when figures such as Marcel Duchamp had acquired reputations for transgressing the norms of the cultural status quo. Within the context of postmodernism, however, this strategy arguably ceased to be truly subversive but resulted rather in the appearance of a new stylistic option in the marketplace for consumers who had tired of those currently available.

Figure 8.5   Ettore Sottsass's 'Carlton' bookcase, designed for the Memphis exhibition in Milan of 1981. Sottsass was the first of a new generation of designers who saw design as being capable of acting as a form of cultural criticism.

The programme undertaken by the Italian company Alessi was significant in this context, as it consciously aligned itself with the commercial face of this new manifestation of 'designer culture'. As part of its strategy to move its image forward and become linked in its customers' minds with a cultural programme the company, which had been producing metal table- and kitchen-ware since the early century, invited a number of well-known international post-modern architects and designers – including Aldo Rossi, Michael Graves, Robert Venturi and Charles Jencks – to create a series of 'tea and coffee-landscapes'. The resulting designs were intended for museum and exhibition purposes only, aiming to reinforce Alessi's cultural programme.[21] The project was part of a more extensive campaign, which lasted for many years. It consisted primarily of the production of books and catalogues to accompany its merchandise, enabling the company to reinforce its self-image of being culturally aware. The link with museum culture was a strategic way of blurring the boundaries between culture and commerce such that the goods which Alessi presented in specialist retail outlets resembled museum objects displayed solely for cultural purposes. The shops in which they chose to retail their goods often looked more like art galleries than shops.

The decision by Alessi to engage with designer culture resulted in a number of designed artefacts the iconic and cultural significance of which went way beyond their utilitarian functions, and which came to represent the idea of the 'designer object' at its most extreme. Michael Graves' and Richard Sapper's kettles, for example, took the concept of design to a new level of meaning such that the objects that embodied it could communicate a complex sociocultural message to a wide community of consumers without ever being used to perform their primary utilitarian function – in this case to boil water. These kettles stood for design-awareness and social aspiration as all those participating in their consumption, whether as purchasers or as the recipients of the objects as gifts, were marking their entrance into a middle-class, culturally aware social grouping. The knowledge that these objects had been created by well-known designers, and manufactured by a design-conscious company which only sold its goods through selected retail outlets, was not visible in the object itself but was shared, nonetheless, by all the participants in the process. Most importantly, in Pierre Bourdieu's term, it 'distinguished' those consumers who possessed that knowledge from those who didn't. The fact that the designs themselves demonstrated the narrative and ironic qualities of what had become to be associated with Italian 'radical' design of this era (even though they hadn't been created by Italian designers) undoubtedly added to their desirability.

The sociocultural potency of Alessi's products was also visible in the work of one of the most media-loved designers of the 1980s and 90s, the Frenchman Philippe Starck.[22] It was also extended to the work of a number of other designers

Figure 8.6   Philippe Starck's 'M5107' television set for Saba, designed in 1994. By the mid-1980s Starck had become a 'super-star' designer, adored by the media. His name attached to a product acted as a form of 'added value'.

who came to the fore in the 1990s and whose personalities were almost as important as the forms they bestowed upon products. The London-based designers Ron Arad and Nigel Coates, for example, created objects which performed a similar sociocultural role to that of Alessi's kettles. Several members of this generation of designers earned reputations as *enfants terribles* through the way they dressed and lived their lives, a strategy which served to sustain the myth that they were linked to members of the early twentieth-century modernist avant-garde. At the end of the twentieth century, however, in the context of postmodernism, the main effect was not one of shocking their audiences but rather of visibility in the media and commercial success. What had been originally conceived as radical gestures in a modernist, fine-art context had, within postmodernism, become normalised and absorbed into the status quo in the form of added value in goods offered up for consumption in the marketplace.

The automobile was one of the last areas of modern, mass-produced material culture to enter 'designer culture' and to utilise what had by the 1990s

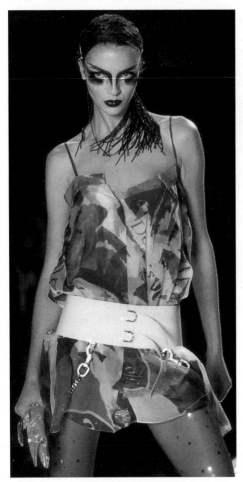

Figure 8.7 John Galliano's dress design for Christian Dior's spring/summer ready-to-wear collection, 2002. Fashion design continued to embrace
the cult of the creative personality as a means of
selling its wares.

become both familiar and effective strategies in a number of other design
areas. Like fashion items, automobiles had long operated within a system of
high stylistic turnover, the annual model change having been introduced in the
1930s. However, unlike fashion design – in which the 'cult of the personality'
epitomised by well-known couturiers from Coco Chanel to Yves Saint
Laurent was highly visible – the names of automotive designers, or 'stylists',

were not in the popular arena. Instead those of the manufacturers – Ford, General Motors, Volkswagen, Fiat, Citroën, Rover and so on – were heavily promoted. As late as the 1980s, only a handful of Italian designers – Battista Pininfarina and Giorgetto Guigiaro among them – who worked in a tradition that was still linked to the individualistic craft-based world of Italian coachbuilding, had achieved public notoriety. In the USA, Germany, Britain, Japan and elsewhere, however, the names of car designers were known only to a very small community.[23]

In the late 1990s that situation changed dramatically, and car designers began to become public property for the first time, appearing in both television and magazine commercials promoting their creations. Peter Schreyer of Audi was one of the first to show his face. This new emphasis coincided with a new marketing focus on the image and identity of cars which, as their technology ceased to be their main attraction, and more women entered the marketplace, increasingly became their key selling point. Mass-produced cars became cultural commodities first and foremost as never before.[24] With this new context the image of the car designer shifted significantly and values that had hitherto been restricted to Alessi kettles and Philippe Starck fruit-juicers were extended to that most ubiquitous of designed artefacts, the motor car. As Ford's head of design, J. Mays – responsible for bringing back and updating the famous 'Thunderbird' model – explained, the task of the automobile designer in the year 2002 was to 'tell stories'. The concept of narrative had finally entered that high-tech object par excellence.[25]

The identification of designers with artefacts gradually came into operation across an increasingly wide spectrum, with traditional decorative objects at one end (Alessi kettles) and new, high-technology goods at the other (Mays' 'Thunderbird'). Even computers and vacuum cleaners became designer goods as the visibility of Jonathan Ives, the creator of the popular iMac computer, in the design press, and James Dyson's growing reputation as a designer of radically different vacuum cleaners – the word 'Dyson' gradually replacing that of 'Hoover' – increased. As cars and products became integrated into designer culture, fashion, the design area that had pioneered the concept of the signature-designer, began to move in a new direction. As mass producers became increasingly efficient at translating catwalk designs into items for the high street, and making them available before the fashion houses could do so themselves, designer fashion lost its appeal to a significant extent, becoming the preserve of a rarefied few. With this crisis came an increasing lack of interest in couture and a new interest in mass fashion. 'Branded' designer fashion became increasingly popular, and labels such as 'Calvin Klein', 'Gucci' and 'Versace' reached new levels of desirability among youth markets. This mass-manufactured, brand-name, designer culture was quick to invade the high street. Moving rapidly beyond clothing, it embraced accessories and perfumes as well creating 'lifestyle' scenarios that appealed to a market in search of new identities. Within this phenomenon the word 'designer' took on a new significance, such that the use of a term such as 'designer jeans' was sufficient to stimulate desire. Based upon a fundamental contradiction implying that people could both belong to a group and be an individual at the same time, the term 'designer' suggested a world of craftsmanship and luxury that was far removed from the reality of mechanised mass production and media-led mass consumption.

Designer culture became completely integrated within 1990s mass-consumer culture, with key designers' names carrying the same level of significance as those of film and TV celebrities. It operated simultaneously within a limited marketplace, which differentiated itself from the mass market immediately below it through association with certain named goods only accessible to one 'taste culture' (this group included designers themselves, who constituted a sizable market by this date), and on the level of designer brands within a wider mass market. Only the designer names were different. Its dynamics were such that names initially familiar and acceptable only to the restricted group moved, within a short space of time, into the wider community of aspiring consumers. The result was the creation of a constantly shifting picture, which allowed new names to enter the frame on continual basis. The art schools provided a flow of new designers as they graduated from their studies, and cultural institutions and media – including, in Britain, London's Design Museum, the specialist design press and Sunday newspaper supplements – helped to disseminate the work and reputations of a constant flow of new names. The cultural capital that designers' names brought with them kept not only the economy but also the sociocultural system in operation. By helping to create constantly new patterns of desire, it fuelled consumption.

While designer culture served to create an illusion of creative individualism within the mass market through the emphasis upon a name, many other designers worked anonymously, outside the 'star system'. Through the 1980s and 90s there was an increasing need for designers to work in a number of new commercial areas, including branding, corporate identity, software, computer games, multimedia, web pages, art direction, exhibitions and events, and lifestyle marketing, within which the input of the individual was considered less important than team work and interdisciplinarity. A number of large interdisciplinary design companies – like IDEO, frogdesign and Imagination – encouraged designers to think flexibly as part of a team. The idea of design work resulting in a 'design icon' only existed at one end of what was an increasingly large spectrum.[26] In this new context the dominance of the architect/artisan was displaced to a significant extent by a generation of young designers who emerged from the ever-expanding arena of graphic and communications design and openly embraced the new opportunities on offer. In this area the individual designer tended to be subsumed by the group. In Britain, as Guy Julier explained, after the recession of the early 1990s

> design consultants would offer an increasing range of services: this meant, for instance, that graphics specialists would offer more three-dimensional orientated facilities such as exhibition stand design, while product designers would diversify to graphic design. Furthermore, some consultancies began to offer other strategic services, carrying out, for instance, design audits of companies, assessing their product and market. Indeed, many of the more prominent design consultancies dropped the word 'design' from their name altogether or added the word 'strategy'.[27]

Thus, as the public became increasingly aware of a cultural concept called 'design', visible in the context of consumption, large numbers of professional designers began to transform their practices and move into new areas of work that were less visible to the general public. The 'added value' they offered was directed less at the consumer in the first instance but and more at the companies, offering them new levels of imagination, increased efficiency and enhanced profits. As their ties with manufacturing decreased, so designers' associations with the world of business grew apace. The disparity that began to appear between 'design' as a form of added value in the marketplace, and

Figure 8.8 A chess set created by the Ingeni design team. This multidisciplinary group of designers, formed in 2002 and based in London's Soho, was put together to work on new models for Ford's eight brands as well a range of sympathetic non-auto products.

as an expanding professional activity within the new communications and leisure-related industries, was reflected in the direction in which design education moved in the last years of the twentieth, and the first years of the twenty-first, centuries. Increasingly boundaries between traditional design specialisms began to be broken down and efforts were made to bring the different design disciplines together.

Designer culture, a hangover from the work of the pioneer American consultant designers of the 1930s, was being replaced by 'experience-culture', within which designers played an even more important role. Although designer culture still filled the pages of mass circulation magazines, and was represented in television adverts promoting a wide range of goods and services, by the early twenty-first century its potency was wearing thin. The language of modernity and the notion of creative individualism, which had been inherited from the era of early modernism and was still going strong eight decades later, remained a powerful way of selling goods, but the culture it represented had a tired look to it even in those areas where it had not been visible before, such as automobiles. Partly as a result of its appropriation by large mass-market retail organisations such as IKEA, the message of design had been diluted, and there was a sense that consumer 'desire' needed to be reinvigorated in new ways.

Chapter 9

POSTMODERNISM AND DESIGN

Modern design in crisis

> Pure function does not eliminate the need for stylistic choice ... A neglect of the vital connection between form and expression is traditional.[1]

From the moment in the early twentieth century when the Viennese architect–designer Adolf Loos proclaimed that 'ornament' should be equated with 'crime', an essentially rationalist approach to modern design began to dominate all other ways of thinking about it. Not only did this view give rise to a highly reductive philosophy of design practice, summed up by the oft-repeated maxim 'form follows function', it also brought with it a minimal aesthetic for designed artefacts characterised by geometric forms, undecorated surfaces and a restricted use of colour. The underlying intention of the modernist architects and designers was both to reject the status-ridden definition of design that had dominated the world of Victorian material culture and to align it with the efficiency culture of mass-production industry, which aimed to continually maximise its outputs and increase profitability. The rationalism that underpinned modernism had its roots in eighteenth-century Enlightenment ideas, which were based on a belief in the power of reason to facilitate social progress.

By the inter-war years, however, there were signs that another model of design was jostling for attention, one that looked to the 'irrational' values of the marketplace and the emotion-laden world of consumption. This was partly the inevitable result of the impossibility of applying the rational, essentially craft-based, philosophy of 'form follows function', which was embraced by educators at the Bauhaus and elsewhere, to the complex consumer artefacts emerging from the new industries – vacuum cleaners, radios and automobiles among them. Rather than revealing their inner structures and basic functions, the seductively simple body-casings of these consumer machines concealed their complex inner workings, thereby explicitly denying the rules of functionalism and positing an alternative definition of modern design based more on 'illusion' than on 'truth'. With the advent of the industrial designer in the inter-war years, the design orthodoxy that had been established by modernist architects was replaced by a more pragmatic approach supporting the creation of simple body-casings for complex products which, in spite of the their creators' claims to be following the high-minded principles of Le Corbusier and others, essentially disguised their functional components.[2] Ironically the real 'machine aesthetic' of these years contradicted the machine-inspired design principles of the early modernists.

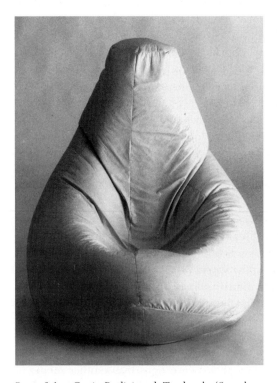

Figure 9.1   Gatti, Paolini and Teodoro's 'Sacco' seat, designed for the Italian manufacturer Zanotta in 1970, which was filled with thousands of small polyurethane balls, epitomised the kind of flexible and formless objects that challenged the static formalism of modernist designs.

In his 1955 essay 'A Throw-away Aesthetic', the design critic Reyner Banham compared a Bugatti Royale Type 41 with a Buick, pointing out that such complex objects defied the simple formula of 'form follows function', and demonstrated that there was no intrinsic link between geometric simplicity and function. 'We live', he explained, 'in a throw-away economy, a culture in which the most fundamental classification of our ideas and worldly possessions is in terms of their relative expendability'.[3] The illusion of 'objectivity' residing in Platonic aesthetics, he went on to argue, had badly misled designers, the concept of objectivity underpinning laws of mechanical engineering did not translate directly to aesthetic laws, and the concept of standardisation had been misunderstood in being equated with an ideal rather than, as in engineering, with a momentary norm.

Banham's words were among the first to acknowledge the dramatic gap that existed between the ideals of the modernists and the realities of design as it operated in the commercial world. Back in the 1940s other commentators, Edgar Kauffmann Jr among them, had realised that, in the same way that jazz had replaced classical music in the popular imagination, popular design values had usurped the place of modernism in the marketplace, but that there had been little recognition of that significant paradigm shift.[4] Banham had opened the lid of a box that had been firmly sealed for several decades. His words were part of a bigger maelstrom, however, created by a number of individuals associated with the worlds of fine art, architecture and design, who came together in the early 1950s to articulate their shared belief that modernism needed to be looked at again in the light of new and exciting ideas and values that had come to the fore through the joint influences of advanced technology and popular culture.

The Independent Group consisted of a number of people linked to the Institute of Contemporary Arts in London through the early 1950s, which included among its members the artists Richard Hamilton and Eduardo Paolozzi, the photographer Nigel Henderson, the art critic Lawrence Alloway and the architectural and design critic Reyner Banham. They set out to debate and document the impact of new technologies and popular culture upon the arts in general. The historians Nigel Whiteley and Anne Massey have both acknowledged the Group's important role in recognising the limitations of modernist thinking and their pioneering work in providing an intellectual basis for understanding design in the years following the Second World War.[5] In essence the Independent Group had wanted to explore the ways in which the notions of ephemerality, popular appeal and desire had redefined the meaning of designed objects. It had also aimed to develop new ways of evaluating the results of cultural practices that resisted modernist reductivism and the rules of 'good taste'. Among the disciplines called upon to help in the task

Figure 9.2   Eduardo Paolozzi's *Dr. Pepper* collage of 1948. Paolozzi
juxtaposed image and icons from the mass media in his search for
an aesthetic that would push beyond the limits of modernism.

of developing a new evaluative methodology was anthropology, useful
because it did not impose a hierarchy upon cultural practices but aimed,
rather, to understand them in context. In his article in *Architectural Review*
entitled 'The Expendable Icon', the Independent Group member John
McCale attempted a value-free analysis of contemporary popular culture
along these lines.[6]

Attempts to define design in an early 'postmodern' context were also
emerging from other countries. In France, for example, the cultural critic

Roland Barthes combined the anthropological ideas of Claude Lévi-Strauss with the semiological work of Ferdinand de Saussure to develop an analytical model for a discussion of such popular cultural manifestations as 'Greta Garbo's face', 'Steak and Chips', and 'The Romans in Films'. The broad picture of contemporary popular culture that he both painted and analysed also embraced material culture in the form of the Citroën DS car and plastic products, both of which he claimed to be potent messengers of contemporary life. For Barthes the Citroën was 'the exact equivalent of the great Gothic cathedrals ... the supreme creation of an era, conceived with passion by unknown artists, and consumed in image if not in usage by a whole population', while plastic represented the 'abolition of a hierarchy of substances'.[7] His emphasis upon the object in the context of consumption, and his interest in the 'image' of the object rather than its 'use', represented an important new direction for material culture studies at that time. Barthes' approach was formulated at a moment when the impact of the mass media on popular culture, including designed artefacts and images, was only just being fully understood. Although designers, it could be argued, had always tacitly understood the significance of the image, the critical rhetoric that had accompanied their work since the early years of the twentieth century had sought to equate their achievements with those of the architect and the engineer and had neither recognised nor acknowledged their skills as image creators and manipulators in the context of the marketplace.

The linguistic underpinning of Barthes' work rapidly became a feature of a more general approach to the analysis of designed artefacts. Through the 1950s several other writers, among them Gillo Dorfles and Abraham Moles, also employed a semiotic approach with which to discuss the meaning of objects, especially ones which did not confirm to the conventional notion of 'good taste'.[8] In Germany teachers at the newly established Hochschule für Gestaltung at Ulm, among them the Argentinian Tomas Maldonado, also sought to develop a linguistic approach to design analysis. The crisis of the theoretical underpinnings of modernism became increasingly apparent as the 1950s progressed and was expressed in a number of different quarters. In the USA, the home of so many of the popular cultural artefacts and images that had inspired the members of the Independent Group, writers also focused upon the cultural shifts that were taking place. David Riesman, for example, noted the changing significance of the individual in the face of the masses, now defined as a set of markets. Objects, he and others explained, were being redefined as images for a society which was increasingly defined by the process of mass consumption. In *The Image*, written in 1961, the writer Daniel J. Boorstin expressed his dismay at this overwhelming tendency, explaining that tempted, like no other generation before us, to believe that we can fabricate our experience – our news, our celebrities, our adventures and our art forms – we finally believe we can make the very yardstick by which all these are to be measured. That we can make our very ideals. This is the climax of our extravagant expectations. It is expressed in a universal shift in our American way of speaking; from talk about 'ideals' to talk about 'images'.[9]

His book pinpointed a significant moment in American mass culture in which, according to Boorstin, the American people had created an image of itself through its high, albeit unrealistic expectations of, for example, 'compact cars which are spacious, luxurious cars which are economical'.[10] What Boorstin did not explain is that these expectations had been partly constructed by advertisers in collaboration with designers, encouraged in their efforts by consumers and their unquenchable desire for goods with which to express their new-found identities and aspirations.

Such was the power of the mass market in the 1950s that it could not be ignored by cultural theorists. The result was the death, or at the least the dramatic transformation, of modernism, and a reduction in the potency of its accompanying rhetoric. Stylistically, of course, modernist design remained one of the options available in the marketplace, but its hegemony was destroyed. The idea that 'good design' – the term that had come to denote that branch of design which was rooted within modernist thought – was in crisis dominated the work of numerous design critics and cultural theorists through the 1950s and 60s. They located the cause of the crisis in the influence of American culture in Britain and in Western Europe. The 'spectre of Americanisation' was manifested in a variety of cultural forms – from food to music to literature to architecture to advertising to designed mass-produced consumer goods. As Peter Masson and Andrew Thorburn explained, 'the years following the Second World War saw an enormously expanded American influence in Europe in terms of economic aid, business concessions, political influence and numbers of personnel'.[11] This new form of 'imperialism' contained a strong cultural component, and it quickly became apparent that the marketing-led approach to design, the consultant design profession, and the stylistic idiom of streamlining had moved across the Atlantic. Although inevitable modifications were made according to local tendencies – streamlining, as we have seen, took on a strongly sculptural quality in Italy for example – America's presence influenced the material culture of post-war Europe, especially on the popular level. Dick Hebdige also described the extent to which British writers and cultural critics – among them George Orwell, Richard Hoggart and Raymond Williams – were suspicious of this

Figure 9.3   Paul Clark's design for a mug from the mid-1960s. The addition of a strong decorative motif on to the surface of a product enhanced the essential 'Pop' strategy of making a strong visual impact, which was not necessarily sustained.

cultural influence, which they saw as a 'levelling down'. As he explained, 'whenever anything remotely "American" was sighted, it tended to be read at least by those working in the context of education or professional cultural criticism as the beginning of the end'.[12]

Although the resistance to Americanisation temporarily prolonged the belief at establishment level in modernism and the concept of 'good design', in Britain a new generation sought new values in their material goods. What has come to be called the 'Pop' movement in design was a spontaneous outburst of expendable forms and materials, bright colours and provocative decoration. It represented a commitment to pleasure and instantaneity. As such it resisted theorisation and remained closely linked to the laws of the marketplace, determined as it was by consumer preference rather than by ideological beliefs. Focused specifically at and largely created by youth, it sought to represent the values of a generation which had not known war-time austerity and which had more expendable income than its parents to spend on clothes, music and other lifestyle accessories. Only a few people attempted to describe it, among them the journalist Corin Hughes-Stanton, who wrote in the mouthpiece of the bewildered Design Council's *Design* magazine that 'it has cheerfully embraced Pop, Op and Surrealist Fine Art, Cottage pinewood furniture, Buckminster Fullerism, amusement arcades, hot dog stands and Archigram'.[13] Reluctantly the chairman of the Design Council, Paul Reilly, also had to admit that Pop design had won the day, and that the language traditionally used to describe design was going to have to be transformed.[14] Although on one level Pop design was a commercially oriented phenomenon which influenced transient lifestyle goods – fashion items, posters and other items of graphic ephemera, and shopfronts in particular – and which failed, with a few notable exceptions, to penetrate the more durable worlds of product design and architecture, its long-term cultural impact was far from trivial. Pop served to break apart what had been seen, within modernism, as the inseparable concepts of form and function, and to demonstrate the possibility that form, or rather image, and expression could, in the context of consumption, be closely linked instead. This seemingly light-hearted design movement served, in fact, as a model for what later came to be known as postmodernist design.

The aesthetic and cultural significance of Pop were strongly felt in Italy in the late 1960s and early 1970s, where groups of radical architects self-consciously adopted many of the spontaneous strategies of the British Pop designers. The Italian groups Archizoom, Superstudio, Gruppo Strum and others stepped sideways from the marketplace in order to demonstrate that design could become its own cultural critic, and that it could ally itself with the political context of the era by helping to break down the bourgeois consumerist ethic which, in turn, had been strongly allied with the Italian modernist design movement of the 1950s and early 60s. The work these groups showed in galleries and at events in the late 1960s acted as cultural irritants and, unlike its somewhat politically naïve British Pop design equivalents, sought to introduce a debate about design in Italy that had wide sociocultural and political ramifications. The work of the Italian designer Ettore Sottsass, undertaken both for Olivetti and on a more individual basis, operated in a similar way. It also employed strategies borrowed from Pop designers – bright colours, strong imagery and transient forms – to achieve its radical ambitions.[15]

The most significant piece of theoretical work of the 1960s to articulate the crisis of modern design was written by the American architect Robert Venturi and entitled *Complexity and Contradiction in Architecture*.[16] It represented the first attempt to provide a theoretical framework for the shift in architectural and design values that had emanated from the impact of popular culture from the 1950s onwards. Modernism had been culturally challenged, not by an articulated counter-theory but by an erosion of its values by the reality of design as it functioned in the marketplace. Theory was, in effect, running to catch up with practice. Some brave attempts were made to renew the impetus of modernism in the post-war years. Germany's Hochschule für Gestaltung at Ulm, as well as the German manufacturer of audio equipment, Braun, tried to revive pre-war rationalism, while the new design movement that emerged in Italy in the 1940s and 50s had a strong element of neomodernist idealism built into it.[17] By the 1960s, however, the power of the market, and of the mass-cultural values embedded within it, ensured that these manifestations of pre-war thinking had lost their rhetorical potency, except as markers of national identity and modernisation. They had lost the power to be messengers of international ideological modernism and had became transformed, instead, into stylish statements, containing a high level of cultural capital, in a world in which consumer choice had become more powerful than design idealism. In response to this market reality, and the new energy that was seen to flow from the material culture emanating from it, critics and designers moved forward in the 1970s and 80s to embrace a range of new ideas that responded to the 'condition of postmodernity'.

Postmodern design

> I have read that under the name of postmodernism, architects are getting rid of the Bauhaus project, throwing out the baby of experimentation with the bath-water of functionalism.[18]

The 1970s and 80s saw the emergence of a body of theoretical writings, emanating from a number of different disciplines, which converged through their shared concern with the concepts of 'postmodernity' and 'postmodernism'.[19] Their roots lay in the cultural shift that had resulted from the growing influence of mass culture on everyday life and the growing disillusionment with modernism. The 1950s had seen modernism dominating the value systems of key cultural institutions which embraced universality, rationality, an aesthetic minimalism and a commitment to the concept of modernity and progress. Where material culture was concerned this had meant an emphasis on 'good design' accompanied by a resistance, amongst the cultural elite, to the effects of the mass media and mass culture.

What has been called, by Jürgen Habermas, the 'project of modernity' was described by many of the theorists of postmodernism as having been initiated in the eighteenth century, the period of the Enlightenment, and as having lasted up until the late 1960s. They saw the uprisings of 1968 as a cultural watershed after which modernism was unable to regain its position of authority.[20] Many of the theorists regretted the end of this era of progress and experimentation and saw postmodernism as a moment when the grand ideals of the past had been abandoned. Positioning themselves within modernism, albeit at its end, they saw postmodernism as a condition in which consumption and the rules of the marketplace held sway and in which old ideas about value had become redundant. Certain writers, feminists among them, were more optimistic, however, and saw within postmodernism an opportunity for what had long been perceived as the 'other' to gain a level of credibility and authority. The sociologist Janet Wolff, for example, welcomed its 'destabilizing effects', explaining that 'the radical task of postmodernism is to deconstruct apparent truths, to dismantle dominant ideas and cultural forms, and to engage in the guerrilla tactics of undermining closed and hegemonic systems of thought'.[21] Andreas Huyssen also saw it as an opportunity for a new space for the 'other', defined by him as wearing a feminine face, to be culturally represented.[22] By extension postmodernism had the potential, many theorists believed, to embrace cultural diversity and make culture available to groups that had previously been excluded from it. The key debate centred on the issue of whether or not the culture (or cultures) in question was worth having. A market-based definition of design was, it could be argued, one of the many faces of the 'other' that was liberated by the crisis of values that rejected 'good design'.

In spite of their anxieties about this new cultural moment the writers in question all recognised the presence of what has been described as a new 'structure of feeling'.[23] At its most simple this related to the emergence of a pluralistic culture which no longer recognised absolute truths but which sought, instead, to embrace a set of 'truths'. The question of value lay at the heart of the debates about postmodernism and a strong fear was expressed that relativism would rule the day and that value judgements would not longer be possible. The most optimistic of the supporters of postmodernism claimed not to want to cease to make value judgments but rather to open up the old rules that eliminated the possibility of different kinds of cultural manifestations being valued equally, albeit according to differing sets of criteria. No longer, they suggested, should one speak about 'good design' but rather about 'appropriate design'.

Nowhere was this debate more relevant than in discussions relating to the sensitive issue of 'taste'. A strict division between what was considered 'tasteful' as opposed to 'tasteless' (or 'kitsch') had long served to maintain class and gender differences within western societies. The idea that all tastes could be considered equally valid, although different, had been anathema to the theorists of the Frankfurt school – Theodor Adorno among them – who had repudiated the idea that mass culture brought new, equally valid, values to the fore: their ideas continued to underpin those of many of the postmodern theorists, Frederic Jameson among them.[24] Work emerging within the social sciences, anthropology in particular, began to consider the concept of taste from a new perspective – one, that is, which analysed it in objective, sociocultural terms rather then judging it. Pierre Bourdieu's publication of 1979, *Distinction: A Social Critique of the Judgment of Taste*,[25] opened up a new discussion about taste, defined as a product of education and a formative factor in class determination.

Postmodernism prioritised the consumption of goods, services, spaces and images over their production. Reversing the modernists' distrust of consumption – which, they had felt, had tended to prioritise the 'irrational' over the 'rational' – the postmodernists looked to it as an arena in which meaning was constructed. This gave rise to an extensive body of theoretical work, emanating once again from a variety of academic disciplines, including anthropology, sociology, psychology, literary criticism, art and design history and cultural geography, and building on other work by theorists such as Thorstein Veblen and George Simmel, to find appropriate analytical tools with which to study consumption. Mary Douglas and Baron Isherwood led the way with the *The World of Goods*, in which they set out to supplement the ideas of economists in this arena, and to explain that consumption was one of the important ways in which social relations were formed.[26] Other studies followed – notable among them Daniel Miller's *Material Consumption and Mass Consumption* of 1987, which adopted a Hegelian perspective, and Grant McCracken's *Culture and Consumption* of 1988, which had the most to say about consumer goods and their meanings in the context of consumption – and by the end of the 1980s a significant body of literature had emerged that took a value-free approach to the subject.[27] The impact of this work, for the designer and for the historian of design, was significant. It helped to prioritise a new set of questions about design's relationship with culture, past and present, and to encourage a much wider discussion about design and its relationship with meaning which had hitherto been restricted to the rather narrow field of product semantics. This new approach did not totally eradicate the need for judgements but it helped to provide a set of new criteria according to which they could be formulated.

One body of theory that grew out of the postmodernism, and which had implications for the practice and understanding of design, was linked to the idea of identity. This line of enquiry developed naturally out of studies of consumption that focused attention on the cultural relationships between designed goods, services, spaces, images and their consumers. In a media-dominated, postmodern environment – characterised by the erosion of traditional social relations and their replacement by mediated, represented experiences – the search for identity, whether of the individual or of the group, was high on the agenda. In his seminal text of 1991, entitled *Modernity and Self-Identity: Self and Society in the Late Modern Age* the sociologist Anthony Giddens outlined the way in which the concept of the self had developed as modernity was itself transformed.[28] Other studies focused on the ways in which identifying cultural categories such as gender, class, ethnicity and nationality functioned within a world in which the mass media (including design) played an ever stronger role in helping to define them and in which the impact of colonialism and the culture it had brought with it was dying away. The work of Edward Said, for example, explored the meaning of Arabic culture in the new, post-imperial environment.[29] As countries became independent, one of the ways in which they sought to create an identity for themselves was through an exploration of their indigenous craft and design traditions.

By the 1990s the bodies of theory that had emerged under the umbrella concept of postmodernism were numerous, each one containing its own internal debates. Ideas emanating from within post-structuralism dominated the literature of cultural analysis and criticismof this time. Much of the work touched, to a lesser or greater extent, on the arenas of material, spatial and material culture, although not necessarily overtly. These subjects were frequently only included within the discourses in question as cultural symptoms and exempla, rather than as active agents. Unlike modernist architectural and design theory – which was largely developed by, and for, architects and designers – postmodern ideas focused on the more general issues of knowledge, culture and politics, only touching on architecture and design when they helped to explain a broad cultural concept. Theory had become much less instrumental and its links with practice were indirect at best. Frederic Jameson was one of the few to acknowledge that a parallel activity was going on within cultural practice, noting, for example, the 'reaction against modern architecture and in particular the monumental buildings of the International Style'.[30] Grant McCracken pinpointed the importance of consumer goods in helping to bridge the gap between the 'ideal' and the 'real' in social life, but was less interested in how that idea might feed back into practice.[31] For the most part, postmodern ideas were linked to design but they did not, as modernism had, provide practitioners with a new set of rules.

In the context of architecture and design ideas emerged that helped provide a new approach to practice but they were was observational and analytical, rather than prescriptive, in nature. In the final analysis, in contrast to their role within modernism – a social and cultural ideal to which architects and designers could 'sign up' and, in their own terms, 'make a difference' – within postmodernism designers were, rather, 'part of the problem'. Inasmuch as they had become an inherent part of the media industry and the process of late capitalism, which were the roots of the 'condition of postmodernity', they were symptomatic of it. As Jameson described it, postmodernism was not an ideal to be aspired towards, however, but rather 'a periodizing concept whose function is to correlate new formal features in culture with the emergence of a new type of social life and a new economic order ... the society of the media or the spectacle, or multinational capitalism.'[32] Design, therefore, was part of the message, impotent to stand outside the system of which it was an inherent part.

Postmodernism did have an impact upon material culture, however, if only on the level of the aesthetic formulation of goods and images. As Jameson rightly observed, the rejection of high modernism opened the door to a radically new aesthetic paradigm that embraced decoration, irony, historicism, eclectism and pluralism. It also served to help validate the 'other', which in the world of material culture was represented by luxury, feminised taste, the decorative arts and the world of craft manufacture. To a significant extent, therefore, the postmodern 'structure of feeling' had a significant impact on the world of material culture. Back in 1966 the architect Robert Venturi had developed ideas about 'both/and' rather than 'either/or' culture in his book *Complexity and Contradiction in Architecture*.[33] He followed it in 1973 with a text entitled *Learning from Las Vegas*, in which he set out to show how Pop culture had developed its own valid aesthetic, one which, he claimed, could act as an inspiration for architects and designers who were seeking a way out of the modernist impasse. The pleasure to be gained from the experience of Pop culture, explained Venturi, came from an appreciation of what it had to offer, namely expendability, decoration, fun, irony, historicism, eclecticism and pastiche – values that directly opposed those embraced by heroic modernism.[34] The appeal to the architectural and design professions of Venturi's ideas was that of a new-found freedom which enabled them to move beyond the rationalism and universalism to which all modernist practitioners aspired. In a world in which popular values were increasingly a part, this new level of pleasure to be found in embracing its forms was very appealing. Inevitably it was criticised as being an 'acceptance culture' embracing relativism and rejecting 'real values'. Ironically, also, architects' and designers' implementation of postmodern ideas did not result in a non-hierarchical culture but, in the final analysis, merely replaced the aesthetic content of goods with a high level of 'cultural capital' from a modernist to a postmodernist one. On one level the shift could be seen as that of one fashionable style succeeding another, a necessary strategy to keep the cogs of industry moving and capital flowing.

In 1977 the architect and theorist Charles Jencks published an influential text entitled *The Language of Post-Modern Architecture*. It was among the first instances of the use of the term in the context of the built environment, and its approach depended on linguistic analysis stressing the rhetorical strategies of architects who were interested in what Jencks called 'multivalence' – the

Figure 9.4   Robert Venturi's 'Queen Anne' chairs designed for Knoll International in 1984. In these 'postmodern' artefacts, Venturi sought to put into practice his ideas about complexity and contradiction about which he had written a couple of decades earlier.

language of architectural eclecticism.[35] In fact the book was written before the production of much of what came to be called 'postmodern' architecture created by Michael Graves in the USA, Quinlan Terry in Britain and others, and Jencks had to use historical examples, for the most part, to elaborate his ideas. References were made to Jørn Utzon's Sydney Opera House and Eero Saarinen's TWA terminal at John Kennedy Airport. The book was prophetic in certain ways as the architecture of 'complexity and contradiction' that Jencks set out was, in fact, realised by many designs of the 1980s and 90s, among them Frank Gehry's design for the Guggenheim Museum in Bilbao. This expressive branch of modern, or rather postmodern, architecture developed an aesthetic language for itself distinguishing it from the neo-modernist work that continued to be created in the same decades.

In spite of the enormous paradigm shift that had occurred from the late 1960s onwards, where design was concerned the effects of postmodernism were primarily stylistic. The term came to be identified with goods which had an overtly cultural self-definition and which, as a result, operated in the arena of high culture rather than, as one might have expected, emerging spontaneously from within popular culture. Nowhere was this better exemplified than in the designs created for the Alessi company in the 1980s. Postmodern design, defined as an antidote to the high-cultural neomodernism of the chic furniture and product designs that had characterised the Italian design phenomenon of the late 1950s and early 1960s, had emerged in Italy in the late 1960s through the work of radical design groups based in Florence and Milan. So potent had the cultural language of designed artefacts become in this country that design had been rendered capable, in the manner of fine art, of acting as its own critic. The result was the emergence of a radical design movement that operated outside the commercial system for a short period, finding its natural home in the art gallery. The Memphis experiment of the early 1980s brought this trajectory to a head and, through the extensive presence in the mass media that accompanied it, was quickly transformed from an avant-garde activity in the early twentieth-century sense of the term – albeit couched in an aesthetic language that rejected high modernist design – into a stylistic alternative to modernism in the market-place. The power of the process of commodification, and of the postmodern condition that prioritised the importance of material goods in the context of consumption, inevitably imbued Memphis products with a level of 'added value'. While, at one level, it remained an elite, gallery-oriented phenomenon – the Memphis designers producing an annual show of handmade pieces – it also penetrated the mass market as its images were 'pillaged' and endlessly reproduced. The couture catwalk show, which served as an inspiration for mass-market fashion producers to create instantly fashionable and rapidly replaced items of clothing, was a direct parallel.

The decision, by Alessi, to ask a range of well-known postmodern archi-tects and designers to create objects for them in the 1980s was part of the same story – exploiting the cultural capital that came with the prestigious names who collaborated with the company – from Richard Sapper to Michael Graves to Ron Arad to George Sowden to Norman Foster to Aldo Rossi to Charles Jencks to Robert Venturi to Frank Gehry to Philippe Starck. It was also a strategic means of ensuring their postmodern objects a high level of cultural status, which was then extended to their non-designer goods as well. In design terms, therefore, the use of the postmodernist aesthetic as a strategy fell short of removing the concept of hierarchical value from goods and of creating a genuine pluralism in which all goods were valued equally. Instead it became a badge that imbued objects with enhanced status and designer-appeal in a market continually in search of novelty and new forms of 'distinction' through the consumption of art. The same strategy was employed by a number of American companies that sought to imbue their products with 'added value' in a similar way. Knoll International launched a set of furniture pieces, created by Robert Venturi, while Swid Powell worked with a number of designers from the Memphis stable, and Formica used similar names to work on its Colorcore series of objects.[36] By the end of the 1980s the concept of postmodern design had become synonymous with a highly self-conscious use of aesthetic languages, involving decoration, by an international group of architect–designers who sought to move beyond the communicative strategies of modernism. Ironically these created new ranges of modern luxury items which aspired to art and were at a considerable distance from the popular culture artefacts that had inspired postmodernism in the first place.

Japan was the only country to witness the emergence of a postmodern design movement that retained links with the complex language and decorative aesthetic of consumer-led, mass-market goods. In the 1970s that rapidly developing country had begun to reject its early mass-marketing strategies of selling its products on the basis of technological virtuosity and to adopt a more culturally oriented view of its goods, as well as a more strategic use of design to capture its home market, especially its wealthy young consumers. This led, in the 1980s, to the emergence of ranges of high-technology goods, produced in a range of highly decorative colour schemes and clearly directed at female and youth markets. These were culturally sophisticated products, which appealed on the level of their carefully selected aesthetic and lifestyle potential rather than on their technological attributes. They were not expensive designer-goods, along the lines of the Alessi model, but were available in the general marketplace for all to buy. It has been suggested that the idea of postmodernism can be closely aligned to the Japanese love of contradiction, which pervades its culture.[37] Japan certainly led the way in injecting a consumption-led aesthetic into its mass-produced products.

By the 1990s the term 'postmodernism' had faded from view, both in the context of theory and in the production of designed goods. Its heritage lingered on, however, both on the level of theory and in the world of design practice. The theoretical studies relating to the themes of identity, post-imperialism and globalism that dominated that decade all had their roots in the paradigm shift from modernism to postmodernism. In the world of design practice the somewhat esoteric work of Alessi was reflected in a general reappraisal of the meaning of designed artefacts such that numerous 'modern' objects – such as cars, refrigerators and vacuum cleaners – began to pull back from the need to

Figure 9.5   Volkswagen's new 'Beetle' of the late 1990s, designed in California by Freeman Thomas and J. Mays. It cleverly combined nostalgic references to the past with a strong sense of 'nowness', thereby appealing to a number of different markets.

express the future and linked themselves, nostalgically, to their own modern traditions. Cars were among those objects of material culture which embraced this tendency. Volkswagen's new 'Beetle', designed by J. Mays and Freeman Thomas, represented a new design hybrid of the present, future and past, as did Chrysler's 'PT Cruiser' and the BMW-produced new 'Mini'. Refrigerators created by Smeg also recalled their own streamlined past and Dyson's vacuum cleaners were as much fashion statements as household tools. A high level of decorative self-reflexivity entered the world of product design, a result of the enhanced emphasis upon consumption and the identity of the consumer. However, as the inspiration for a set of new, fashionable styles, visible in the upmarket world of decorative arts, postmodernism had a limited life and, by the early 1990s, had vanished from sight. As a more profound cultural shift it has had a longer life. Indeed the new sensibility that it spawned can be seen to have generated much of the material and visual culture that dominates life in the early years of the twentieth century. Arguably it still underpins the bewildering eclecticism of goods, images and spaces that surround us; the cultural importance of heritage within the post-industrial world; the consumer-led approach of designers; the close link between design and marketing; the dominance of the image over the object; and that of the 'representation' over 'reality', which characterise everyday life in the late capitalist world.

Chapter 10

REDEFINING IDENTITIES

Redefining the nation

As in the pre-war years, so after 1945 design continued to carry with it the potential to represent nation-states and their desire to project their identities on to the world at large. This was the case both for those countries which sought to cast off their links with pre-war Fascism, and those which had had democratic systems in place before the war. Thus Germany, Italy and Japan all embraced 'modern design' as a means of forging new, post-war identities for themselves, ones within which the concept of modernity was uppermost, while Britain, the USA and Sweden, among other countries, also focused on it as a key strategic means of enabling them to enter new international market-places and of encouraging the mass of their indigenous populations to consume modernity. In all cases these countries had developed sophisticated programmes of war-time propaganda and they sought to use them in the context of peace. They understood that the promise of a new lifestyle, provided by the consumption of new modern goods, was an important means of uniting their populations and of moving forward into a new era.

Several studies of design have focused on its national manifestations, seeking to identify key characteristics suggesting a direct correlation between individual nations and taste cultures. Frederique Huygen's *British Design: Image and Identity*, which documented the whole of the twentieth century, highlighted a number of themes understood by the author to be specifically 'British'. The first chapter, entitled 'The Britishness of British Design', characterised its subject as being 'sane and forthright, ordinary, solid, not extreme, honest, modest, homely'. 'The postwar Design Council', maintained Huygen,

Figure 10.1   J.F.K. Henrion's all-aluminium sewing-machine was exhibited at the 'Britain Can Make It' exhibition of 1946, held at London's Victoria and Albert Museum. The exhibition set out to present the British public with an optimistic picture of the future, made possible by designed goods.

'considered good, solid and useable design to be of paramount importance.'[1] The present author's edited collection of essays, published in 1986 to mark the fortieth anniversary of the 'Britain Can Make It' exhibition, held at the Victoria and Albert Museum, also set out to capture what was particular about British design as it was manifested in the early post-war years. The questions posed by this study were less aimed to arrive at a set of epithets that would link design to the British 'character', however, than with an attempt to find out 'how design influenced everyday life' and 'what role it played in influencing the way in which Britain had evolved since the war, economically, socially and culturally'.[2] In this context the role of the Design Council was examined in depth, especially in relation to its agency in the 1946 exhibition, its links with industry and its campaign to raise the level of taste at home. The Design Council, it was suggested, played an essentially paternalistic role up until the mid-1960s when the upsurge of popular taste of that decade threw into question the soft modernist model of design that the Council, under Gordon Russell and Paul Reilly, had been promoting for two decades. The model of 'good design' they backed had been linked to the familiar Arts-and-Crafts-derived rhetoric relating to 'fitness to purpose', while the artefacts approved of by the Council had ranged from simple items of wooden and metal furniture pieces to restrained products that avoided the excesses of American streamlining. Both Huygen's and Sparke's books emphasised the influence of Scandinavia on British 'good' design; the important role played by retailing within British material culture (epitomised by the opening of Terence Conran's 'Habitat' store in 1964); and the strong tradition of exhibition and graphic design in Britain that went back to the work of the wartime Ministry of Information.

Figure 10.2   The Festival of Britain, held on the South Bank of the River Thames in 1951, represented a further attempt to unite the British nation through its appreciation of the bright new future offered by a modern, designed environment. Robin Day's steel rod chairs take pride of place in this image.

They also highlighted the use of modern design to reinforce national identity for a country's home population in these years, achieved through the
creation of a sense of national cohesion and optimism which was uppermost at
Britain's Festival of Britain, held in 1951. Conceived by a Labour government, although realised by a Conservative one, it sought to unite the nation in
a shared experience of modern material culture. A range of didactic displays
providing accounts of Britain's past, present and future aimed to demonstrate
that the 'Contemporary' style heralded a bright new future but maintained
one foot in the past as well. The Festival successfully created a shared vision
that worked for a number of years, manifested in projects such as the
construction of new towns around the country, but its message was ultimately
diluted by the emergence of the youth-oriented popular culture of the 1960s
which was sceptical of centrally controlled modern visions and preferred to
find its own voice in the chaos of the marketplace.[3]

Scandinavia's contribution to post-war design has been documented by a
number of studies, including David McFadden's *Scandinavian Modern Design*.[4]
The very concept of Scandinavian design – an amalgamation of the modern
design traditions of Sweden, Denmark, Finland, Norway and Iceland – was a
construction, or rather a strategic alliance, which functioned effectively for
purposes of trade and public relations outside the countries concerned, but
which was less meaningful within the individual countries, each of which had
its own indigenous traditions and future trajectories. The concept was formed
for an exhibition that toured the USA and Canada from 1954 to 1957, the
main purpose of which was to promote the craft-based modern designs from
the Nordic countries in those buoyant economies. Organised by 'the heads of
the crafts and design organisations in each participating country' (Iceland was
not represented), the exhibition's patrons included the presidents of the
United States and Finland and the kings of Norway, Sweden and Denmark. It
proved highly effective in bringing 'Scandinavian' material culture to the
notice of the American public and it served to unify a broad range of multifarious material objects and to create a new design 'brand' that was highly influential internationally through the rest of the decade.[5] Through its chapter
headings, which emphasised craft areas – ceramics, glass, textiles, metal,
furniture, and so on – Ulf Hard af Segerstad's *Scandinavian Design*, published
in 1961, made it very clear that this newly constructed design movement was
craft-based and defined by its faith in the human hand to transform natural
materials into objects of integrity and democracy.[6] It was a clear and attractive
message to a world that had to come to terms with the concepts of the mass
media, mass consumption and the impact of advanced technologies. Scandinavian design promised the possibility of traditional values being combined with
an image of modernity. Through the 1950s, Scandinavian artisans and

designers exhibited their work at important international venues, such as the Milan Triennales, delighting audiences wherever it was shown.

Among the numerous studies of national design movements in modern democracies, Arthur Pulos's two-volume account of design in the USA has an important place. *The American Design Ethic*, covering the years up to 1940, was followed by *The American Design Adventure*, which documented American design in the period 1940–75.[7] The second volume began with an account of the dream offered to the American public in 1939 in the form of the New York World's Fair. The American public continued to be invited to confront design through the medium of the exhibition in the 1940s and 50s. None of the post-war events, held at New York's Museum of Modern Art, was conceived on the same scale, or communicated the same level of popular excitement, as the 1939 Fair. Nevertheless the post-war years presented to the American public a concept of 'good modern design' which, they were told, would improve their lives significantly. The 'good design' campaign was not managed by federal Government but was in the hands of the 'culture industry', which took on the task of helping manufacturers and retailers to persuade consumers to use discretion in their choice of purchases. Culture and commerce worked closely in collaboration with each other, the Museum of the Modern Art with the Merchandising Mart in Chicago for example. In 1950, the Director of the Department of Industrial Design at the Museum, Edgar Kauffmann Jr, responded to a request from the Mart to help them publicise the notion of good, modern design to manufacturers and consumers. The result was the series of six annual 'Good Design' shows. They proved very popular with the American public and provided an opportunity for the concept to be debated in the press. Furniture and domestic items dominated the exhibition and a large percentage of them was either Scandinavian of origin, or heavily influenced by the Scandinavian craft-based aesthetic. Two cultures of design were clearly emerging in post-war USA, one destined for the living room, which was strongly influenced by Europe with a clear social cachet attached to it, and the other, a more indigenous movement, with more popular origins and appeal, visible in the street and in the kitchen and manifested in the forms of automobiles and bulbous refrigerators. The Museum of Modern Art tried to bridge the cultural gap between these two school of American design by holding two exhibitions, in 1951 and 1953, dedicated to the automobile. Its selection process, however, reflected its taste in furniture, as the cars selected for exhibition all had a strong European flavour.

The countries that sought to renew their national identities in the post-war years and to throw off their links with earlier totalitarian regimes – Germany, Italy and Japan in particular – also utilised the concept of design as a means through which to create new identities, find new trading partners, and renew

Figure 10.3   Gio Ponti's little 'Superleggera' chair, created for Cassina in 1956, combined a reference to traditional, vernacular furniture with a strikingly modern aesthetic, which showed the way forward for the Italian nation as a whole.

their populations' commitment to a democratic, modern future fuelled by the wide availability of attractive and accessible consumer goods. The 1980s saw the publication of a number of accounts of these nations' achievements, including the present author's accounts of Italian design and Japanese design.[8] Both set out to chart the ways in which these two very different countries evolved a post-war national identity that involved defining a particular approach to the concept of design. Neither country had a concerted plan of action, nor were their governments directly involved. Rather the efforts of manufacturers, practising designers and their professional organisations combined to develop a commercial and creative culture that supported the

rise of a modern design movement. Much depended on what had gone on in
the pre-war years – the influence of the Bauhaus was seminal in both countries, for example, as was that of the European architectural Modern Movement. These forces had to be balanced with the American model of mass
production, modern styling and private consumption, however, which was
disseminated world wide in the post-1945 years and which had a strong presence in both countries. The result was a successful marriage of the cultural
and the commercial that produced strong identities for their products and for
their trading faces. Although both countries responded to these same stimuli,
and used the same strategies with which to develop modern design cultures
and identities for themselves, they grew in quite distinct ways, dependent
upon local conditions: while Italy emphasised its fine art orientation, Japan
depended more heavily upon its advanced technology. The emergence of
post-war design cultures in both Italy and Japan represented attempts to
develop nationally specific cultural and commercial identities. Both countries
successfully resisted the wholesale adoption of the American Fordist model to
a considerable extent, Italy through its craft traditions of small, family-based
manufacturing and Japan through its ability to combine small manufacturing
concerns with very large ones using a system of subcontraction.[9] In the
decades following the war modern design proved itself to be a powerful tool
for both countries in terms as a means of developing a new identity, and in
offering their own populations an opportunity to embrace modernity through
consumption.[10]

Figure 10.4   Dieter Ram's late-1950s design for hi-fi system for the German company
Braun. The hard-edged, high-tech, engineered look created by Rams came to represent the
image of efficiency and industrial know-how that Germany embraced in the post-war years.

Germany also used design as a means of creating its post-war identity. The strategy was implemented at governmental level as well as by the private manufacturing sector. The Rat für Formgebung was established to mastermind a series of *Gute Form* (good form) exhibitions, which built on the achievements of the Bauhaus. A number of manufacturers, including Braun AG and Bosch AG, also played a key role in defining the rational, technologically proficient character of modern Germany and its material culture both at home and abroad. The collaboration of Braun with the designer Dieter Rams, in particular, reinforced Germany's reputation as a producer of well-engineered, well-designed, neomodern technological consumer goods. The continuing work of leading pre-war designers, Wilhelm Wagenfeld among them, served to bridge the gap between the pre-war and post-war years and to develop the modern aesthetic of the products of the German decorative arts industries, while electrical appliance companies, such as AEG, applied the same level of aesthetic rationalism to the 'high-tech' products that they had in the early century, helping to earn Germany an international reputation for the creation of 'well-designed' modern products. The image of German design at the Milan Triennale of 1954 suggested a highly efficient, hard-working country determined to provide all the members of its population with high-quality goods.

It was not only nations that were quick to utilise the visual and ideological rhetoric of design as a means of creating instant identities in the years after 1945, however. Multinational companies also saw in design the potential to define global identities that would enable them to control markets on a worldwide basis. Indeed, since the turn of the century, companies such as AEG had understood that a harmonious, modern-looking identity that extended beyond buildings and products into graphic design was a huge asset. While the post-war emphasis on nations as key political, economic and cultural units remained strong, a number of corporations were beginning to define themselves as transnational entities. This was especially true in the USA, as the economy became increasingly dependent upon global sales. Nowhere was this more apparent than in the case of the Coca-Cola company which, since its origins in 1886, had continually expanded to embrace world markets. Indeed the term 'cocacolonisation' was frequently used to describe the impact of American culture on the rest of the world after the Second World War. Described as a 'megabrand', the Coca-Cola product – a sweet liquid – was highly dependent upon design for its identity, both through packaging but also, more subtly, through the image of the company as a whole.[11] Much effort had gone into advertising and promoting the product and the brand both before and during the war, but the pace quickened after 1945 to concentrate on the product's position within a lifestyle. As an advertisement explained, 'Creative entertaining is part of today's good life ... and you can count on Coca-Cola to make its own contribution to the good taste of your arrangements'.[12] This was an example of design doing its work without objects, an evocation of the concept of 'good taste' in the abstract, linked to a cold drink. As Stephen Bayley explained 'By 1969 Coca-Cola was very much more than a drink. It was a talisman.'[13] Although Coca-Cola was international it was also, paradoxically, American. This national/international ambiguity characterised a number of corporate products and services in the post-war years and established a model that remains in existence today – for example in the form of a company, such as IKEA, that trades internationally on the basis of its inherent Swedishness.

In the 1950s companies such as the American multinational IBM also embraced the concept of 'good design', employing Eliot Noyes, hitherto Head of the Design Department at New York's Museum of Modern Art, to design its typewriters and oversee its total corporate identity. In Italy, Olivetti, a patron of modern design since the inter-war years, employed the graphic designer Marcello Nizzoli to create its office machines thereby buying into the internationally understood concept of 'good design' while retaining its Italian identity at the same time. The German company Braun worked with Dieter Rams in a similar way, although he was not directly employed by them. Unlike Coca-Cola, these engineering-based companies depended upon a production-oriented, modernist definition of design with which to sell their consumer machines. Arguably, though, in the eyes of consumers these engineered goods were equally talismanic, and suggestive of the 'good life' aspired to by Coca-Cola drinkers.

One product that was sold on the basis of overtly national characteristics, if not stereotypes, and which had strongly national characteristics but was increasingly becoming part of a global industry, was the automobile. Swedish 'safety' vied with German 'technical efficiency', French 'idiosyncrasy', and Italian 'elegance' in the international marketplace, each image representing almost a caricature of national identity. This was design semantics at its richest, the creation of a set of design languages that communicated to consumers more than mere 'fitness for purpose' in the products they accompanied. The example of the automobile industry also demonstrated the growing significance of national identity in the context of global trading. As the global context threatened their demise, the meaning of 'local' and 'national' were intensified. By 1970 the concept of national identity in design – one that had had a high level of meaning in the immediate post-war years at a time when new nations were redefining themselves after the trauma of a world war and were, by necessity, vying for positions in the international marketplace – had become little more than a set of linguistic devices that could be manipulated at will to influence the market. The 'real' links, if they had ever existed, between material culture and a set of particular conditions and characteristics determining national identity, had been displaced by an ever-expanding globalism. The former existed only as strategic marketing ploys, used to create an illusion of identity in a world in which, through the growing influence of the mass media, the process of identity formation was changing at a rapid pace.

After 1970 a number of newly formed countries joined in the activity of creating national identities for themselves through modern design – France, Spain (or rather Catalonia), and the former countries of the Eastern bloc among them – demonstrating that the acceptance of modernism, albeit with a local dialect, had become an intrinsic element of the process of national modernisation. As more and more countries underwent the experience 'real' local and national characteristics and variations were lost and replaced by constructed ones. In their place consumers were offered a variety of national versions of the 'modern dream', which were, in the end, all part of the same dream – that of a modern lifestyle, accessed through consumption.

Redefining lifestyles

The use of design as a tool, by nation-states and corporations alike, with which to project their identities had been a widespread activity from the mid-nineteenth century right through to the years following the Second World War. As the mass media increasingly replaced the role of the public exhibition after 1970, however, that means of expressing national identities through design gradually faded from view. Sporadic World's Fairs and a few large-scale international events, such as the Olympic Games, continued to make an impact upon an international audience, and design inevitably played an important part in them, but, for the most part, the era of exhibition-visiting had come to an end, replaced by the role of the mass media as the dominant form of mass communication, and the redefinition of audiences as consumers. In this transformation design expanded its role to become not only a medium through which nations and corporations could communicate express identities, but, perhaps more importantly, a force underpinning the formation of new kinds of identities constituted at a number of levels, whether nationally, globally, locally, or defined by a wide range of cultural categories, gender, race, ethnicity, age and religious persuasion among them. Increasingly people came to be defined less as citizens than by their memberships of consumer groups or 'taste cultures'. In response to these transformations, design, working hand-in-hand with commerce, strengthened its self-conscious links with identity formation and with the concept of the 'brand'.

Increasingly, through the twentieth century, identities linked to place – the nation in particular – came to be determined less and less by inherited cultural ideas and more and more by new patterns of consumption. Thus nations became linked, both within their boundaries but more frequently from outside them, with tastes and products with which they were culturally identified, usually stereotypically. These were frequently food, clothing, and lifestyle related. Thus England, for example, became identified with the upper-class image suggested by Burberry mackintoshes, cashmere sweaters and Jaguar cars, while Italy was seen as the home of the steel pasta maker, and France that of the cafetière and the products of the luxury industries, couture fashion and perfume among them. While, to some extent, these were traditional identities linked to real practices with real origins, in some instances they were 'invented' traditions, which took on equally powerful roles.[14] As countries industrialised and sought modern identities for themselves, the notion of modern design became increasingly significant as a means of giving them a visual face. Although modern design shared broad characteristics across boundaries it developed distinct local inflections, which served to reinforce national differences. Thus, in the 1950s, Scandinavia was linked with simple craft products made of natural materials while, in the following decade, Italy was associated with slick shiny plastic products and sophisticated furnishing items in modern materials and forms. References to Italian traditions were retained – the use of marble in many of Italy's modern products for example – but for the most part this was a constructed new image developed to show new levels of modernity and competitiveness.

A few European countries felt the need to re-brand themselves in the 1980s and 90s as they emerged as new traders in the global marketplace. They did so understanding that identity and consumption had become strongly interdependent. During the presidency of François Mitterand – and following the lead of his culture minister, Jack Lang – France, for example, made huge efforts to promote modern design in the 1980s, conscious that it had fallen behind countries such as Italy. In addition to the architectural works they commissioned (referred to as the 'Grands Projects') their initiatives included the formation, in 1979, of VIA (Valorisation de l'Innovation de l'Ameublement), which served to finance individual furniture designers; in 1982, of ENSCI (Ecole Nationale Supérieure de Création Industrielle), a new school for design; and of APCI (l'Agence de Promotion de la Création Industrielle). Their efforts generated a strong, internationally visible, modern French design movement in which a number of designers, Pascal Mourgue and Philippe Starck among them, achieved near 'super-star' status.[15] The country's new national, design-conscious 'brand' was widely promoted at exhibitions at home and abroad and in magazines worldwide. As a deliberate strategy to renew France's image as a modern late twentieth-century state with a strong link between culture and commerce it was a great success.

Another example of government and industry working together to renew the image of a locality – this time a city within a distinctive region, rather than a nation-state occurred in Barcelona during the 1980s and 90s. Following the collapse of the Fascist regime, Spain initiated a programme of modernisation that was similar to the one pursued by Italy nearly three decades earlier. While Italy had modernised its identity within the context of late modernism, however, Barcelona underwent a similar process in a global, postmodern context that was post-industrial and consumer-oriented. Catalonia sought to differentiate itself from the rest of Spain, taking advantage of its past reputation for progressive design and of Barcelona's position as a centre of production. More significantly, however, it understood the importance of consumption and of servicing a wealthy middle-class market which, under the Fascist regime, had been deprived of the experience of consuming modernity. Barcelona's economic and cultural regeneration was a complex process involving private and public collaborations and innovations in the design of products, retail environments and public spaces. It was a thoroughgoing exercise, which benefited significantly from the decision to hold the Olympic Games in the city in 1990. This provided the leverage for a wholesale revamping of the city.[16] Most significantly, however, fundamental change was achieved through a re-branding exercise and the encouragement of new patterns of consumption. The new brand was based on an image of technological competence, but it was couched in a global language with local inflections. The work of Oscar Tusquets was symptomatic in this context. He dubbed one of his chair designs 'Gaulino' – a mixture of the names of Antonio Gaudí – Barcelona's indigenous, 'modernista' architect–hero – and of Carlo Mollino, an important designer within Italy's cultural reconstruction of the 1940s.

Barcelona's re-branding, which was totally dependent upon a notion of design containing a high level of cultural capital, was an expression of late modernity expressed in a postmodern context. Many of the changes Britain made to its image in the 1980s, however, were symptomatic of the post-industrial, postmodern age, depending as they did upon the concept of 'heritage'. Returning to Britain in 1979 after time spent in Canada, Patrick Wright remarked, 'I had come back to a country which was full of precious and imperilled traces – a closely held iconography of what it is to be English – all of them appealing in one covertly projective way or another to the historical and sacrosanct identity of the nation'.[17] From the 1980s onwards the work of the National Trust, of British Heritage and of a number of other government agencies was intensified as they took on the task of protecting and renovating many of Britain's crumbling historical sites. Two years after the publication of Wright's book, Robert Hewison explained that there were, at that time, over

Figure 10.5   Mail-order catalogues – such as the one depicted here, *Art*Room – encouraged people to consume nostalgic objects from the comfort of their own homes. These 'Art Deco' objects were rendered more desirable by the blockbuster exhibition held at the Victoria and Albert Museum on the subject.

forty-one Heritage Centres in Britain.[18] They included the Wigan Pier and Heritage Centre; the Ironbridge Gorge Museum; Beamish Museum; and the renovated the Albert Docks in Liverpool. The challenge of this work to designers was no less great than that of working within modernism to create an environment of the present and near future. From the 1980s onwards the skills of many of Britain's designers were applied to the task of creating experiences, whether within a museum setting or in a regenerated city centre. With the decline of manufacturing industry in that country, many designers moved into a new interdisciplinary mode of working, crossing the traditional areas of interior design, exhibition design, furniture and product design and graphic design. Film-making and script-writing were also undertaken on many occasions. The result was a new kind of designer, one who was more flexible and team-conscious than ever before. The same skills were demanded of designers working in other expanding areas, among them design for film and television and the world wide web. In Britain and elsewhere, the 1990s saw a shift away from a focus on the object towards one that emphasised the 'experience' and the 'immaterial', symptomatic of a culture that was more consumption- than production-oriented.

Design played a role in the re-branding of many nations and localities in the years after 1980. The opening up of Eastern Europe provided an opportunity for Hungary, Poland, East Germany, the Czech Republic, Slovakia and a number of other countries to use design both to reinforce and communicate their craft traditions and to develop a modern face to show to the rest of the world.[19] In the Far East, countries such as Korea, Singapore, Taiwan and China, among others, followed Japan's lead in using modern design as a way of re-branding themselves, of modernising their cultures and of entering into international trade. Countries such as Canada, Australia, India and South Africa also began to develop their own modern design traditions as one of the ways of moving beyond their imperial pasts, as did many of the countries of Latin America. By the end of the century the USA/Europe axis, which had tended to dominate the development of modern design in the first half of the twentieth century was becoming less and less dominant culturally as many other countries in other parts of the world negotiated modernism as a means of demonstrating their desire to become part of the modern, developed world. Following the models of Sweden and Italy in the immediate post-war years, many countries that were new to design now used it as a means of expressing their intentions.

Design's role in the creation of identities of place, nations in particular, accompanied the part it played in the formation of global identities which, although linked originally to specific localities, were usually experienced 'at home'. A number of definitions of globalisation have been put forward, among them that of Anthony Giddens, who described it as 'an intensification of worldwide social relations which link distant localities in such a way that local happenings are shaped by events occurring many miles away and vice versa.'[20] Another way of thinking about globalisation was as the result of new technologies and mobilities which either brought experiences to people in new ways or took people to them. It occurred through the homogenisation of products, industries and technologies, and, most significantly, through homogenised patterns of commodified consumption (of products – both material and immaterial – services, images and experiences), but it also, para-doxically, recognised diversity, making it available beyond the geographical boundaries of its origins. The latter process has been called 'glocalisation'. It encompassed the essentially contradictory character of globalisation, which makes possible both 'sameness' and 'difference', the important thing being that the consumption of both is dramatically transformed.[21]

Although globalisation occurred prior to the 1990s, most writings about it emerged during that decade. It had developed gradually throughout the course of the twentieth century as a result of the expansion of commercial life; the opening up of international markets; the expansion of the media; and

Figure 10.6   Jonathan Ives' colourful, translucent iMac computer for Apple Computers Inc. appealed to an international 'taste culture' that sought to integrate its technological possessions into its lifestyle.

transformations in the nature of both elite and mass consumption. The cultural changes that lay beneath the last – the shift from class-based, 'trickle-down' consumption to the emergence of what Zygmunt Bauman called 'neo-tribes', or lifestyle, consumption, and the accompanying emergence of 'taste cultures', which cross the conventional cultural classifications of class, age, gender, ethnicity and nationality (among others) – were fundamental to the growth of globalisation and closely linked to developments in design.[22]

One of the most visible ways in which design and globalisation joined hands was in the concept of the corporate brand. Much work has been undertaken in analysing the effects of multinational branding, such as that of Coca-Coca, which, as we have seen, brought American culture to the rest of the world.[23] More recently, studies have been made of the Italian fashion producer/retailer Benetton and of the Japanese producer of electronic goods Sony in attempts to unpack the complex working of the brand in the late twentieth century. Both Pasi Falk and Celia Lury have published work about Benetton that attempts to get beneath the surface of the company's brand strategies.[24] In her essay on the subject Lury explained that the brand functions through the way 'in which it can recoup the effects of the subject or consumer's action, consti-tuting these effects as the outcome of the brand's own powers through the repetitive assertion of its ability to motivate the branded object's meaning and

EVERYONE
HAS THE RIGHT
TO LEAVE ANY COUNTRY,
INCLUDING HIS OWN,
AND TO RETURN
TO HIS COUNTRY
(art.13)

FIFTIETH ANNIVERSARY
OF THE UNIVERSAL
DECLARATION
OF HUMAN RIGHTS

UNITED COLORS
OF BENETTON.

Figure 10.7   In the 1990s the Italian fashion retailer Benetton developed a number of sophisticated advertising campaigns, which focused on the cultural pluralism of the Benetton consumers who were united by the 'taste culture' to which they all belonged.

uses'.[25] She suggested that although the product is absent the brand anticipates it. It can work so well, she argued, because we have seen 'an intensification of the imaging of the object' through the twentieth century such that we know it even if it is not there. When we see the Coca-Cola logo, for example, we imagine the bottle and the drink without needing to see them. Benetton's brand was made visible in the last decade of the twentieth century through a programme of progressive global advertising that took globalisation, rather than the company's products, as its main theme. A number of advertisements moved away from a representation of its products to depictions of its worldwide consumers shown as young, happy people from a number of ethnic origins. Lury was critical of the implications of the advertisements, claiming that they set out to 'naturalise' racial difference, making it appear to be a matter of skin colour only.

While Lury concentrated on analysing globalisation as represented by the 'text' of the advertising that forms part of the brand, in their study of the Sony Walkman Paul du Gay, Stuart Hall, Linda Janes, Hugh Mackay and Keith Negus looked at the globalisation strategies of that Japanese company from technological and marketing perspectives as well.[26] Sony launched its product locally in Japan at first, then introduced it into a range of countries using a different product name in each. In the early 1980s it decided to stand-ardise the name globally. In order to sell the Walkman internationally, however, Sony had to make it technologically consistent and guarantee its repair or replacement across the world. The company also decided to set up local manufacturing operations in a number of different countries, as a means of entering local marketplaces. Thus the company's process of globalisation worked on a number of fronts: from a design perspective the product was standardised in the first instance, but variants were quickly developed to ensure the Walkman a constant flow of customers. Those variants were directed at global niche taste cultures across the globe, however, rather than at different local markets.

Many other companies developed along the lines that Sony and others pioneered. Japanese companies were especially keen to establish local plants. This was especially evident in the car industry and, from the 1970s onwards, Japanese cars competed favourably alongside those of the USA and Europe in the international marketplace. Indeed, cars had long operated on a global basis – Ford, General Motors and Chrysler set up foreign manufacturing in the inter-war years in imitation of the earlier electrical industries General Elec-tric, Westinghouse and Siemens. It was natural for the products of the new technology industries to pave the way for international trade as they had no cultural traditions behind them to work against. With the gradual homogeni-sation of the environment, however, came the taste for 'difference' and a desire for the exotic on the part of consumers who had experienced foreign travel and wanted to continue the experience at home. The success of retailers, such as Terence Conran with his Habitat store in the 1960s, was the recognition of this need for culturally diverse goods, which came, like all commodities, to find their place within the fashion system such that their appeal was necessarily temporary but there was always another example of 'exotica' to take their place.

Globalisation of production and consumption was inevitably followed by the same process taking place within the design profession, and by the mid-twentieth century it had become commonplace for design consultancies to set up branches in countries where they had clients. Raymond Loewy's French firm was a case in point, as was the movement of British consultancies around the globe in the 1980s. The 1990s saw the collapse of many of those firms, however, and the design industry reformed itself with an expansion of in-house design. Britain continued to be a focus for international design, however, a fact that was confirmed by the American Ford Motor Company's formation of a design centre in London in 2002. Named 'Ingeni' the group was located in a building designed by the architect Richard Rogers and described as 'a laboratory and a shop window all at the same time'.[27] The group's brief was to create products that would be marketed as part of the Ford brand. London was selected, as it was seen to be the most internationally oriented of the world's major cities.

The creation of national identities for countries, and of brand identities for global corporations, through the strategic use of design positioned closely alongside politics and marketing, was a striking phenomenon in the twentieth century. Both depended strongly on the concept of branding and the role that design played within it. The cultural spin-off of both processes was the formation of identities for consumers, whether acquired through a sense of belonging, through consumption, through an association with a particular place, or through a link with a lifestyle promulgated by a commercial brand. A number of other cultural categories, among them gender and age, were also represented by designed artefacts in the marketplace such that consumers could use them as a means of constructing individual and group identities for themselves. Just as national identities reasserted themselves when they were under threat from globalism, so overt representations of femininity and masculinity became more apparent in the marketplace as, in everyday life, those gendered identities became less distinctive. Publications such as Pat Kirkham's group of edited essays, *The Gendered Object*, and Katherine Martinez and Kenneth L. Ames' *The Material Culture of Gender: The Gender of Material Culture*, were symptomatic of that tendency.[28] The first covered a wide range of products, both past and present, from guns to Barbie dolls to perfume, describing the subtle, and not so subtle, ways in which commodities played, and continued to play, a role in gender-identity formation. Pat Kirkham and Alex Weller's account of the male and female coding in the advertising of Clinique cosmetic products, for example, showed how the former communicated a rational and objective message that was less apparent in the female equivalent, which, according to the authors, contained less information. 'By the time they are old enough to afford Clinique products', they explained, 'they [girls] do not need [like the men] to be "educated" about them'.[29] In her essay on the subject of 'Perfume' Angela Partington explained that 'it [perfume] represents the *contingencies* of identity' and that 'the consumer produces something real – new ways of relating as gendered subjects – and design provides the raw material' thus showing, very succinctly, the way in which design helped form identities, in this instance gendered ones.[30] Martinez and Ames' book adopted a more historically oriented approach to a similar subject and focused on the fact that material culture had long played a role in gendered identity formation. This cultural truism, one author explained, represented one of the dominant ways in which consumers related to the constructed material and spatial world.

Figure 10.8   By the late 1990s shopping for designed goods, seen here taking place in New Street, Birmingham, England, had become the most important form of identity formation for the majority of people living in the industrialised world.

In its capacity as a cultural force with the potential to fill the gap left by the move away from traditional social relations, design had clearly come to play a fundamental role within everyday life by the end of the twentieth century. As a tool to convey the power of nations it had moved a long way from the nineteenth-century exhibitions filled with huge halls displaying early production machinery. National identity had come to be on display in the marketplace. It was embedded within the mass media and experienced on a daily basis. As individuals, consumers had learnt to negotiate their identities and their sense of 'belonging', aware that it was made up of many elements defined by multiple categories, including gender, age, ethnicity, lifestyle and locality. Aided by the consumption of the designed goods, services, spaces and images available at any one moment in the marketplace, individuals could negotiate their own identities, and play an active part in the construction of modern, or indeed postmodern, life in the everyday world.

NOTES

Introduction

1 Foster, H. *Design and Crime* (London and New York: Verso, 2002), p. 22.
2 McCracken, G. *Culture and Consumption: New Approaches to the Symbolic Character of Consumer Goods and Activities* (Bloomington and Indianapolis: Indiana University Press, 1990), p. xi.
3 Huyssen, A. *After the Great Divide: Modernism, Mass Culture and Postmodernism* (Bloomington and Indianapolis: Indiana University Press, 1986) and Bourdieu, P. *Distinction: A Social Critique of the Judgement of Taste* (London and New York: Routledge and Kegan Paul, 1986).

Chapter 1   Consuming modernity

1 Saisselin, R.G. *Bricobracomania: The Bourgeois and the Bibelot* (London: Thames and Hudson, 1985), p. 64.
2 McKendrick, N., Brewer, J., Plumb, J.H. (eds) *The Birth of Consumer Society: The Commercialization of Eighteenth-Century England* (London: Hutchinson, 1982); Campbell, C. *The Romantic Ethic and the Spirit of Modern Consumerism* (Oxford: Basil Blackwell, 1987); Weatherill, L. *Consumer Behaviour and Material Culture in Britain 1660–1760* (London and New York: Routledge, 1988); and Vickery, A. *The Gentleman's Daughter: Women's Lives in Georgian England* (New Haven and London: Yale University Press, 1998).
3 Weatherill, 1988, p. 77.
4 See Logan, T. *The Victorian Parlour: A Cultural Study* (Cambridge: Cambridge University Press, 2001). Davidoff, L. and Hall, C. *Family Fortunes: Men and Women of the English Middle Class 1780–1850* (London: Routledge, 1987).
5 Girling Budd, A. 'Comfort and gentility, furnishings by Gillows, Lancaster 1840–1855', in McKellar, S. and Sparke, P. (eds), *Interior Design and Identity* (Manchester: Manchester University Press, 2004).
6 Fraser, W.H. *The Coming of the Mass Market, 1850–1914* (London and Basingstoke: Macmillan, 1981).

 7 Bushman, R.L. The *Refinement of America: Persons, Houses, Cities* (New York: Vintage Books, 1993).

 8 Bronner, S.J. *Consuming Visions: Accumulation and Display of Goods in America, 1880–1920* (Wintherthur, DE: The Henry Francis du Pont Wintherthur Museum, 1989).

 9 Hultenen, K. 'From parlor to living room: domestic space, interior decoration, and the culture of personality' in Bronner, 1989, pp. 157–89.

10 Walkowitz, J. *Prostitution and Victorian Society: Women, Class and the State* (Cambridge: Cambridge University Press, 1980) and Rappoport, E.D. *Shopping for Pleasure: Women in the Making of London's West End* (Princeton, NJ: Princeton University Press, 2000).

11 Wolff, J. 'The culture of separate spheres: the role of culture in 19th century public and private life', in *Feminine Sentences: Essays on Women and Culture* (Cambridge: Polity, 1990).

12 Wilson, E. *The Sphinx in the City* (London: Virago, 1991).

13 Leach, W. *Lands of Desire: Merchants, Power and the Rise of a New American Culture* (New York: Vintage Books, 1994).

14 These include Bowlby, R. *Just Looking: Consumer Culture in Dreiser, Gissing and Zola* (New York: Methuen, 1985) and Miller, M.B. *The Bon Marché: Bourgeois Culture and the Department Store 1869–1920* (New Jersey: Princeton Univesity Press, 1981).

15 Bronner, 1989, p. 8.

16 Giedion, S. *Mechanisation Takes Command: A Contribution to Anonymous History* (New York: W.W. Norton and Co., 1948).

17 Giedion, 1948.

18 Sparke, P. *A Century of Car Design* (London: Mitchell Beazley, 2002), p. 10.

19 Greenhalgh, P. (ed.) *Art Nouveau, 1890–1914* (London: V & A Publications, 2000).

20 Wharton, E. and Codman Jr, O. *The Decoration of Houses* (London: Batsford, 1898).

21 Milan, S. 'Refracting the gaselier: understanding Victorian responses to domestic gas lighting', in Bryden, I. And Floyd, J. (eds), *Domestic Space: Reading the Nineteenth-century Interior* (Manchester and New York: Manchester University Press, 1999).

22 Wilson, E. *Adorned in Dreams: Fashion and Modernity* (London: Virago, 1985) and Breward, C. *The Hidden Consumer, Masculinities, Fashion and City Life* (Manchester: Manchester University Press, 1999).

23 Barthes, R. *Mythologies* (London: Jonathan Cape, 1983).

24 Veblen, T. *The Theory of the Leisure Class* (London: Unwin, 1970 [originally 1899]).

25 Wulf, K.H. (ed.) *The Sociology of Georg Simmel* (Glencoe: The Free Press, 1950).

26 Beetham, M. *A Magazine of Her Own: Domesticity and Desire in the Woman's Magazine, 1800–1914* (New York and London: Routledge, 1996) and Scanlon, J. *Inarticulate Longings: The Ladies' Home Journal and the Promises of Consumer Culture* (New York and London: Routledge, 1995).

27 Hine, T. *The Total Package* (Boston: Little Brown, 1995).

28 Strasser, S. *Satisfaction Guaranteed: The Making of the American Mass Market* (New York: Pantheon Books, 1989).

29 Slater, D. *Consumer Culture and Modernity* (Cambridge: Polity Press, 1997).

30 Alexander, S. 'Becoming a Woman in London in the 1920s and 1930s', in Alexander, S. (ed.), *Becoming a Woman and Other Essays in Nineteenth- and Twentieth-Century Feminist History* (New York: New York University Press), pp. 203–24.

31 Harrison, H.A. (ed.) *Dawn of a New Day: The New York World's Fair, 1939/40* (New York: New York University Press, 1980).

32 See Strasser, 1989, and Tedlow, R.S. *New and Improved: The Story of Mass Marketing in America* (New York: Basic Books, 1990).

33 Forde, K. 'Celluloid dreams: the marketing of Cutex in America, 1916–1935', *Journal of Design History* (vol.15, no.3, 2002), pp. 175–90.

34 Scanlon, 1995.

35 Forde, 2002, p. 178.

36 Peiss, K. *Hope in a Jar: The Making of America's Beauty Culture* (New York: Henry Holt & Co. Inc., 1998).

37 See Bayley, S. *Harley Earl* (London: Trefoil, 1990) and Clarke, S. 'Managing design: the art and colour section at General Motors, 1927–1941', *Journal of Design History* (vol.12, no.1, 1999), pp. 65–79.

38 Clarke, 1999.

39 Frederick. C. *Selling Mrs Consumer* (New York: Business Bourse, 1929).

40 Frederick, 1929. p. 22.

41 Swiencicki, M.A. 'Consuming brotherhood: men's culture, style and recreation as consumer culture, 1880–1930', in Glickman, L.B. (ed.), *Consumer Society in American History: A Reader* (Ithaca and London: Cornell University Press, 1999), p. 207.

42 Swiencicki, 1999, p. 226.

43 Gartman, D. *Auto Opium: A Social History of American Automobile Design* (New York and London: Routledge, 1994).

44 Jeremiah, D. 'Filling up: the British experience, 1896–1940', *Journal of Design History* (vol.8, no.2, 1995), pp. 97–116.

45 Lewis, D.L. and Goldstein, L. (eds) *The Automobile and American Culture* (Michigan: University of Michigan Press, 1983).

46 O'Connell, S. *The Car in British Society: Class, Gender and Motoring, 1896–1939* (Manchester: Manchester University Press, 1998), p. 43.

47 Gronberg. T. *Designing Modernity: Exhibiting the City in 1920s Paris* (Manchester: Manchester University Press, 1998), p. 62.

48 Gieben-Gamal, E. 'Feminine spaces, modern experiences: the design and display strategies of British hairdressing salons in the 1920s and 1930s', in McKellar, S. and Sparke, P. (eds), *Interior Design and Identity* (Manchester: Manchester University Press, 2004).

49 Clarke, C. *Tupperware: The Promise of Plastic in 1950s America* (Washington and London: Smithsonian Institution Press, 1999).

50 Light, A. *Forever England: Femininity,Literature and Conservatism Between the Wars* (London and New York: Routledge, 1991).

51 Ryan, D.S. *The Ideal Home through the Twentieth Century* (London: Hazar Publishing, 1997).

52 Massey, A. *Hollywood Beyond the Screen* (Oxford: Berg, 2000).

53 Fine, B. and Leopold, E. *The World of Consumption* (London: Routledge, 1993).

Chapter 2   The impact of technology

1 Ford, H. 'Mass production', in *Encyclopaedia Britannica* (Chicago: Chicago University Press, 1926).

2 For a longer discussion see Fine, B. and Leopold, E. *The World of Consumption* (London: Routledge, 1993) in which the authors outline the concept of 'systems of provision' which cross the production/consumption divide.

3 Examples such as James Nasmyth's steam hammer of 1838 and James Wyatt's pumping engine of 1783 were among the many tools developed to exploit this new source of power.

4 Clark, H. *The Role of the Designer in the Early Mass Production Industry* (unpublished PhD thesis, University of Brighton, 1982).

5 Habakkuk, H.J. *American and British Technology in the Nineteenth Century: The Search for Labour-Saving Inventions* (Cambridge: Cambridge University Press, 1962).

6 Giedion, S. *Mechanisation Takes Command: A Contribution to Anonymous History* (New York: W.W. Norton and Co., 1969 [1948]).

7 Hounshell, D.A. *From the American System to Mass Production 1800–1932* (Baltimore and London: Johns Hopkins Press, 1984).

8 The Austrian Postal Savings Bank building of 1904–06 and the office building for the *Die Zeit* newspaper of the same years both used aluminium. For more examples of early work in aluminium see Nichols, S. (ed.) *Aluminum by Design* (New York: Harry Abrams, 2000).

9 Attfield, J. *Wild Things: The Material Culture of Everyday Life* (Oxford and New York: Berg, 2000), pp. 16–18.

10 Clifford, H. and Turner, E. 'Modern Metal', in Greenhalgh, P. (ed.), *Art Nouveau 1890–1914* (London: V&A Publications, 2000).

11 Friedel, R. *Pioneer Plastic: The Making and Selling of Celluloid* (Wisconsin: University of Wisconsin Press, 1983).

12 The interior decorator Elsie de Wolfe was responsible for this innovation.

13 Frederick W. Taylor developed a system of rationalisation through the analysis of work, which came to be known as 'time and motion studies'.

14 Beecher, C. and Stowe, H.B. *The American Woman's Home* (New York: J.B. Ford and Co., 1869).

15 Cowan, R.S. *More Work for Mother: The Ironies of Household Technology from the Open Hearth to the Microwave* (New York: Basic Books, 1983) and Strasser, S. *Never Done: A History of American Housework* (New York: Pantheon Books, 1982).

16 Frederick, C. *The New Housekeeping: Efficiency Studies in Home Management* (New York: Garden City, Doubleday Page, 1913).

17 Stage, S. and Vincenti, V.B. (eds) *Rethinking Home Economics: Women and the History of a Profession* (Ithaca and London: Cornell University Press, 1997).

18 See Bullock, N. 'First the kitchen – then the façade', *Journal of Design History* (vol.1, nos.3 and 4, 1988), pp. 177–92.

19 Sparke, P. 'Cookware to cocktail shakers: the domestication of aluminum in the United States 1900–1939', in Nichols, 2001.

20 Forty, A. *Objects of Desire* (London: Thames and Hudson, 1986).

21 Habakkuk, 1962.

22 Sparke, P. *Electrical Appliances* (London, Bell and Hyman, 1987).

23 Frankl, P. *New Dimensions* (New York: Payson & Clarke, 1928), p. 23.

24 Kwint, M., Breward, C., and Aynsley, J. *Material Memories: Design and Evocation* (Oxford: Berg, 1999).

25 Barthes, R. *Mythologies* (London: Jonathan Cape, 1983), p. 97.

26 Friedel, 1983.

27 Meikle, J.L. *American Plastic: A Cultural History* (New Brunswick, NJ: Rutgers University Press, 1995), p. 6.

28 Meikle, 1995, p. 106.

29 Meikle, 1995, p. 118.

30 Bayley, S. *In Good Shape: Style in Industrial Products 1900–1960* (London: Design Council, 1979).

31 Nichols, 2000.

32 See Sparke, 2000.

33 D. Dohner, 'Modern technique of designing', *Modern Plastics* (14 March 1937), p. 71.

34 Grief, M. *Depression Modern: The Thirties Style in America* (New York: Universe Books, 1975).

35 Pulos, A. *American Design Ethic: A History of Industrial Design to 1940* (Cambridge, MA: MIT Press, 1983), pp. 348–53.

36 Drexler, A. Introduction to *Mies van der Rohe: Furniture and Furniture Drawings* (New York: Museum of Modern Art, 1977), and Frampton, K. *Le Corbusier* (London: Thames and Hudson, 2001).

37 Davies, K. 'Finmar and the furniture of the future: the sale of Alvar Aalto's plywood furniture in the UK, 1934–1939', *Journal of Design History* (vol.11, no.2, 1998), pp. 145–56.

38 See Ierley, M. *The Comforts of Home: The American House and the Evolution of the Modern Convenience* (New York: Three Rivers Press, 1999).

39 Handley, S. *Nylon: The Manmade Fashion Revolution* (London: Bloomsbury, 1999).

Chapter 3   The designer for industry

1 Clark. H. *The Role of the Designer in Early Mass Production Industry* (unpublished PhD thesis, University of Brighton, 1986).

2 Forty, A. *Objects of Desire* (London: Thames and Hudson, 1986).

3 Atterbury, P. and Irvine, L. *The Doulton Story* (London: Victoria and Albert Museum, 1979).

4 Sparke, P. *Electrical Appliances* (London: Bell and Hyman, 1987).

5 Quoted in Naylor, G. *The Arts and Crafts Movement: A Study of its Sources, Ideals and Influence on Design Theory* (London: Studio Vista, 1971).

6 Halen, S. *Christopher Dresser* (Oxford: Phaidon, 1990).

7 Schwartz, F. 'Commodity signs: Peter Behrens and the AEG, and the trademark', *Journal of Design History* (vol.9, no.3, 1996), pp. 153–84.

8 Aynsley, J. *A Century of Graphic Design: Graphic Design Pioneers of the 20th Century* (London: Mitchell Beazley, 2001), p. 6.

9 Hine, T. *The Total Package* (Boston: Little, Brown and Company, 1995), p. 84.

10 Hine, 1995, p. 87.

11 Leach, W. *Lands of Desire: Merchants, Power and the Rise of a New American Culture* (New York: Vintage Books, 1994).

12 Walker, L. 'Women and architecture', in Attfield, J. and Kirkham, P. (eds), *A View from the Interior: Feminism, Women and Design* (London: The Women's Press, 1989).

13 Howe, A.H. *et al. Herter Brothers: Furniture and Interiors for a Gilded Age* (New York: Harry N. Abrams, 1994).

14 Peck, A. and Irish, C. *Candace Wheeler: The Art and Enterprise of American Design 1875– 1900* (New Haven and London: Yale University Press, 2002).

15 Hampton, M. *Legendary Decorators of the Twentieth Century* (New York: Doubleday, 1992).

16 Kirkham, P., Sparke, P. and Gura, J.B. '"A woman's place ..."?: women interior designers', in Kirkham, P. (ed.), *Women Designers in the USA 1900–2000: Diversity and Difference* (New Haven and London: Yale University Press, 2000).

17 Pevsner, N. *Pioneers of Modern Design* (Harmondsworth: Penguin, 1968), pp. 34–5.

18 McConnell, P. 'SID – American hallmark of design integrity', *Art and Industry* (vol.47, 1949), p. 84.

19 Sloan, A.P. *My Years with General Motors* (New York: Mcfadden-Bartell, 1965).

20 Sloan, 1965, p. 269.

21 Meikle, J.L. *Twentieth Century Limited: Industrial Design in America, 1925–1939* (Philadelphia: Temple University Press, 1979).

22 Meikle, 1979, p. 8.

23 See Sparke, P. 'From a lipstick to a steamship: the growth of the American industrial design profession', in Bishop, T. (ed.), *Design History: Fad or Function?* (London: Design Council, 1978), pp. 10–16.

24 Ewen, S. *All Consuming Images: The Politics of Style in Contemporary Culture* (New York: Basic Books, 1988).

25 Ewen, 1988, p. 45.

26 Teague, W.D. *Design This Day: The Technique of Order in the Machine Age* (London: The Studio Publications, 1940).

27 Bel Geddes, N. *Horizons* (Boston: Little, Brown and Company, 1932).

28 Forty, 1986.

29 Bourdieu, P. *Distinction: A Social Critique of the Judgement of Taste* (London and New York: Routledge, 1986).

30 Bel Geddes Archive, Humanities Index, University of Texas, Austin, USA, File 199.

31 See Sparke, P. *Consultant Design: The History and Practice of the Designer in Industry* (London: Pembridge Press, 1983).

32 Wilk, C. *Marcel Breuer: Furniture and Interiors* (New York: Museum of Modern Art, 1981).

33 Aynsley, 2001, p. 15.

34 Rothschild, J. (ed.), *Design and Feminism: Revisioning Spaces, Places and Everyday Things* (New Brunswick, NJ, and London: Rutgers University Press, 1999).

35   Seddon, J. and Worden, S. (eds) *Women Designing: Redefining Design in Britain between the Wars* (Brighton: University of Brighton, 1994).

36   Sparke, P. *As Long as It's Pink: The Sexual Politics of Taste* (London: Pandora, 1995).

Chapter 4   Modernism and design

1   Dorfles, G. *Introduction à l'industrial design* (Paris: Casterman, 1974), p. 15.

2   Foster, H. *Design and Crime* (London and New York: Verso, 2002), p. 18.

3   Pevsner, N. *Pioneers of Modern Design* (Harmondsworth: Penguin, 1960).

4   Banham, P.R. *Theory and Design in the First Machine Age* (London: Architectural Press, 1960).

5   Banham, 1960, p. 14.

6   Banham, 1960, p. 27.

7   Banham, 1960, p. 46.

8   Bourke, J. 'The great male renunciation: men's dress reform in inter-war Britain', *Journal of Design History* (vol.9, no.1, 1996), pp. 23–33), and Burman, B. 'Better and brighter clothes: the men's dress reform party', *Journal of Design History* (vol.8, no.4, 1995), pp. 275–90).

9   Naylor, G. *The Arts and Crafts Movement* (London: Studio Vista, 1971).

10   McCarthy, F. *A History of British Design 1830–1970* (London: Allen and Unwin, 1917), p. 8.

11   Steadman, P. *The Evolution of Designs* (Cambridge: Cambridge University Press, 1979), p. 33.

12   Durant, S. *Victorian Ornamental Design* (London: Academy Editions, 1972).

13   Schaefer. H. *Nineteenth-Century Modern: The Functional Tradition in Victorian Design* (London: Studio Vista, 1970).

14   Hounshell, S. *From the American System to Mass Production 1800–1932: The Development of Manufacturing Technology in the U.S.* (Baltimore and London: Johns Hopkins University Press, 1990).

15   Giedion, S. *Mechanisation Takes Command* (New York: Norton, 1948).

16   Frederick, C. *The New Housekeeping: Efficiency Studies in Home Management* (New York: Garden City, Doubleday Page, 1913).

17   Greenough, H. *Form and Function: Remarks on Art, Design and Architecture* (Berkeley: University of California Press, 1947).

18   Greenough, 1947, p. 131.

19   Loos, A. 'Ornament and crime', reprinted in Conrads, U. (ed.), *Programmes and Manifestoes on Twentieth-Century Architecture* (London: Lund Humphries, 1970).

20   Colomina, B. *Sexuality and Space* (Princeton, NJ: Princeton Architectural Press, 1992).

21   Greenhalgh, P. (ed.) *Art Nouveau 1890–1914* (London: V&A Publications, 2000).

22   Naylor, 1971, p. 184.

23   Tschudi-Madsen, S. *Art Nouveau* (London: Wiedenfeld and Nicholson, 1967), pp. 54–5.

24 Collins, P. *Changing Ideals in Modern Architecture* (London: Faber and Faber, 1965), pp. 267–8.

25 Greenhalgh, P. (ed.) *Modernism and Design* (London: Reaktion Books, 1990).

26 See Bojko, S. *New Graphic Design in Revolutionary Russia* (New York/Washington: Praeger Publishers, 1972).

27 Troy, N. *The De Stijl Environment* (Cambridge, MA: The MIT Press, 1983), p. 5.

28 Overy, P. *De Stijl* (London: Thames and Hudson, 1991).

29 Overy, 1991, p. 32.

30 Naylor, G. 'Swedish grace … or the acceptable face of modernism', in Greenhalgh, 1990, pp. 164–83, and Sparke, P. 'Swedish modern: myth or reality', in Bishop, T. (ed.), *Svensk Form* (London: Design Council, 1981), pp. 15–20.

31 Sparke, 1981, p. 16.

32 Gropius, W. *The New Architecture and the Bauhaus* (London: Faber and Faber, 1935), p. 19.

33 Gropius, 1935, p. 51.

34 Klee, P. *Pedagogical Sketchbook* (London: Faber and Faber, 1953).

35 Gropius, 1935, p. 71.

36 De Zurko, E.R. *Origins of Functionalist Theory* (New York: Columbia University Press, 1957).

37 Collins, 1965.

38 Le Corbusier *Towards a New Architecture* (London: The Architectural Press, 1974 [1927]), p. 7.

39 Le Corbusier, 1974, p. 22.

40 Rietveld built the Schroeder house in 1924/5 while Le Corbusier's Villa Savoie was created in 1927.

41 Bullock, N. 'First the kitchen – then the façade', *Journal of Design History* (vol.1, nos.3 and 4, 1988), pp. 177–92.

42 Thomson, E.M. '"The science of publicity": an American advertising theory, 1890–1920', *Journal of Design History* (vol.9, no.4, 1996), pp. 253–69.

43 Bourke, 1996, pp. 23–33, and Burman, 1995, pp. 275–90.

44 Greenhalgh, 1990, p. 9.

45 Gropius, 1935, p. 92.

46 Sparke, P. *As Long as It's Pink: The Sexual Politics of Taste* (London: Pandora, 1995).

47 Sparke, 1995, p. 118.

Chapter 5   Designing identities

1 McCarthy, F. *A History of British Design 1830–1970* (London: George Allen and Unwin Ltd, 1979), and Pevsner, N. *Pioneers of Modern Design* (Harmondsworth: Penguin, 1968).

2 Heskett, J. *Design in Germany 1870–1918* (London: Trefoil, 1986).

3 Heskett, 1986. p. 58.

4 Greenhalgh, P. *Ephemeral Vistas: The Expositions Universelles, Great Exhibitions and World's Fairs 1851–1939* (Manchester: Manchester University Press, 1988).

5   See Naylor, G. *The Arts and Crafts Movement* (London: Studio Vista, 1971).

6   Ernyey, G. *Made in Hungary: The Best of 150 Years in Industrial Design* (Budapest: Rubik Innovation Foundation, 1993).

7   Exhibition catalogue *Josef Hoffmann 1870–1956: Architect and Designer* (London: Fischer Fine Art Gallery, 1977), pp. 5–6.

8   See Crowley, D. 'Budapest: international metropolis and national capital', in Greenhalgh, P. (ed.), *Art Nouveau 1890–1914* (London: V&A Publications, 2000).

9   Ernyey, 1993.

10 Ernyey, 1993, p. 24.

11 Lamarova, M. 'The new art in Prague', in Greenhalgh, 2000.

12 Campbell, J. *The German Werkbund: The Politics of Reform in the Applied Arts* (Princeton, NJ: Princeton University Press, 1978), Burckhardt, L. *The Werkbund: Studies in the History and Ideology of the Deutscher Werkbund* (London: Design Council, 1980), and Schwartz, F. *The Werkbund: Design Theory and Mass Culture before the First World War* (New Haven and London: Yale University Press, 1996).

13 Campbell, 1978, p. 10.

14 Schwartz, 1996.

15 McFadden, D. *Scandinavian Modern Design 1880–1980* (New York: Harry Abrams, Inc, 1982).

16 Opie, J. 'Helsinki: Saarinen and Finnish Jugend', in Greenhalgh, 2000, p. 375.

17 See Moller, S.E. (ed.) *Danish Design* (Copenhagen: Det danske Selskab, 1974).

18 Silverman, D.L. *Art Nouveau in Fin-de-Siècle France: Politics, Psychology and Style* (Berkeley: University of California Press, 1989).

19 Tiersten, L. *Marianne in the Marketplace: Envisioning Consumer Society in Fin-de-Siecle France* (Berkeley: University of California Press, 2001).

20 Hobsbawm, E.J. *Nations and Nationalisms since 1780* (Cambridge: Cambridge University Press, 1990), p. 141.

21 Hobsbawm, 1990, p. 141.

22 See Hitchcock, H.-R. and Johnson, P. *The International Style* (New York: W.W. Norton and Co. Inc., 1966).

23 Newman, G. 'A survey of design in Britain, 1915–1939', in *British Design* (Milton Keynes: The Open University, 1975).

24 Greenhalgh, 2000.

25 Gronberg, T. *Designs on Modernity: Exhibiting the City in 1920s Paris* (Manchester: Manchester University Press, 1998), p. 11.

26 Gronberg, 1998, p. 30.

27 Dell, S. 'The consumer and the making of the *Exposition Internationale des Arts Décoratifs et Industriels Modernes*, 1907–1925', *Journal of Design History* (vol.12, no.4, 1999), pp. 311–25.

28 Doordan, D. *Twentieth-Century Architecture* (London: Lawrence King, 2001).

29 Ewen, S. *Captains of Concsiousness: Advertising and the Social Roots of Cinsumre Culture* (New York: McGraw Hill, 1977).

30 Bowlby, R. *Shopping with Freud* (London: Routledge, 1993).

31 Frederick, C. *Selling Mrs Consumer* (New York: Business Bourse, 1929).

32 Sheldon, R. and Arens, E. *Consumer Engineering: A New Techique for Prosperity* (New York: Arno Press, 1932), p. 154.

33 'Building the world of tomorrow', *Art and Industry* (vol.26, no.154, April 1939), p. 126.

34 Susman, W.I. 'The People's Fair: cultural contradictions of a consumer society', in *Dawn of a New Day: The New York World's Fair, 1939/40* (New York: New York University Press, 1980), p. 17.

35 Susman, 1980, p. 27.

36 See Woodham, J. 'Images of Africa and design in British Empire exhibitions between the wars', *Journal of Design History* (vol.2, no.1, 1989), pp. 15–33.

37 Woodham, 1989, p. 22.

38 Examples include the De La Warr Pavilion in Bexhill, London Zoo's penguin pool, and the Highpoint, Quarry Hill and Lawn Road housing schemes.

39 Ryan, D.S. *The Ideal Home through the 20th Century* (London: Hazar Publishing, 1997).

40 See Light, A. *Forever England: Femininity, Literature and Conservatism Between the Wars* (London and New York: Routledge, 1991).

41 Elliott, D. Introduction to *Devetsil: Czech Avant-garde Art, Architecture and Design of the 1920s and 1930s* (Oxford and London: Museum of Modern Art, 1990), p. 6.

42 *Design Process: Olivetti, 1908–1983* (Italy: Olivetti, 1983), p. 16.

Chapter 6   Consuming postmodernity

1 Hopkins, H. *The New Look: A Social History of the Forties and Fifties* (London: Secker and Warburg, 1964), p. 231.

2 See Hebdige, D. 'Towards a cartography of taste 1935–1962', in *Hiding in the Light* (London and New York: Routledge, 1988), pp. 45–76.

3 De Grazia, V. 'Changing consumption regimes in Europe', in Strasser, S., McGovern, C. and Judt, M. (eds), *Getting and Spending: European and American Consumer Societies in the Twentieth Century* (Cambridge: Cambridge University Press, 1998), p. 61.

4 Merkel, I. 'Consumer culture in the GDR', in Strasser, McGovern and Judt, 1998, pp. 282–3.

5 Hopkins, 1964.

6 Galbraith, J.K. *The Affluent Society* (Harmondsworth: Penguin, 1958), and Carter, E. *How German is She? National Reconstruction and the Consuming Woman in the FRG and West Berlin 1945–1960* (Ann Arbor, MI: University of Michigan, 1996).

7 Williams, R. *Culture and Society 1780–1950* (London: Chatto and Windus, 1958).

8 See writings by Theodor W. Adorno and Max Horkeheimer on the subject, among them *Dialect of Enlightenment* (London: Verso, 1979 [1944]).

9 Williams, R. *Communications* (Harmondsworth: Penguin, 1968), p. 99.

10 Williams, 1968, p. 85.

11 Marling, K.A. *As Seen on TV: The Visual Culture of Everyday Life in America in the 1950s* (Cambridge, MA: Harvard University Press, 1994).

12   See McDermott, C. 'Popular taste and the campaign for contemporary design in the 1950s', in Sparke, P. (ed.), *Did Britain Make It? British Design in Context, 1946–1986* (London: Design Council, 1986), pp. 156–64.

13   Wilson, R. *Only Halfway to Paradise, Women in Postwar Britain, 1945–1968* (London and New York: Tavistock Publications, 1980), p. 38.

14   Riesman, D. *The Lonely Crowd: A Study of the Changing American Character* (New Haven and New York: Yale University Press, revised edition, 1970).

15   1948 Newson report quoted in Wilson, 1980.

16   Mort, F. 'Boy's own? Masculinity, style and popular culture', in Chapman, R. and Rutherford, J. (eds), *Male Order* (London: Lawrence and Wishart, 1993).

17   Hine, T. *Populuxe: The Look and Life of America in the 1950s and 1960s, from Tailfins and TV Dinners to Barbie Dolls and Fallout Shelters* (New York: Alfred A. Knopf, 1986).

18   During, S. (ed.) *Cultural Studies Reader* (London and New York: Routledge, 1993), p. 62.

19   Massey, A. *The Independent Group: Modernism and Mass Culture in Britain, 1945–1959* (Manchester: Manchester University Press, 1995), and Whiteley, N. *Pop Design: Modernism to Mod* (London: Design Council, 1987).

20   Attfield, J. 'Inside Pram Town: a case study of Harlow House Interiors, 1951–1961', in Attfield, J. and Kirkham, P. (eds), *A View From the Interior: Feminism, Women and Design* (London: The Women's Press, 1989), pp. 215–38.

21   Wright, L. 'Objectifying desire: the stiletto heel', in Attfield and Kirkham, 1989, p. 17.

22   Hebdige, D. 'Object as image: the Italian scooter cycle', in Hebdige, 1988, pp. 77–115.

23   See Clarke, A. *Tupperware: The Promise of Plastic in 1950s America* (Washington and London: Smithsonian Institution Press, 1999), and Peiss, K. *Hope in a Jar* (New York: Metropolitan Books, 1998).

24   See Moller, S.E. (ed.) *Danish Design* (Copenhagen: Der Danske Selskab, 1974).

25   See Venturi, R. *Complexity and Contradiction in Architecture* (New York: The Museum of Modern Art, 1966).

26   Venturi, 1966, p. 23.

27   Sparke, P. *Theory and Design in the Age of Pop* (unpublished PhD thesis, University of Brighton, 1975).

28   Lyotard, F. *The Postmodern Condition: A Report on Knowledge* (Manchester: Manchester University Press, 1984), p. 81.

29   Haug, W.H. *Critique of Commodity Aesthetics: Appearance, Sexuality and Advertising in Capitalist Society* (Oxford: Polity Press, 1986), p. 45.

30   Lehtonen, T.-K. and Maenpaa, P. 'Shopping in the East Centre Mall', in Falk, P. and Campbell, C. (eds), *The Shopping Experience* (London: Sage, 1997).

32   Baudrillard, J. *Simulations* (New York: Semiotext[e], 1983).

32   Mort, F. *Cultures of Consumption: Masculinities and Social Space in Late Twentieth-century Britain* (London and New York: Routledge, 1996).

33   Entwhistle, J. '"Power dressing" and the construction of the career woman', in Nava, M., Blake, A., MacRury, I. and Richards, B. *Buy This Book: Studies in Advertising and Consumption* (London and New York: Routledge, 1997).

34 Lunt, P. and Livingstone, S.M. *Mass Consumption and Personal Identity: Everyday Economic Experience* (Buckingham and Philadelphia: Open University Press, 1992).

35 Douglas, M., and Isherwood, B. *The World of Goods: Towards an Anthropology of Consumption* (Harmondsworth: Penguin, 1978), p. 59.

36 Du Gay, P., Hall, S., Mackay, H. and Negus, K. (eds), *Doing Cultural Studies: The Story of the Sony Walkman* (Milton Keynes: The Open University, 1997).

37 Bauman, Z. quoted in Warde, A. 'Consumers, identity and belonging: reflections on some theses of Zygmunt Bauman', in Keat, R., Whiteley, N. and Abercrombie, N. (eds), *The Authority of the Consumer* (London and New York: Routledge, 1994).

38 Pavitt, J. (ed.) *Brand New* (London: V&A Publications, 2000).

39 Klein, N. *No Logo* (London: Flamingo, 2001), p. 4.

40 Dyson, J. *Against the Odds: An Autobiography* (London: Orion, 1997).

41 Hewison. R. *The Heritage Industry: Britain in a Climate of Decline* (London: Methuen, 1987), Wright, P. *On Living in an Old Country: The National Past in Contemporary Britain* (London: Verso, 1985), and Samuel, R. *Theatres of Memory, Vol. I: Past and Present in Contemporary Culture* (London: Verso, 1995).

42 Urry, J. *Consuming Places* (London and New York: Routledge, 1995).

43 Wright, 1985, p. 5.

44 Urry, 1995, p. 177.

45 Eco, U. *Travels in Hyperreality* (New York: Harcourt Brace Jovanovich, 1986).

46 Zukin, S. *Landscapes of Power: From Detroit to Disneyland* (Berkeley: University of California Press, 1992).

Chapter 7   Technology and design: a new alliance

1 *Dupont: The Autobiography of an American Enterprise* (Wilmington, DE: E.I. Du Pont de Nemours & Company, 1952), p. 119.

2 Hine, T. *Populuxe: The Look and Life of America in the '50s and '60s, from Tailfins and TV Dinners to Barbie Dolls and Fallout Shelters* (New York: Alfred A. Knopf, 1986), p. 70.

3 Hine, 1986, p. 128.

4 See Hogan, M.J. *The Marshall Plan: America, Britain and the Reconstruction of Western Europe, 1947–1952* (Cambridge: Cambridge University Press, 1987).

5 Sparke, P. *Italian Design: 1870 to the Present* (London: Thames and Hudson, 1988).

6 Sparke, 1988 and Sparke, P. *Japanese Design* (London: Michael Joseph, 1987).

7 Sparke, P. 'The straw donkey: tourist kitsch or proto-design? Craft and design in Italy, 1945–1960', *Journal of Design History* (vol.11, no.1, 1998), pp. 59–69.

8 Palmer, A. *Couture and Commerce: The Transatlantic Fashion Trade in the 1950s* (Toronto: UBC Press, 2001).

9 Palmer, 2001, p. 20.

10 Pulos, A.J. *The American Design Adventure 1940–1975* (Cambridge, MA: MIT Press, 1988).

11 Pulos, 1988, p. 79.

12 Jackson, L. *Robin and Lucienne Day: Pioneers of Contemporary Design* (London: Mitchell Beazley, 2001).

13   Catterall, C. 'Perceptions of plastics: a study of plastics in Britain 1945–1956', in Sparke, P. (ed.), *The Plastics Age: From Modernity to Postmodernity* (London: V&A Publications, 1990), pp. 68–9.

14   Sparke, P. 'Plastics and pop culture', in Sparke, 1990, pp. 92–104.

15   Attfield, J. 'The tufted carpet in Britain: its rise from the bottom of the pile, 1952–70', *Journal of Design History* (vol.7, no.3, 1994), pp. 205–16.

16   Pile, S. 'The foundation of modern comfort: latex foam and the industrial impact of design on the British rubber industry, 1948–1958', in *One-Off: A Collection of Essays by Postgraduate Students on the V&A/RCA Course in the History of Design* (London: Victoria and Albert Museum, 1997).

17   Clarke, A.J. *Tupperware: The Promise of Plastic in 1950s America* (Washington and London: Smithsonian Institution Press, 1999).

18   Clarke, 1999, p. 10.

19   Handley, S. *Nylon: The Manmade Fashion Revolution* (London: Bloomsbury, 1999).

20   Sparke, 1988.

21   Blaszczyk, R. *Imagining Consumers: Design and Innvoation from Wedgwood to Corning* (Baltimore and London: Johns Hopkins University Press, 2000).

22   Blaszczyk, 2000, p. 275.

23   Kron, J. and Slesin, S. *High Tech* (New York: Potter, 1978).

24   Du Gay, P., Hall, S., Janes, L., Mackay, H. and Negus, K. (eds) *Doing Cultural Studies: The Story of the Sony Walkman* (Milton Keynes: The Open University, 1997).

25   Postman, N. *Technopoly: The Surrender of Culture to Technology* (New York: Vintage Books, 1993).

26   Postman, 1993, p. 7.

27   Ive, J. 'The apple bites back', *Design* (no.I, Autumn 1998), pp. 36–41.

28   Hounshell, D. *From the American System to Mass Production 1800–1932: The Development of Manufacturing Technology in the US* (Baltimore and London: Johns Hopkins University Press, 1982).

29   Sparke, 1987.

30   Sabel, C.F. *Work and Politics: The Division of Labor in Industry* (Cambridge: Cambridge University Press, 1982).

31   Wajcsman, J. *Feminism Confronts Technology* (Cambridge: Polity, 1991), p. 137.

32   Scharff, V. 'Gender and genius: the auto industry and femininity', in Martinez, K. and Ames, K.L. (eds), *The Material Culture of Gender, the Gender of Material Culture* (Winterthur, DE: Henry Francis du Pont Winterthur Museum, 1997), p. 137.

33   Horowitz, R. *Boys and their Toys? Masculinity, Class and Technology in America* (New York/London: Routledge, 2001).

34   Manzini, E. *The Material of Invention: Materials and Design* (Milan: Arcadia, 1986), p. 66.

35   Manzini, 1986, p. 68.

36   Antonelli, P. 'Aluminum and the new materialism', in Nichols, S. (ed.), *Aluminum by Design* (New York: Harry N. Abrams, 2000), p. 185.

Chapter 8 Designer culture

1 See Jackson, L. *The New Look: Design in the Fifties* (London: Thames and Hudson, 1991), Jackson, L. *The Sixties: Decade of Design Revolution* (London: Phaidon, 2000), and Hines, T. *Populuxe: The Look and Life of America in the '50s and '60s, from Tailfins to TV Dinners to Barbie Dolls and Fallout Shelters* (New York: Alfred A. Knopf, 1986).

2 Day, R. 'At the Robin Days', in *Daily Mail Ideal Home Yearbook 1953–54* (London: Daily Mail Publication, 1954).

3 Race, E. 'Design in Modern Furniture', in *Daily Mail Ideal Home Book 1952–53* (London: Daily Mail Publication, 1953), p. 62.

4 Hard af Segerstad, U. *Scandinavian Design* (Stockholm: Nordisk Rotogtavyr, 1961), p. 16.

5 Sparke, P. *Italian Design: 1870 to the Present* (London: Thames and Hudson, 1988).

6 Kirkham, P. *Charles and Ray Eames: Designers of the Twentieth Century* (Cambridge, MA, and London: MIT Press, 1995).

7 Kirkham, 1995, p. 61.

8 Kaufmann Jr, E. *Introductions to Modern Design* (New York: The Museum of Modern Art, 1950), p. 9.

9 Kaufmann, 1950, p. 8.

10 Bayley, S. *Art and Industry* (London: Boilerhouse Project, 1982).

11 *Kenneth Grange at the Boilerhouse: An Exhibition of British Product Design* (London: Boilerhouse Project, 1983).

12 See Aloi, R. *L'arredamento moderno* (Milan: Hoepli, 1955).

13 See Murgatroyd, K. *Modern Graphics* (London: Studio Vista, 1969), and Aynsley, J. *A Century of Graphic Design* (London: Mitchell Beazley, 2001).

14 Banham, R. (ed.) *The Aspen Papers: Twenty Years of Design Theory from the International Design Conference in Aspen* (London: Pall Mall Press, 1974).

15 Packard, V. *The Hidden Persuaders* (Harmondsworth: Penguin, 1957), Packard, V. *The Status Seekers* (Harmondsworth: Penguin, 1963), and Packard, V. *The Waste-Makers* (London: Longmans, 1961).

16 Ambasz, E. (ed.) *Italy: The New Domestic Landscape, Achievements and Problems of Italian Design* (New York: The Museum of Modern Art, 1972).

17 Foster, H. *Design and Crime* (London and New York: Verso, 2002).

18 Dyer, R. *Stars* (London: British Film Institute, 1992).

19 McDermott, C. *Street Style: British Design in the '80s* (London: Design Council, 1987).

20 Radice, B. and Sottsass, E. *Ettore Sottsass: A Critical Biography* (New York: Rizzoli, 1993).

21 *Alessi Design Factory* London: Academy Editions, 1998), and Sweet, F. *Alessi: Art and Poetry* (London: Thames and Hudson, 1998).

22 Boissière, O. *Philippe Starck* (Munich: Taschen, 1991) and Sweet, F. *Philippe Starck: Subverchic Design* (London: Watson-Guptil, 1999).

23 See Sparke, P. *A Century of Car Design* (London: Mitchell Beazley, 2002).

24 See Wollen, P. and Kerr, J. (eds) *Autopia: Cars and Culture* (London: Reaktion Books, 2002).

25 J. Mays, lecture given at the Design Museum, London, 15 August 2002.

26 Kelley, T., Littman, J., and Peters, T. *The Art of Innovation: Lessons in Creativity from IDEO, America's Leading Design Firm* (New York: Doubleday, 2001).

27 Julier, G. *The Culture of Design* (London: Sage, 2000), pp. 22–3.

Chapter 9 Postmodernism and design

1 Arnheim, R. 'From function to expression', *The Journal of Aesthetics and Art Criticism* (Fall, 1964), p. 31.

2 Raymond Loewy, Norman Bel Geddes and others claimed to be following in the footsteps of the European modernists whom they admired.

3 Banham, R. 'A throw-away aesthetic', in Sparke, P. (ed.), *Reyner Banham: Design by Choice* (London: Academy Editions, 1980) pp. 90–3.

4 Kaufmann Jr, E. 'Borax or the chromium-plated calf', *Architectural Review* (August 1948), pp. 88–93.

5 Whiteley, N. *Pop Design: Modernism to Mod* (London: Design Council, 1987), Massey, A. *The Independent Group: Modernism and Mass Culture in Britain 1945–59* (Manchester: Manchester University Press, 1995), Massey, A. and Sparke, P. 'The myth of the Independent Group', *Block* (Middlesex University, 10, 1985), pp. 48–56, and Hebdige, D. 'In poor taste: notes on Pop', in *Hiding in the Light* (London and New York: Routledge, 1988), pp. 116–43.

6 McCale, J. 'The expendable icon', *Architectural Review* (London: Feb/March, 1959).

7 Barthes, R. *Mythologies* (London, Jonathan Cape, 1972), pp. 88 and 99.

8 Dorfles, G. *Kitsch* (London: Studio Vista, 1969), and Moles, A. *Le Kitsch* (Paris: Maison Mame, 1971).

9 Boorstin, D.J. *The Image* (London: Weidenfeld and Nicholson, 1962), p. 186.

10 Boorstin, 1962, p. 16.

11 Masson, P. and Thorburn, A. 'Advertising: the American influence on Europe', in Bigsby, C.W.E. (ed.), *Superculture: American Popular Culture and Europe* (London: Paul Elek, 1975), p. 98.

12 Hebdige, D. 'Towards a cartography of taste 1935–62', in Hebdige, 1988, p.52.

13 Hughes-Stanton, C. 'What comes after Carnaby Street?' *Design* (February 1968).

14 Sparke, P. *Theory and Design in the Age of Pop* (unpublished PhD thesis, Brighton University, 1975).

15 Sparke, P. *Ettore Sottsass* (London: Design Council, 1982).

16 Venturi, R. *Complexity and Contradiction in Architecture* (New York: Museum of Modern Art, 1966).

17 Lindinger, H. Introduction to *Hochschule für Gestaltung, Ulm: Die Moral der Gegenstande* (Berlin: Ernst & Sohn, 1987).

18 Lyotard, J.F. *The Post-modern Condition: A Report on Knowledge* (Manchester: Manchester University Press, 1984).

19 These included Jean-François Lyotard's *The Postmodern Condition*, originally published in 1979 by Editions de Minuit, Hal Foster (ed.) *The Anti-Aesthetic: Essays on Postmodern Culture* (Port Townsend: Bay Press, 1983), Jameson, F. 'Postmodernism, or the

cultural logic of late capitalism', *New Left Review* (vol.146, July/August 1984), pp. 53–92, Huyssen, A. *After the Great Divide: Modernism, Mass Culture and Postmodernism* (London: Macmillan, 1986), Harvey, D. *The Condition of Postmodernity* (Oxford: Blackwell, 1989), and Hutcheon, L. *The Politics of Postmodernism* (London and New York: Routledge, 1989).

20 See Habermas, J. 'Modernity – an incomplete project', in Foster, 1983.

21 Wolff, J. *Feminine Sentences: Essays in Women and Culture* (Cambridge: Polity Press, 1990), p. 87.

22 Huyssen, 1986.

23 Harvey, 1989, p. 39.

24 Jameson, 1984.

25 Bourdieu, P. *Distinction: A Social Critique of the Judgment of Taste* (London and New York: Routledge, 1986 [1979]).

26 Douglas, M. and Isherwood, B. *The World of Goods: Towards an Anthropology of Consumption* (London and New York: Routledge, 1996 [1979]).

27 Miller, D. *Material Culture and Mass Consumption* (Oxford: Basil Blackwell, 1987), McCracken, G. *Culture and Consumption: New Approaches to the Symbolic Character of Consumer Goods* (Bloomington and Indianapolis: Indiana University Press), and Featherstone, M. *Consumer Culture and Postmodernism* (London: Sage, 1983).

28 Giddens, A. *Modernity and Self-Identity: Self and Society in the Late Modern Age* (California: Stanford University Press, 1991).

29 Said, E. *Culture and Imperialism* (New York: Vintage Books, 1994).

30 Jameson, F. 'Postmodernism and consumer society', in Foster, 1983, p. 111.

31 McCracken, 1988, p. 105.

32 Jameson, 1983, p. 113.

33 Venturi, 1966.

34 Venturi, R., Scott-Brown, D., and Izenour, S. *Learning from Las Vegas: The Forgotten Symbolism of Architecural Form* (Cambridge, MA: MIT Press, 1972).

35 Jencks, C. *The Language of Post-Modern Architecture* (London: Academy Editions, 1977), p. 96.

36 See Collins, M. and Papadakis, A. *Post-Modern Design* (London: Academy Editions, 1989).

37 See Sparke, P. *Japanese Design* (London: Michael Joseph, 1987).

Chapter 10   Redefining identities

1 Huygen, F. *British Design: Image and Identity* (London: Thames and Hudson, 1989), pp. 19 and 23.

2 Sparke, P. (ed.) *Did Britain Make It? British Design in Context, 1946–86* (London: The Design Council, 1986).

3 Oram, S. 'Constructing contemporary: common-sense approaches to "going modern" in the 1950s', in McKellar, S. and Sparke, P. (eds), *Interior Design and Identity* (Manchester: Manchester University Press, 2004).

4 McFadden, D. *Scandinavian Modern Design* (New York: Harry N. Abrams, 1982).

5   McFadden, 1982, p. 21.

6   Hard Af Segerstad, U. *Scandinavian Design* (London: Studio Books, 1961).

7   Pulos. A. *The American Design Ethic* (Cambridge, MA: MIT Press, 1983), and *The American Design Adventure* (Cambridge, MA: MIT Press, 1988).

8   Sparke, P. *Italian Design, 1879 to the Present* (London: Thames and Hudson, 1988), and *Japanese Design* (London: Michael Joseph, 1987).

9   Sabel, C.F. *Work and Politics: The Division of Labour in Industry* (Cambridge: Cambridge University Press, 1982).

10 Sparke, P. 'Nature, craft, domesticity and the culture of consumption: the feminine face of design in Italy 1945–60', *Modern Italy* (vol.4, no.I, 1999).

11 See Bayley, S. *Coca-Cola 1886–1986: Designing a Megabrand* (London: The Boilerhouse, 1986).

12 Bayley, 1986, p. 63.

13 Bayley, 1986, p. 62.

14 Hobsbawm, E. *The Invention of Tradition* (Cambridge: Cambridge University Press, 1992).

15 *Design français 1960–1990* (Paris: Centre Georges Pompidou, 1990).

16 Narotzky, V. *An Aquired Taste: The Consumption of Design in Barcelona, 1975–1992* (unpublished PhD thesis, Royal College of Art, London, 2003).

17 Wright, P. *On Living in an Old Country: The National Past in Contemporary Britain* (London: Verso, 1985), p. 2.

18 Hewison, R. *The Heritage Industry: Britain in a Climate of Decline* (London: Methuen, 1987), p. 24.

19 Crowley, D. *National Style and National State: Design in Poland from the Vernacular Revival to the International Style* (Manchester: Manchester University Press, 1992).

20 Quoted in Franklyn, S., Lury, C. and Stacey, J. *Global Nature, Global Culture* (London: Sage, 2000), p. 2.

21 Franklyn, Lury and Stacey, 2000, p. 3.

22 Zygmunt Bauman's term 'neo-tribes' is referred to in Warde, A. 'Consumers, identity and belonging: reflections on some theses of Zygmunt Bauman', in Keat, R., Whiteley, N. and Abercrombie, N. (eds), *The Authority of the Consumer* (London and New York: Routledge, 1994), p. 58.

23 Oliver, T. *The Real Coke: The Real Story* (London: Elm Tree, 1986), Pendergrast, M. *For God, Country and Coca-Cola* (London: Weidenfeld and Nicholson, 1993), and Miller, D. 'Coca-Cola: a black sweet drink from Trinidad', in Miller, D. (ed.), *Material Cultures: Why Some Things Matter* (London: UCl Press, 1998).

24 Falk, P. *The Consuming Body* (London: Sage, 1994) pp. 180–2, and 'The Benetton–Toscani effect: testing the limits of conventional advertising', in Nava, M., Blake, A., MacRury, I. and Richards. B. (eds), *Buy This Book: Studies in Advertising and Consumption* (London: and New York: Routledge, 1997), and Lury, C. 'The United Colors of Diversity', in Franklyn, Lury and Stacey, 2000, pp. 146–87.

25 Lury, 2000, p. 167.

26 Du Gay, P., Hall, S., Janes. L., Mackay, H. and Negus, K. (eds) *Doing Cultural Studies: The Story of the Sony Walkman* (Milton Keynes: The Open University Press, 1997).

27 *Newdesign* Magazine (London: Design Council, July/August, 2002), p. 22.

28 Kirkham, P. (ed.), *The Gendered Object* (Manchester and New York: Manchester University Press, 1996), and Martinez, K. and Ames, K.L. (eds) *The Material Culture of Gender: The Gender of Material Culture* (Winterthur, DE: The Henry Francis de Pont Wintherthur Museum, 1997).

29 Kirkham, P. and Weller, A. 'Cosmetics: a Clinique case study', in Kirkham, 1996, p. 199.

30 Partington, A. 'Perfume: pleasure, packaging and postmodernity', in Kirkham, 1996, p. 205.

GLOSSARY

Aalto, Alvar (1898–1976) A Finnish architect–designer best known for his humanistic buildings executed in a modern, organic style (e.g., Viipuri Library, 1927–35 and Paimio Sanitorium, 1929–1933); his furniture, which was made from wood moulded into two-dimensional curves; his curvaceous glass vases; and his textiles.

Anti-Design The name given to the Italian movement of the 1960s, and its revival in the 1980s, which set out to disassociate design from commerce and position it within the cultural area. The term Radical Design was used interchangeably. Ettore Sottsass played a key role in the movement from the 1960s onwards.

Arad, Ron (1951–) An Israeli designer who made his impact in London, where he settled in 1974, selling his idiosyncratic designs through his shop in Covent Garden. He was associated with the High-Tech movement in the 1970s and he formed a company called One-Off. His best-known design is the Rover chair, made from a recycled car seat. He is Professor of Design at the Royal College of Art.

Archizoom An Italian architectural group, formed in 1966 in Florence, which participated in the Anti-Design movement. Its early members included Andrea Branzi and Paolo Deganello, and the group created a number of visionary environments and some fantasy furniture as part of its attempt to move Italian design away from its preoccupations with consumerism and high style.

Art Deco The name of a design movement that emerged in France in the 1920s, taking its name from the 1925 *Exposition des Arts Décoratifs* , held in Paris. Although it was a term associated with exclusive objects in the first instance it moved into the popular arena in the 1930s through its mass production and dissemination and its alliance with new materials, such as plastics.

Art Nouveau The name of an international architectural and decorative arts movement which came into being in the 1890s but which had disappeared by 1914. It was characterised by its flowing, organic forms in France, Spain and elsewhere but it had more rectilinear manifestations in Scotland and Austria. It has been described as the first modern design style.

Arts and Crafts Movement A British architectural and design movement, based on the ideas of John Ruskin and William Morris in Britain, which sought to eliminate the bad effects of industrialisation on material culture and revert to a pre-industrial model in which hand-making played a part. The ideas and designs of the Arts and Crafts protagonists – C.F.A. Voysey and C.R. Ashbee among them – were enormously influential abroad and influenced the early development of modernism internationally.

Banham, Peter Reyner (1922–88) A British architectural and design historian, theorist and critic who wrote prolifically in the 1950s and 60s about the Modern Movement and its demise. A member of the Independent Group in the 1950s he introduced the topics of mass culture and design to its meetings. He taught at a number of institutions, including the University of Los Angeles at Santa Cruz where he was Professor of Art History.

Bauhaus The most influential design school of the twentieth century, the Bauhaus was formed in 1919 in Weimar by Walter Gropius and it subsequently moved to Dessau. It took a radical approach to design education, starting from scratch and developing forms in craft workshops in collaboration with fine artists. It was closed by the Nazis in 1933.

Behrens, Peter (1868–1940) Peter Behrens was an architect–designer who worked in the Art Nouveau idiom in Darmstadt before becoming a consultant to the AEG Company, for which he designed a complete corporate identity in 1907. Walter Gropius, Mies van der Rohe and Le Corbusier all spent time in his studio.

Bel Geddes, Norman (1893–1952) Norman Bel Geddes began his career as a portrait painter before moving into stage design, shop-window display and finally consultant industrial design. His 'streamlined' fantasies for transport designs were the most expressive of the 1930s, but his work for production was more mundane by comparison.

Bellini, Mario (1935–) The Milanese architect–designer Mario Bellini is best known for his elegant typewriters and office machines, which he created for Olivetti in the 1960s and 70s, as well as for his stylish furniture designed for Cassina. An innovative product designer he also created a wedge-shaped tape-deck for the Japanese firm Yamaha. He was much admired and widely emulated in the 1970s.

Brandt, Marianne (1893–1983) A German painter, designer and metalworker who established her reputation through her work at the German Bauhaus, where was a graduate. She went on to become the head of the metal workshop and she designed some highly geometric objects there, including a small teapot, which have become classic designs.

Branzi, Andrea (1938–) A Florentine architect–designer who was a member of Archizoom in the 1960s and who moved later to Milan to play a central role in the second phase of Italian Radical design, which emerged at the the end of the 1970s. He is also a teacher and writer.

Breuer, Marcel (1902–81) The Hungarian architect–designer Marcel Breuer was trained at the German Bauhaus Weimar, where he designed his famous tubular-steel chairs. He went on to teach at that institution and, on its closure by the Nazis, came to England to work for Jack Pritchard's Isokon company, for which he developed chairs made from bent plywood. In 1937 Breuer went to the USA to join Walter Gropius at Harvard.

Brody, Neville (1957–) Born in London the graphic designer Neville Brody worked on *The Face* magazine in the 1980s developing radically new typefaces and lay-outs. He combined early modernist ideas with images emanating from contemporary subculture to create a new look that was highly influential. Brody moved on to work on record covers and a wide range of graphic design projects.

Castiglioni, Achille (1918–2002) Of the three Castiglioni brothers, Pier Giacomo (1910–1968), Livio (1912–1952), and Achille it was the last, a Milan-based designer, who had the greatest influence on twentieth-century design. His designs for furniture, lighting and appliances – among them the Tractor Seat (Mezzadro) for Zanotta and his Arco light for Floa – won him numerous prizes and made him an important force both in Italy and elsewhere.

Chanel, Coco (1883–1971) The French fashion couturier Coco Chanel was a pioneer in the field, opening her first millinery shop in 1909 and moving on to create a highly influential fashion house in the inter-war years. She anticipated the idea of selling clothes as part of a lifestyle and launched her perfume Chanel No. 5, to accompany her clothes, in 1923.

Cliff, Clarice (1899–1972) A British ceramic designer who came out of the Stoke-on-Trent tradition but who went on to make a reputation for herself as a result of her brightly painted ceramics, which she sold through her own firm. Her pattern named 'Bizarre' was among her most successful designs. Her work is avidly collected.

Coates, Wells (1895–1958) Born in Tokyo, Wells Coates came to Britain in 1929 and became a major figure in the British architectural and design modern movement. After working on shop interiors he went on to design an apartment block for Jack Pritchard's Isokon firm and he pioneered modern industrial design through his work for the Ekco Radio Company.

Colombo, Joe (1930–71)   One of the most influential of the super-star Italian designers of the 1960s Colombo is especially remembered for his brightly coloured plastic products designed for Kartell. He began life as a painter but went on to produce influential furniture and product designs for several Italian manufacturers, including Zanotta, Elco and Stilnovo.

Conran, Terence (1931–)   Trained as a furniture designer in London, Terence Conran's impact on post-war British, and international, design was through his role as a retailer of lifestyle products. He opened Habitat in London's Fulham Road in 1964 and went on from there to influence post-war taste and aspirations through his numerous retailing achievements. Latterly he has moved into developing restaurants.

Constructivism   The name given to the modern movement in art, architecture and design which is linked to the abstract work that emanated from Russia in the years around the 1917 Revolution. It took its lead from engineering, seeking to move away from the decorative traditions of the applied arts.

Contemporary Style   A term used to describe the modern yet decorative domestic style of furniture and furnishings that emerged in the years after the Second World War in Britain. The work exhibited at the 1951 Festival of Britain was highly influential on this essentially popular style, which was characterised by its biomorphic forms and bright colours.

Cooper, Susie (1902–95)   A British ceramic artist and business woman who, like Clarice Cliff, grew out of the Stoke-on-Trent tradition but who moved on to sell her own highly abstract, modern work. Her Curlew shape of 1933 was among her best known. In the 1960s her company was absorbed by Wedgwood.

Coray, Hans (1906–91)   The Swiss designer Hans Coray is best known for his all-aluminium chair, which was shown at the Zurich exhibition of 1939 and is still in production today.

Day, Robin (1915–) and Lucienne (1917–)   Robin Day was one of Britain's leading furniture designers in the 1950s and 60s, working with the Hille Company, while his wife, Lucienne, was known for her textile designs, retailed through Heals. They collaborated on several interiors, notably at the Milan Triennale of 1954.

De Lucchi, Michele (1951–)   The Milan-based architect–designer, de Lucchi,played a leading role in the Memphis project of the early 1980s. He went on to combine his work for Olivetti, and for other international product manufacturers, with his own experimental work in which he continued to push the cultural role of design into new areas.

De Stijl   The De Stijl Movement, which took its name from a Dutch magazine of the same name, was formed during the First World War in

Holland. It combined the fine-art work of Piet Mondrian with the design, graphic and architectural work of several others, all of whom sought to find a new abstract, geometric aesthetic for their practices.

De Wolfe, Elsie (1865–1950)   A pioneer American interior decorator, who worked from both New York and Paris, who created a new consultant profession that entailed supplying interior furnishings to clients as a means of increasing the level of taste in their homes. She was one of the first to understand the close link, for consumers, between design, taste and lifestyle.

Dior, Christian (1905–57)   The French fashion designer Dior launched his first collection with what he called the New Look in 1947. It had an enormous impact and he helped establish Paris as the headquarters of post-war haute couture. Following his sudden death, Yves Saint Laurent took over the design direction of his fashion house. In 1996 the British designer John Galliano became the chief designer at Dior.

Dresser, Christopher (1834–1904)   Dresser was an English designer who began his career as a botanist but moved later into product design. His metalwork and textiles were greatly influenced by Japan (which he visited in 1877) and he became one of the first designers internationally to work with manufacturing industry on a freelance basis.

Dreyfuss, Henry (1902–72)   From his background in the theatre prop business, Dreyfuss, like Norman Bel Geddes, was a stage designer before he became a consultant industrial designer. His early clients included the Bell Telephone Company; the Hoover Company; and the New York Central Railroad. He wrote about his anthropometric approach to design in his book *Designing for People*, published in 1955.

Deutscher Werkbund   One of the first European modern design reform bodies, created in Germany in 1907 as a state and industry partnership, which set out to promote modern design as a key component of trade and national identity. The Werkbund sponsored the Cologne Exhibition of 1914 and a number of others in later years. It provided a model that several other countries emulated.

Eames, Charles (1907–78) and Ray (1912–88)   The American architect–designer Charles Eames first came to public notice when his moulded plywood furniture, designed with Eero Saarinen, won a competition at the Museum of Modern Art in New York in 1944. He had a one-man show there two years later at which he introduced furniture that combined moulded plywood with steel rod. He went on to design a number of even more innovative furniture items through the 1950s and 60s, as well as venturing, with his wife Ray, who worked collaboratively with him from the 1940s onwards, into experimental film-making.

Earl, Harley (1893–1969)　Earl began his career as a coach-builder in Hollywood but was employed by Alfred. P. Sloan of General Motors (GM) in 1926 to make the company's mass-produced automobiles look more attractive. The 1927 Cadillac Lasalle made automotive history in this respect and Earl went on to head the Styling Section at GM until the 1950s.

El Lizzitsky (1890–1940)　A Russian graphic designer who worked for various architects up to 1917 and who subsequently became involved with the artistic propaganda of the Revolution. His work was executed in the Suprematist style, pioneered by the Russian artist Kasimir Malevich, and he is best known for his 'Proun' compositions of the early 1920s.

Esslinger, Hartmut (1945–)　The founder of the German design consultancy frogdesign, which was based in his home town of Altensteig. In 1982, the consultancy opened a Californian office and Apple Computer became an important client, for whom frogdesign created the first all-white computer. Other clients have included Villeroy and Bosch, and Sony.

Fowler, John (1906–77)　A British interior decorator who adopted a historicist approach from the inter-war years onwards. He worked with the National Trust in the years following the Second World War, restoring dilapidated country houses with chintz fabrics. He was a partner, with Nancy Lancaster, in Colefax and Fowler.

Franck, Kay (1911–88)　A Finnish ceramicist, textile, and glassware designer who took a more subtle, everyday approach than that of his contemporary 'super-star' designers. He was a designer at the Arabia pottery for many years, responsible for numerous simple, practical wares, including his 1952 *Kilta* tableware.

Frank, Josef (1885–1947)　An Austrian modernist architect who settled in Sweden in 1934 and who became the chief designer for the Stockholm furnishings company Svenskt Tenn. He modified his earlier purist aesthetic to include pattern and texture in his later furniture, lights and fabrics. An early exponent of the style known as 'Swedish Modern', he remained with Svenskt Tenn until his death.

Fuller, Richard Buckminster (1895–1983)　An American designer and visionary who embraced design, and wrote and lectured extensively about it, as part of advanced technology in the service of mankind. He designed a Dymaxion house in 1927, a Dymaxion car in 1932 and, later, a series of geodesic domes.

Functionalism　A term used by design theorists to describe the ideas of the protagonists of the early twentieth-century Modern Movement in architecture, who sought to derive their forms through an abstract consideration of their object's function, a process akin to that of an engineer, rather than by adding decoration to its surface to make it desirable.

Gaudí, Antonio (1852–1926) A Spanish architect and designer, based in Barcelona, who evolved his own idiosyncratic version of Art Nouveau. His buildings – including the Sagrada Familia of 1903–26, the Casa Vicens of 1878–80, and his Parque Guell, begun in 1900 – all displayed the same fantastic aesthetic as his furniture designs.

Giacosa, Dante (1905–96) A designer–engineer who worked for the Italian automobile manufacturer Fiat from the late 1920s into the 1970s. His most influential designs included the Fiat 500 of 1936 and the little 600 of 1956. He approached the problem of style as an engineer and, as a result, worked very differently from his contemporary car stylists in the USA.

Giedion, Siegfried (1888–1968) A Swiss art historian who, under the tutorship of Heinrich Wolfflin, developed an approach to 'anonymous' history, which he articulated in his major study *Mechanisation Takes Command*, published in 1948. The book became an important modernist design-historical text.

Grange, Kenneth (1929–) A British product designer who worked in the neofunctionalist style for, among others, the Kenwood company, from the late 1950s onwards. In 1972 he joined the Pentagram design consultancy in London, becoming its first product designer. He went on to work for many clients, including a number in Japan.

Giugiaro, Giorgio (1938–) An Italian car designer who set up his own firm, Italdesign, in 1968. Since then Guigiaro has designed a number of very significant cars, including the Alfa Romeo Akfa Sud (1971), the Volkswagen Golf (1974) and the Fiat Panda (1980). He has also worked as a product designer creating, among other goods, a camera for Nikon.

Gray, Eileen (1878–1976) An Irish architect–designer who did most of her work while living in Paris, where she settled in 1907. From a background in luxurious, lacquered furniture she went on to participate in the Modern Movement, creating a number of seminal furniture designs including models in steel and leather in the 1920s. From the 1930s she dedicated her self to architecture.

Gropius, Walter (1883–1969) The German modernist architect Walter Gropius began his career in partnership with Adolf Meyer in 1910 – with whom he designed the Fagus Factory in the following year – and became the first director of the German Bauhaus in 1919. He went on to become Professor of Architecture at Harvard in the USA in 1937.

Gugelot, Hans (1920–65) The Dutch designer Hans Gugelot set up his own office in 1950 after having worked with Max Bill and collaborated with the Ulm design school, in his capacity as head of its development group, on designs for the Braun company in the mid-1950s. His work was neofunctionalist in style.

Heal, Ambrose (1872–1959) The British designer Ambrose Heal joined the family furniture business in 1893. He became linked to the Arts and Crafts Movement and began designing in 1896. The Heal's store was established in 1840 and Ambrose moved its emphasis from reproduction to simple, modern furniture. He became chairman of the business in 1913 and played a role in the formation of the Design and Industries Association in 1915.

Henrion, F.H.K. (1914–90) Graphic designer of French origin who came to Britain in the 1930s and worked there, throughout the war and the post-war period, as one of the country's leading graphic designers.

High-Tech An interior and furniture aesthetic popular among the young and stylish in the 1970s, which borrowed its look and its materials from the industrial sector and applied them to the domestic arena. Shelves made from scaffolding epitomised this brutal aesthetic.

Hille The British furniture manufacturing company Hille developed from a small business set up in the early part of the twentieth century to become a substantial firm after the Second World War sponsoring modern furniture. Robin Day, Roger Dean and Fred Scott all worked for Hille, which was dissolved in 1983. Day's polypropylene chair of the early 1960s is the company's most influential product.

Hoffmann, Josef (1870–1956) An Austrian architect and designer who worked in the studio of Otto Wagner but went on to become a founder member of the Viennese Secession and an influential designer of furniture and decorative objects executed in a strikingly modern, geometric style. He worked across of range of products destined for the domestic sphere.

Honda The Japanese motor cycle company Honda was founded in 1948. Its first important product was the Super-Cub step-through motor cycle, which succeeded, through the aggressive marketing that accompanied it, in conquering the American market. Since then the company has diversified into power appliances and motor cars. The Civic, Prelude, Accord and, more recently, the Insight eco-car are all examples of successful Honda designs

Issigonis, Sir Alec (1906–88) A British car designer who is best known for his designs for the 1948 Morris Minor, the 1959 Austin Mini and the 1962 Morris 1100. Of them the Mini made the greatest impact on world markets.

Itten, Johannes (1888–1967) Itten was largely responsible for the preliminary course at the Bauhaus. His ideas were too mystical for Walter Gropius, who dismissed him in 1923. He went on to form his own school in Berlin and, later, to become the director of the art schools in Zurich and Krefeld.

Jacobsen, Arne (1902–71) The work of the Danish architect and designer Arne Jacobsen is synonymous with the concept of Danish modernism. He was influenced by Le Corbusier and created highly influential bentwood furniture items in the 1950s – Ant and Swan being the best known. His Cylinda Line stainless steel tableware for Stelton remains much admired internationally.

Jiricna, Eva (1938–) A Czech architect–designer who came to London in 1968 and became known through her retail interiors for the fashion-shop owner Joseph Ettedgui. Her simple modernist work became identified with the High-Tech style and was characterised by its use of glass and chrome. She went on to collaborate with several modernist architects on the interiors of their buildings.

Jugendstil The German name for the French term Art Nouveau, Judendstil was used to describe the revolutionary, new, turn-of-the-century style that swept across Europe at that time. The term is used to describe its extensive manifestations in countries of the former Eastern Bloc.

Kåge, Wilhelm (1889–1960) Trained as a fine artist, Kåge began working for the Swedish ceramic company Gustavsberg in 1917 and was responsible for encouraging it to use modern, democratic designs. In the 1930s he produced several ceramic ranges including Praktika and Pyro, but in 1949 he returned to painting.

Kiesler, Frederick (1896–1965) Associated with the Viennese Secession group, the Dadaists and the De Stijl Group in Holland, Kiesler left Europe and went to the USA in the late 1920s, continuing to work as an artist–architect–designer in that country. His numerous designs included a range of aluminium furniture which he created in the 1930s.

Klint, Kaare (1888–1954) A Danish architect and furniture designer, working in the 1920s in Copenhagen, who developed an anthropometric approach to designing furniture. His 1933 deck chair is based on a vernacular model, as were several of his other designs. Rud Rasmussen produced many of his designs.

Knoll The Knoll furniture company was formed in the USA in the late 1940s by a German cabinet-maker, Hans Knoll, and his wife, Florence Schust, a graduate of the Cranbrook Academy. From the beginning they used modern designers, including Eero Saarinen and Harry Bertoia, and established a reputation as a manufacturer of progressive furniture designs.

Kuramata, Shiro (1934–91) A Japanese furniture and interior designer who opened his own office in Tokyo in 1965. Kuramata combined traditional

Japanese minimalist ideas with contemporary influences to create his highly original furniture designs. He created interiors for a number of the shops of the Japanese fashion designer Issey Miyake.

Le Corbusier (1887–1968) Born Charles Edouard Jeanneret, this Swiss architect become one of the leading figures of the Modern Movement in architecture and design. His 1920s buildings were typically white and flat-roofed in imitation of Mediterranean architecture, and he achieved a simplicity of form in all his work. Where his design is concerned, he is best known for his Grand Confort chair and his chaise longue.

Loewy, Raymond (1893–1986) Born in France, Loewy went to the USA in 1919 and became one of the city's first consultant industrial designers. His first client was Sigmund Gestetner, for whom he restyled a duplicator in 1929. Through the 1930s, 40s and 50s he went on to design many products for a number of clients including the Hupp Motor Company, Frigidaire, Lucky Strike and Studebaker.

Loos, Adolf (1870–1933) An Austrian architect who, in 1908, wrote a much-quoted article entitled 'Ornament and Crime' in which he outlined what he believed to be the decadence of architectural ornament. His own designs from the early century included the Steiner House and the Müller house.

Mackintosh, Charles Rennie (1868–1928) A Scottish architect who worked as part of a group known as the Glasgow Four. He created a number of buildings, interiors, furniture pieces and decorative items in what was seen at the time as a Scottish version of Art Nouveau. His designs were very influential in Vienna.

Magistretti, Vico (1920–) An Italian architect and furniture designer who was trained in Milan and worked there, after the Second World War, particularly for the Arflex and Cassina furniture companies. His brightly coloured, plastic moulded chairs of the early 1960s were among the first of their kind. He has continued to design influential furniture items, including his Sindbad chair of 1981.

Maldonado, Tomas (1922–) Born in Buenos Aires, the design theoretician Maldonado was invited by Max Bill to take over the directorship of the Hochschule für Gestaltung at Ulm, where he remained until the mid-1960s. Maldonado favoured a systematic approach to the design process.

Marimekko A Finnish fabric company and shop, established by Armi Ratia in Helsinki in 1951. Marimekko (which means Mary's Frock) is best known for its bold printed fabrics which are made up into simple clothing.

Mathsson, Bruno (1907–88) A Swedish furniture designer who, with G.A. Berg and Josef Frank, was responsible for creating the Swedish

Modern design movement. He used wood and hemp webbing rather than tubular steel and leather and his most famous chair, created in 1934, is still produced today by Dux Mobel.

Maugham, Syrie (1879–1955) An English interior decorator who took the ideas of Elsie de Wolfe forward in a British context. Maugham was known for her all-white rooms and for her use of modernist components, including rugs by Marion Dorn. She had a number of high-class clients, Wallis Simpson among them.

Mellor, David (1930–) A British designer, based in Sheffield, who established his own cutlery and product manufacturing company, and kitchen-equipment retail outlets. Trained at the Royal College of Art in the 1950s Mellor is best known for his designs for cutlery: 'Pride' won him a Design Council award in 1959.

Memphis Led in Milan by Ettore Sottsass, and supported by a group of international colleagues and young associates, the Memphis project launched itself with a show of Pop-inspired furniture prototypes in Milan in 1981. Annual shows continued into the 1990s. The group's aim was to revitalise design as a cultural concept rather than one which was led by industry and commerce.

Mendini, Alessandro (1931–) A participant in the Italian Radical Design movement, Mendini began his professional career working for the architectural group Nizzoli Associates. He went on to edit a number of design magazines, among them *Casabella*, *Modo* and *Domus*.

Mies van der Rohe, Ludwig (1886–1969) A German architect who, along with Walter Gropius and Le Corbusier, is one of the most renowned exponents of the Modern Movement in architecture and design. Mies was the last director of the Bauhaus. From there he went to the USA, where he worked in Chicago. In design terms he is best known for his steel and leather furniture items, especially his Barcelona chair of 1929.

Miyake, Issey (1935–) Trained in Paris as a graphic designer, the Japanese fashion designer Miyake opened his own studio in Tokyo in 1970. He cleverly combined French couture (the influence of Vionnet was strong) with Japanese dress to create an internationally appealing new fashion idiom, as at home on the stage as the catwalk.

Modernism The general term used to describe the cultural phenomenon of the early years of the twentieth century that sought to ally cultural practice and the aesthetic it embraced with the flow of modern life and its influences. It was especially strong in the arena of architecture and design, which constituted the material stuff of modernity.

Modern Movement A term, coined by Nikolaus Pevsner in 1936, to describe the collective efforts of architects and designers to develop a new philosophy and aesthetic that was in tune with the spirit of modernity, especially the realities of mass production and the dominance of the machine.

Moholy-Nagy, László (1895–1946) Born in Hungary, Moholy-Nagy moved to Berlin in 1920. In 1922 he became a staff member at the Bauhaus in Weimar. Influenced by Eastern European Constructivism be worked as a painter and photographer and went to Chicago in the 1930s to set up the New Bauhaus, later known as the Insitute of Design.

Mollino, Carlo (1905–73) An Italian furniture designer, based in Turin, who created furniture pieces in the 1940s and 50s, which he described as 'streamlined-surreal'. His baroque, wooden forms contrasted sharply with the more rational designs emerging from Milan in those years.

Morrison, Jasper (1959–) A British furniture and product designer who introduced a new, slightly nostalgic but eminently modern aesthetic into design in the 1980s. Morrison has worked with many international clients including FSB in Germany and Cappellini in Italy.

Murray, Keith (1892–1981) A New Zealander by origin, the architect-trained Keith Murray turned to designing ceramic and glass products in the 1930s, working with James Powell's Whitefriars Glassworks and Wedgwood, among others. His simple, geometric designs contrasted strongly with many others which emerged at that time.

Muthesius, Hermann (1861–1934) A German diplomat who travelled to England at the end of the nineteenth century and wrote a book, *Das Englische Haus* (1905), about the architecture he discovered there. He was a major force behind the formation of the German Werkbund and did much to promote German design for industry in the early twentieth century.

Nelson, George (1907–86) The American architect and designer George Nelson, who began his career as an architectural journalist, created numerous modern artefacts for progressive clients, including Herman Miller. He is best known for his Storagewall and his office designs from the years immediately following the Second World War.

Neo-Functionalism A term used to describe the return to an austere, rational geometric aesthetic that occurred in Germany in the years after 1945. it was epitomised by the work of Dieter Rams for the Braun company and by many of the designs emerging from the design school at Ulm.

Newson, Marc (1963–) Australian by birth the product designer finally settled in London and formed his own studio in the late 1990s. His characteristic organic form was injected into a wide range of products, from furniture to a car for Ford. He also created a number of interior spaces for shops and restaurants in a similar style.

Nike The Nike training shoe manufacturer, based in the USA, was among the first to embrace the idea of developing many different stylistics in its products at any one time in order to make running shoes part of an ever-changing lifestyle choice on the part of the consumer. It was a marketing philosophy that depended upon rapid stylistic turn-over and automated manufacturing.

Nizzoli, Marcello (1887–1969) Trained as a graphic designer, Nizzoli was hired by Adriano Olivetti in 1938. He worked on the Italian company's electrical machines and produced some elegant typewriters in the 1940s and 50s – among them the Lexicon 80 and the Lettera 22. He also designed the Mirella sewing machine for the Necchi company in 1956.

Noyes, Eliot (1910–77) An American industrial designer who worked as a curator for the Museum of Modern Art in New York and was subsequently hired by Thomas Watson, the son of the founder of the IBM Company. From 1956 he worked, with the graphic designer Paul Rand, as the corporate design director creating a number of striking office machines.

Nurmesniemi, Antti (1927–2003) and Eskolin, Vuokko (1930–)
Husband and wife designers. Nurmesniemi was a Finnish interior and industrial designer, and his wife is a textile designer, who markets her fabrics under the name of Vuokko. Nurmesniemi set up his own design office in Finland in 1956 and worked on interiors for many clients, sometimes in collaboration with his wife and sometimes alone.

Olivetti, Camillo (1868–1943) and Adriano (1901–60) The former was the founder of the Olivetti Office Machinery Company in 1908. He designed the first typewriter himself. His son, Adriano, took over the reins of the company in the 1920s and was responsible for hiring some of the designers who worked with Olivetti, including Marcello Nizzoli and Ettore Sottsass.

Panton, Verner (1926–98) A Danish architect and designer, working in Switzerland, who is best known for his furniture designs from the 1960s. He created the first one-piece, cantilever plastic chair and his 1960 Stacking Chair was produced by Herman Miller.

Paulsson, Gregor (1889–1964) The Swedish architect Paulsson was the first Director of the Swedish design society – the Svenska Sjlödföreningen. In 1919 he wrote a book about design entitled *More Beautiful Everyday Things*, which was highly influential in Sweden. He made a significant contribution to the organisation of the 1930 Stockholm Exhibition.

Pentagram A British design consultancy that was established in 1971 on the basis of a graphic design consultancy from the 1950s called Fletcher, Forbes and Gill. Among several the product designers, Kenneth Grange and Daniel Weil joined the group in the 1970s and 1990s respectively.

Perriand, Charlotte (1903–99) Between 1927 and 1937 the French designer Charlotte Perriand worked with Le Corbusier on his furniture designs, making a significant input. Later she visited Japan and became an adviser on arts and crafts to that country. She continued to design after the Second World War, focusing on interiors.

Pesce, Gaetano (1939–) An Italian architect–designer who has worked in a highly individual way since the 1960s producing, among other designs, nihilistic, 'decaying' objects. He has worked with the Cassina company on several occasion and divides his time between Venice and New York, where he continues to practise and teach.

Pevsner, Nikolaus (1902–83) A German-born art historian whose writings about modern architecture and design have been very influential. He helped to define, and championed, the idea of the Modern Movement in his book of 1936 *Pioneers of the Modern Movement* (later *Pioneers of Modern Design*).

Pininfarina, Battista (1893–1966) With his roots in coach-building, the Italian car manufacturer and designer Pininfarina embraced a sculptural approach to his craft. His creations for Alfa Romeo and Lancia – including the Lancia Aprilia of 1937 – were ahead of their time stylistically and led into dramatic post-war designs such as the 1947 Cisitalia.

Ponti, Gio (1891–1979) An Italian architect–designer, and editor of *Domus* magazine, Ponti worked as a designer of architecture, furniture and decorative objects from the 1920s. He sustained his own, highly individualistic aesthetic through these years and his many clients include Fontana Arte, Arflex and Cassina.

Pop The Pop design movement was a spontaneous British phenomenon of the mid-1960s. It focused on fashion and lifestyle accompaniments and stressed instant impact and ephemerality. It was a reaction, on one level, to the timeless forms of modernism.

Porsche A Stuttgart-based car company, named after its founder, Ferdinand Porsche, the designer of the Volkswagen 'Beetle'. Known for its upmarket, stylish products the company created a number of what became classic cars from the 1960s onwards, including the models 911 (designed by 'Butzi' Porsche), the 928 and, most recently, the Boxster, designed by Harm Lagaay.

Postmodernism The catch-all name given to all the architectural and design manifestations of the late 1980s onwards which deliberately sidestepped the strategies of high modernism and sought to relate to the sphere of consumption, rather than that of production. It was expressed in a number of different ways, from nostalgia to the use of strongly expressive forms of many kinds.

Race, Ernest (1913–64)   Trained initially as an architect, the British furniture designer Ernest Race established Race Furniture Ltd in 1946, the same year in which he designed an influential, aluminium-framed chair. He went to create a range of steel rod chairs for the 1951 Festival of Britain.

Rams, Dieter (1932–)   A German product designer who made a name for himself working with the Braun Company, from 1955. He created for them a number of domestic machines that came to typify the sparse, geometric style of much post-war German design.

Rationalism   The term used to describe Italy's contribution to inter-war architectural and design modernism, as expressed by Guiseppe Terragni and others. For a short period of time Mussolini flirted with Rationalism as his official style but he moved away from it towards a more classically inspired Italian modern style, known as Novecento.

Reich, Lilly (1885–1947)   A German interior and furniture designer, working in the modernist idiom, who collaborated with Mies van der Rohe from 1927. Their first project was for the Weissenhof exhibition of that year. She also worked with him two years later on the Barcelona exhibition and taught him at the Bauhaus from 1932.

Riemerschmid, Richard (1868–1957)   A German designer, based in Munich, who developed a range of standardised furniture for serial production in the first decade of the twentieth century. He was an early member, with Peter Behrens, of the Deutscher Werkbund.

Rietveld, Gerrit (1888–1964)   Born in Utrecht and trained as a cabinet-maker, the Dutch architect–designer became a member of the De Stijl group and created a number of highly influential chairs, among them the Red-Blue chair of 1917/18 and the Zig-Zag chair of 1934. Both have become classic designs.

Rodchenko, Alexander (1891–1956)   A Russian Constructivist sculptor–designer who – with his wife, the textile designer Stepanova, and others – worked on interiors and street constructions at the time of the 1917 Russian Revolution. In the 1920s he moved closer to Tatlin's idea of the 'artist-engineer' and began designing utility items, such as furnishings and clothing.

Rosenthal   A German ceramics manufacturing company, founded in Bavaria in 1897. Through the latter half of the twentieth century Rosenthal encouraged a number of international designers – Tapio Wirkkala, Raymond Loewy and Walter Gropius among them – to work with them on products presented as part of its Studio range.

Ruhlmann, Jacques-Emile (1879–1933)   An exponent of the exclusive, French decorative style of the 1920s Ruhlmann used exotic woods in his furniture and interiors. His Hôtel du Collectionneur pavilion at the 1925 Paris 'Exhibition of Decorative Arts' exposed his luxurious style to a large audience.

Saarinen, Eero (1910–61)   The son of Eliel Saarinen, the Finnish architect–designer Eero Saarinen went to the USA with his father in 1923. He studied architecture at Yale and, in 1940, he worked with Charles Eames on a range of moulded plywood furniture pieces. In the 1950s Knoll manufactured his furniture designs, among them the famous Tulip chair.

Sapper, Richard (1932–)   A German-born designer who gravitated towards Italy, worked in Milan in the office of Marco Zanuso, collaborating with him on a number of projects for Brionvega, and set up his office there in the mid-1970s. His lighting designs have been especially influential and his Tizio desk-light is a design classic.

Sarpaneva, Timo (1926–)   A Finnish designer of glass, ceramics, textiles and metalwork who was employed by the Iittala Glassworks in 1950 and who showed his work at the Milan Triennale exhibitions of the 1950s, winning several prizes. He helped make the world aware of modern Finnish design.

Sason, Sixten (1912–69)   A Swedish consultant product designer who trained as a silversmith and who went on to work for Electrolux, Hasselblad and Saab Motors, for whom he designed the stylish Saab 92 automobile.

Sipek, Boris (1949–)   A Czech designer who settled in Holland, where he now works. Sipek is known for his designs for domestic objects, which combine modernism with luxurious decoration. His glass and ceramic designs, in particular, manifest a baroque quality .

Sony   The Japanese consumer electronics manufacturer that was the first to think about the aesthetic design of its products as well as their advanced technology. The Sony Walkman, launched in the early 1980s, combined innovative design and technology with an understanding about lifestyle.

Sottsass, Ettore (1917–)   An Italian architect–designer who set up a consultant practice in Milan in the years after the Second World War and who went on to become the leading figure in the world of Radical Design in Italy. He was a consultant for many years for Olivetti and masterminded the Memphis experiment of the 1980s.

Streamform   The name given to the organic style of American automobile and products of the inter-war years the forms of which had been determined by 'streamlining' – making them aerodynamic and fast-moving. In static objects, such as irons and fruit juicers, the style was transferred metaphorically to denote futurity.

Superstudio Formed in Florence in 1966 Superstudio was one of the architectural and design groups that spearheaded the Radical Design movement in Italy in those years. The group worked on a number of experimental projects and designed a table that was manufactured by Zanotta.

Swatch A Swiss watch manufacturer, which rejected the idea of 'a watch for life' and introduced, in its place, the concept of the fashion watch that changed according to the clothes and tastes of its wearers.

Swedish Modern The term coined at the New York World's Fair of 1939 to describe the soft, humanistic version of modernism that was evolved by the Swedish designers such as Bruno Mathsson and Josef Frank. It became a very influential style in the post-war years.

Tatlin, Vladimir (1885–1953) A Russian Constructivist sculptor who turned, after the 1917 Revolution, to working on functional projects such as clothing. He is best known for his Monument to the Third International of 1919–20, in the creation of which he set out to work like an engineer in the service of the Revolution.

Teague, Walter Dorwon (1883–1960) A pioneer American consultant industrial designer of the 1930s, Teague is often called the 'dean of industrial design'. His office worked with Eastman Kodak for many years, among other clients, and he chaired the Board of Design for the New York World's Fair of 1939, as well as designing a number of its exhibits.

Hochschule für Gestaltung, Ulm A German design school, founded in 1953, as a revival of the pre-war Bauhaus. The Swiss designer Max Bill was the first director of the school and he was replaced at the end of the decade by Tomas Maldonado. In the 1960s the school was divided by strong internal ideological differences and it was forced to close in 1968.

van de Velde, Henry (1863–1957) A Belgian Art Nouveau architect and designer who moved to Germany in 1900 to run the Weimar School of Applied Arts. He was influenced by William Morris, wrote extensively about design and was a founder member of the Deutscher Werkbund.

Van Doren, Harold (1895–1957) An American consultant industrial designer who, like his colleagues, worked with a number of companies throughout the 1930s, including Philco and Goodyear. He moved into this new profession from the museum world and in 1940 he published a book entitled *Industrial Design: A Practical Guide*.

Venturi, Robert (1925–) An American architect who, in 1966, wrote his influential book *Complexity and Contradiction in Architecture*, which heralded the advent of postmodernism in architecture and design. Through the 1960s and 70s he worked on a number of Pop architectural projects, and he designed a range of furniture pieces for Knoll in the early 1980s. More recently he designed an extension for London's National Gallery.

Wagenfeld, Wilhelm (1900–79) A German Bauhaus graduate who worked at the Lausitzer Glassworks from 1935 to 1947 and who went on to run his own design studio in Stuttgart. Considered one of Germany's leading designers, he worked on a wide range of products, from glass to ceramics to cutlery to lighting.

Wagner, Otto (1841–1918) An Austrian proto-modernist architect–designer who, in the 1890s, worked at the edge of Art Nouveau but who showed more classical tendencies by the end of the decade. He pioneered the use of aluminium in buildings – for example, in his design for the Post Office in Vienna and for the feet of some of his furniture designs from the turn of the century.

Westwood, Vivienne (1941–) A British fashion designer who emerged from the subculture of Punk in the 1970s and who has remained a subversive figure in spite of her commercial success. She is known for her nostalgic clothes and her unconventional approach towards fashion and the fashion industry.

Wirkkala, Tapio (1915–85) One of Finland's super-star designers of the post-war era, who was employed by the Iittala glass company in 1947 and who went on to create striking decorative art objects and designs through the next three decades. He came to international recognition through his work that was exhibited at the Milan Triennales in the 1950s. Outside Finland he worked both for Venini and Rosenthal.

Wright, Russel (1904–76) An American product designer who made his name through his ceramic dinner services created in the 1930s, which were marketed under the name American Modern. He was one of the first to use aluminium in a progressive manner, again in hospitality objects. His furniture designs also reached a large audience.

BIBLIOGRAPHY

Introduction

Since the first edition of this book appeared in 1986 the subjects of 'design' and 'material culture' have been discussed more widely in the English-speaking world than they had been before that date, and a number of books have emerged that take a broad, analytical/critical approach to the subjects. They include the following.

Attfield, J. *Wild Things: The Material Culture of Everyday Life* (Oxford and New York: Berg, 2000).

Dormer, P. *The Meanings of Modern Design: Towards the Twenty-First Century* (London: Thames and Hudson, 1990).

Foster, H. *Design and Crime (and other Diatribes)* (London and New York: Verso, 2002).

Heskett, J. *Toothpicks and Logos: Design in Everyday Life* (Oxford: Oxford University Press, 2002).

Julier, G. *The Culture of Design* (London: Sage, 2000).

Kwint, M., Breward, C., and Aynsley, J. *Material Memories: Design and Evocation* (Oxford: Berg, 1999).

Margolin, V. (ed.) *Design Discourse: History, Theory, Criticism* (Chicago: University of Chicago Press, 1989).

Margolin, V. *The Politics of the Artificial: Essays on Design and Design Studies* (Chicago and London: Chicago University Press, 2002).

Walker, J. *Design History and the History of Design* (London: Pluto Press, 1989).

A number of overviews of design in the twentieth century have also emerged, most of them focusing on a single design discipline. They include the following.

Aynsley, J. *A Century of Graphic Design* (London: Mitchell Beazley, 2001).

Breward, C. *Fashion* (Oxford: Oxford University Press, 2003).

Calloway, S. *Twentieth-Century Decoration: The Domestic Interior from 1900 to the Present Day* (London: Weidenfeld and Nicholson, 1988).

Crowley, D. and Jobling, P. *Graphic Design: Reproduction and Representation since 1800* (Manchester: Manchester University Press, 1996).

Doordan, D. P. *Twentieth-Century Architecture* (London: Lawrence King, 2001).

Edwards, C. *Twentieth-Century Furniture: Materials, Manufacture and Markets* (Manchester: Manchester University Press, 1994).

Forty, A. *Objects of Desire: Design and Society 1750–1980* (London: Thames and Hudson, 1986).

Massey, A. *Interior Design of the 20th Century* (London: Thames and Hudson, 1990).

Pile, J. *A History of Interior Design* (New York: John Wiley & Sons, 2000).

Sparke, P. *A Century of Car Design* (London: Mitchell Beazley, 2002).

Woodham, J. *Twentieth-Century Design* (Oxford: Oxford University Press, 1997.

Much of the work in the areas of design history and material culture undertaken since the 1980s has adopted a cultural slant. While the focus has been on a wide range of cultural issues, that of 'identity' has tended to dominate debates, especially in relation to gender, but also, albeit to a lesser extent to date, in relation to race and ethnicity, especially in the context of post-imperialism and the unification of Europe. The importance of class issues to design-historical work remain important as well. Work on the relationship between women, design and material culture, influenced by concurrent work being undertaken within cultural studies, has been especially visible in the last two decades. Publications in this area include the following.

Attfield, J. 'Feminist critiques of design', in Walker, J. (ed.), *Design History and the History of Design* (London: Pluto Press, 1989).

Attfield, J. and Kirkham, P. *A View from the Interior: Feminism, Women and Design* (London: The Women's Press, 1989).

Buckley, C. 'Made in patriarchy: towards a feminist analysis of women in design', *Design Issues* (vol.3, no.2, 1986), pp. 251–62.

Davis, F. *Fashion, Culture and Identity* (Chicago: Chicago University Press, 1992).

De Grazia, V. and Furlough, E. *The Sex of Things* (Berkeley: University of California Press, 1996).

Evans, C. and Thornton, M. *Women and Fashion: A New Look* (London: Quartet, 1989).

Ferguson, M. *Forever Feminine; Women's Magazines and the Cult of Femininity* (London: Heinemann, 1983).

Kirkham, P. (ed.) *The Gendered Object* (Manchester and New York: Manchester University Press, 1996).

Martinez, K. and Ames, K.L. *The Material Culture of Gender: The Gender of Material Culture* (Winthertur, DE: Henry Francis du Pont Wintherthur Museum, 1997).

McKellar, S. and Sparke, P. (eds) *Interior Design and Identity* (Manchester: Manchester University Press, 2004).

Sparke, P. *As Long as It's Pink: The Sexual Politics of Taste* (London: Pandora, 1995).

Most significantly, in relation to this publication, an enormous body of theoretical work emanating from tangential disciplines – including cultural studies, sociology, consumption theory, anthropology, social psychology, literary studies and cultural geography – has had a dramatic impact on the way in which work on the subjects of design and material culture has been undertaken. Among the many – too numerous to list here – important and useful studies are the following.

Apparudai, A. (ed.) *The Social Life of Things: Commodities in Cultural Perspective* (Cambridge: Cambridge University Press, 1986).

Baudrillard, J. *The System of Objects* (London: Verso, 1996).

Bourdieu, P. *Distinction: A Social Critique of the Judgement of Taste* (London and New York: Routledge, 1986).

Campbell, C. *The Romantic Ethic and the Spirit of Modern Consumerism* (London: Basil Blackwell, 1987).

Dittmar, H. 'Gender Identity: relation meanings of personal possessions', *British Journal of Social Psychology* (28, 1989), pp. 159–71.

Douglas, M. and Isherwood, B. *The World of Goods: Towards an Anthropology of Consumption* (London and New York: Routledge, 1996).

Ewen, S. *All Consuming Images: The Politics of Style in Contemporary Culture* (New York: Basic Books, 1988).

Falk, P. *The Consuming Body* (London: Sage, 1994).

Fine, B. and Leopold, E. *The World of Consumption* (London and New York: Routledge, 1993).

Fiske, J. *Understanding Popular Culture* (London: Routledge, 1989).

Haug, W.F. *Critique of Commodity Aesthetics* (Cambridge: Polity, 1986).

Hebdige, D. *Hiding in the Light: On Images and Things* (London and New York: Routledge, 1988).

Huyssen, A. *After the Great Divide: Modernism, Mass Culture and Postmodernism* (London: Macmillan, 1986).

Lund, P. and Livingstone, S.M. *Mass Consumption and Personal Identity: Everyday Economic Experience* (Buckingham and Philadelphia: Open University Press, 1992).

McCracken, G. *Culture and Consumption: New Approaches to the Symbolic Character of Consumer Goods* (Bloomington and Indianapolis: Indiana University Press, 1988).

McDowell, L. *Gender, Identity and Place: Understanding Feminist Geographies* (Cambridge: Polity, 1999).

Miller, D. *Material Culture and Mass Consumption* (Oxford: Basil Blackwell, 1987).

Mort, F. *Cultures of Consumption: Masculinities and Social Space in Late Twentieth-Century Britain* (London and New York: Routledge, 1996).

Stewart, S. *On Longing: Narratives of the Miniature, the Gigantic, the Souvenir, the Collection* (Durham and London: Duke University Press, 1993).

The emergence of two important journals – *Design History Journal* (Oxford University Press) and *Design Issues: History, Theory, Criticism* (MIT Press) – has helped to provide an outlet for work in this area

Chapter 1   Consuming modernity

RECOMMENDED READING

Many books deal with the relationship between consumer culture, material culture and modernity. While some focus on it through a single area of material culture, be it advertising, magazines, retailing or fashion, others, such as Don Slater's *Consumer Culture and Modernity* (Cambridge: Cambridge University Press, 1997) provide useful overviews; Simon J. Bronner's book of edited essays, *Accumulation and Display of Goods in America, 1880–1920* (New York and London: W.W. Norton & Company, 1989) shows how consumer culture and material culture worked together in the USA; Elizabeth Wilson's two books – *Adorned in Dreams; Fashion and Modernity* (London: Virago, 1985) and *The Sphinx in the City: Urban Life, the Control of Disorder and Women* (London: Virago, 1991) – deal with issues relating to fashion, gender, the urban landscape and modernity; in *Lands of Desire: Merchants, Power and the Rise of a New American Culture* (New York: Vintage Books, 1994), William Leach focuses on the impact of the visual culture of the department store on the American urban landscape; while Thad Logan, in *The Victorian Parlour; A Cultural Study* (Cambridge: Cambridge University Press, 2001), provides a model for a cultural analysis of a room in the private sphere.

FURTHER READING

Adburnham, E.S. *Shops and Shopping 1800–1914* (London: Allen and Unwin, 1981).

Beetham, M. *A Magazine of her Own: Domesticity and Desire in the Woman's Magazine, 1800–1914* (London and New York: Routledge, 1996).

Berman, M. *All That is Solid Melts into Air: The Experience of Modernity* (New York: Simon and Schuster, 1982).

Bowlby, R. *Shopping with Freud* (London: Routledge, 1993).

Bowlby, R. *Carried Away: The Invention of Modern Shopping* (London: Faber and Faber, 2000).

Bryden, I. and Floyd, J. (eds) *Domestic Space: Reading the Nineteenth-century Interior* (Manchester and New York: Manchester University Press, 1999).

Bushman, R. *The Refinement of America: Persons, Houses, Cities* (New York: Vintage Books, 1993).

Chaney, D. 'The department store as a cultural form', *Theory, Culture and Society* (vol.1, no.3, 1983) pp. 22–31.

Davidoff, L. and Hall, C. *Family Fortunes: Men and Women of the English Middle Class, 1780–1850* (London: Routledge, 1987).

Ewen, S. *Captains of Consciousness: Advertising and the Social Roots of Consumer Culture* (New York: McGraw Hill, 1977).

Forde, K. *Hope in a Jar: The Making of America's Beauty Culture* (New York: Henry Holt & Co. Inc., 1998).

Fraser, W.H. *The Coming of the Mass Market, 1850–1914* (London and Basingstoke: Macmillan, 1981).

Frederick, C. *Selling Mrs Consumer* (New York: Business Bourse, 1929).

Frisby, D. *Fragments of Modernity: Theories of Modernity in the Work of Simmel, Kracauer and Benjamin* (Cambridge: Polity, 1985).

Glickman, L.B. (ed.) *Consumer Society in American History: A Reader* (Ithaca and London: Cornell University Press, 1999).

Grier, K.C. *Culture and Comfort: People, Parlors and Upholstery 1850–1930* (New York: The Stron Museum, 1988).

Harris, N. 'The drama of consumer desire', in *Cultural Excursions: Marketing Appetites and Cultural Tastes in Modern America* (Chicago: University of Chicago Press, 1990).

Hine, T. *The Total Package* (Boston: Little, Brown and Company, 1995).

Jeffreys, J.B. *Retail Trading in Britain 1850–1950* (Cambridge: Cambridge University Press, 1954).

Laermans, R. 'Learning to consume: early department stores and the shaping of the modern consumer culture (1860–1914)', *Theory, Culture and Society* (vol.10, no.4, November 1993), pp. 79–102.

Marchand, R. *Advertising the American Dream: Making Way for Modernity 1920–1940* (Berkeley: University of California Press, 1985).

Mason, R. *Conspicuous Consumption: A Study of Exceptional Consumer Behaviour* (Hampshire: Gower, 1981).

Miller, M.B. *The Bon Marché: Bourgeois Culture and the Department Store, 1869–1920* (Princeton: Princeton University Press, 1981).

Rappaport, E.D. *Shopping for Pleasure: Women in the Making of London's West End* (Princeton: Princeton University Press, 2000).

Richards, T. *The Commodity Culture of Victorian England: Advertising and Spectacle 1851–1914* (London and New York: Verso, 1990).

Saint, A. Introduction to *London Suburbs* (London: Merrill Holberton, 1999).

Scanlon, J. *Inarticulate Longings: The Ladies Home Journal, Gender and the Promise of Consumer Culture* (New York and London: Routledge, 1995).

Strasser, S. *Satisfaction Guaranteed: The Making of the American Mass Market* (New York: Pantheon Books, 1989).

Tester, K. (ed.) *The Flaneur* (London and New York: Routledge, 1994).

Veblen, T. *The Theory of the Leisure Class* (London: Unwin, 1970).

Chapter 2   The impact of technology

RECOMMENDED READING

The most important book to deal with the story of American industrialisation and its effect upon material culture is, without doubt, David Hounshell's *From the American System to Mass Production 1800–1932: The Development of Manufacturing Technology in the US* (Baltimore and London: Johns Hopkins University Press, 1982), although he stops short of an analysis of 'design'. S. Giedion's *Mechanization Takes Command: A Contribution to Anonymous History* (New York: Norton, 1949) was an early attempt to look back at the effects of industrialisation on the material culture of the USA. Ruth Schwartz Cowan's 'The industrial revolution in the home: household technology and social change in the 20th century', in *Technology and Culture* (vol.17, no.1, January 1976) provides a useful overview of the effects of technology in the domestic sphere. On the subjects of materials and modernity the two most useful books are J. Meikle's *American Plastic: A Cultural History* (New Brunswick: Rutgers University Press, 1995) and S. Nichols' *Aluminum by Design* (New York: Harry N. Abrams, 2000), pp. 12–140. Robert Friedel's book *Pioneer Plastic: The Making and Selling of Celluloid* (Wisconsin: University of Wisconsin Press, 1983) is also an important source.

FURTHER READING

Arnold, E. and Burr, L. 'Housework and the appliance of science', in Failkner, W. and Arnold, E. (eds), *Smothered by Invention* (London: Pluto Press, 1985).

Bayley, S. *Harley Earl* (London: Trefoil, 1990).

Beecher, C. and Stowe, H.B. *The American Woman's Home* (New York: J.B. Ford and Co., 1870).

Bullock, N. 'First the kitchen – then the façade', *Journal of Design History* (vol.1, nos.3 and 4, 1988), pp. 177–92.

Clifford, H. and Turner, R. 'Modern metal', in Greenhalgh, P. (ed.), *Art Nouveau 1890–1914* (London: V&A Publications, 2000).

Cowan, R.S. *More Work for Mother: The Ironies of Household Technology from the Open Hearth to the Microwave* (New York: Basic Books, 1983).

De Wolfe, E. *The House in Good Taste* (New York: Century, 1913).

Dubois, J.H. *Plastics History USA* (Boston: Cahners, 1972).

Frederick, C. *The New Housekeeping: Efficiency Studies in Home Management* (New York: Garden City, Doubleday Page, 1913).

Frederick, C. *Household Engineering and Scientific Management in the Home* (Chicago: American School of Home Economics, 1919).

Horowitz, R. and Mohun, A. (eds) *His and Hers: Gender, Consumption and Technology* (Charlottesville and London: The University of Virginia Press, 1998).

Ierley, M. *The Comforts of Home: The American House and the Evolution of Modern Convenience* (New York: Three Rivers Press, 1999).

Katz, S. *Plastics: Design and Materials* (London: Studio Vista, 1978).

Kaufman, M. *The First Century of Plastics* (London: Plastics Institute, 1963).

Lupton, E. and Abbott Miller, J. *The Bathroom, the Kitchen and the Aesthetics of Waste: A Process of Elimination* (Cambridge, MA: MIT Press, 1992).

MacKenzie, D. and Wajcman, J. *The Social Shaping of Technology* (Milton Keynes and Philadelphia: Open University Press, 1985).

Mayr, O. and Post, R.C. (eds) *Yankee Enterprise: The Rise of the American System of Manufactures* (Washington: Smithsonian Institution Press, 1981).

Meikle, J. 'New Materials and Technologies', in Benton, T. and C., and Wood, G. *Art Deco 1910–1919* (London: V&A Publications, 2003).

Sparke, P. *Electrical Appliances* (London: Bell and Hyman, 1987).

Stage, S. and Vincenti, V.B. (eds) *Rethinking Home Economics: Women and the History of a Profession* (Ithaca and London: Cornell University Press, 1997).

Strasser, S. *Never Done: A History of American Housework* (New York: Henry Holt and Co., 1982).

Chapter 3 The designer for industry

RECOMMENDED READING

There is a paucity of literature on the important subject of the emergence of the designer for industry and the cultural ramifications of that modern phenomenon. My book *Consultant Design: The History and Practice of the Designer in Industry* (London: Pembridge Press, 1983), offers a brief, albeit dated, introduction to the subject, while my essay, 'From a lipstick to a steamship:

the growth of the American industrial design profession', in Bishop, T. (ed.) *Design History: Fad or Function?* (London: Design Council, 1978), serves to open up the discussion about the origins about the modern industrial designer. Jeffrey Meikle's *Twentieth-Century Limited: Industrial Design in America 1925–1939* (Philadelphia: Temple University Press, 1979) is still the best source on the inter-war American designer for industry seen from a cultural perspective, while Gregory Votolato's *American Design in the Twentieth Century* (Manchester: Manchester University Press, 1998) is a good complement to it. Isabelle Anscombe's *A Woman's Touch: Women in Design from 1860 to the Present Day* (London: Virago, 1984) is a useful introduction to all the female designers who have been left out of the picture.

FURTHER READING

Atterbury, P. and Irvine, L. *The Doulton Story* (London: V&A Publications, 1979).

Bel Geddes, N. *Horizons* (New York: Dover Publications, 1977).

Buckley, C. 'Design, femininity, and modernism: interpreting the work of Susie Cooper', *Journal of Design History* (vol.7, no.4, 1994), pp. 277–93.

Callen, A. *Angel in the Studio: Women in the Arts and Crafts Movement* (London: Astragal Books, 1979).

Campbell, N. and Seebohm, C. *Elsie de Wolfe: A Decorative Life* (London: Aurum Press, 1992).

Cheney, S. and M. *Art and the Machine* (New York: McGraw Hill, 1936).

Clark, H. *The Role of the Designer in the Early Mass Production Industry* (unpublished PhD thesis, University of Brighton, 1982).

De la Haye, A. and Tobin, S. *Chanel: The Couturière at Work* (London: Overlook Press, 1994).

De Marly, D. *Worth: Father of Haute Couture* (London: Elm Tree Books, 1980)

Dreyfuss, H. *Designing for People* (New York: Viking Press, 1955).

Flinchum, R. *Henry Dreyfuss, Industrial Designer: The Man in the Brown Suit* (New York: Cooper-Hewitt, National Design Museum and Rizzoli, 1997).

Halen, S. *Christopher Dresser* (London: Phaidon, 1990).

Hampton, M. *Legendary Decorators of the Twentieth Century* (New York: Doubleday, 1992).

Howe, K.S. *et al. Herter Brothers, Furniture and Interiors for a Gilded Age* (New York: Harry N. Abrams, 1995).

Loewy, P. *Never Leave Well Enough Alone* (New York: Simon and Schuster, 1951)

Naylor, G. *The Arts and Crafts Movement: A Study of its Sources, Ideals and Influence on Design Theory* (London: Studio Vista, 1971).

Peck, A. and Irish, C. *Candace Wheeler: The Art and Enterprise of American Design 1875–1900* (New York: The Metropolitan Museum of Art, 2002).

Pulos, A. *The American Design Ethic* (Cambridge, MA: MIT Press, 1983).

Richards, C. *Art in Industry* (New York: Macmillan, 1922).

Schwartz, F. 'Commodity signs: Peter Behrens, the AEG and the trademark', *Journal of Design History* (vol.9, no.3, 1996), pp. 153–84.

Seddon, J. and Worden, S. *Women Designing: Redefining Design in Britain between the Wars* (Brighton: University of Brighton, 1991).

Sloan, A.J. *My Years at General Motors* (New York: Macfadden-Bartell, 1965).

Teague, W.D. *Design This Day: The Technique of Order in the Machine Age* (London: Studio Publications, 1946).

Thomson, E.M. '"The science of publicity": an American advertising theory', *Journal of Design History* (vol.9, no.4, 1996), pp. 253–72.

Van Doren, H. *Industrial Design: A Practical Guide* (New York: McGraw Hill, 1940).

Weltge, S.W. *Bauhaus Textiles: Women Artists and the Weaving Workshop* (London: Thames and Hudson, 1998).

Chapter 4   Modernism and design

RECOMMENDED READING

The literature relating to the subject of modern architecture and its theoretical underpinnings is extensive but that relating to modern design is less so. Because early twentieth-century design thinking took its lead from architecture, a dependency on that literature exists to a significant extent. Thus Reyner Banham's *Theory and Design in the First Machine Age* (London: Architectural Press, 1960) is a seminal text on this context as is T. and C. Benton and D. Sharp (eds) *Form and Function: A Source Book for a History of Architecture and Design 1890–1939* (London: Crosby, Lockwood and Staples, 1975), which, although written some time ago, still provides a useful introduction to a study of modernist design. Paul Greenhalgh's book of edited essays, *Modernism and Design* (London: Reaktion Books, 1990), is the only one to focus directly on the relationship between this broad-based cultural movement and design, while Mark Wigley's *White Walls, Designer Dresses: The Fashioning of Modern Architecture* (Cambridge, MA: MIT Press, 1995) is a more critical, retrospective analysis of architectural and design modernism.

FURTHER READING

Bojko, S. *New Graphic Design in Revolutionary Russia* (New York and Washington: Praeger, 1972).

Bourke, J. 'The great male renunciation: men's dress reform in inter-war Britain', *Journal of Design History* (vol.9, no.1, 1996), pp. 23–33.

Burnam, B. 'Better and brighter clothes: the men's dress reform party', *Journal of Design History* (vol.8, no.4, 1995), pp. 275–90.

Collins, P. *Changing Ideals in Modern Architecture, 1750–1950* (London: Faber And Faber, 1965).

Colomina, B. *Sexuality and Space* (Princeton: Princeton Architectural Press, 1992).

Colomina, B. *Privacy and Publicity: Modern Architcture as Mass Media* (Cambridge, MA: MIT Press, 1994).

Conrads, U. (ed.) *Programmes and Manifestoes on Twentieth-Century Architecture* (London: Lund Humphries, 1970).

De Zurko, E.R. *Origins of Functionalist Theory* (New York: Columbia University Press, 1957).

Frampton, K. *Modern Architecture: A Critical History* (London: Thames and Hudson, 1985).

Greenhalgh, P. (ed.) *Art Nouveau 1890–1914* (London: V&A Publications, 2000).

Greenough, H. *Form and Function: Remarks on Art, Design and Architecture* (Los Angeles: University of Californian Press, 1969).

Gropius, W. *The New Architecture and the Bauhaus* (London: Faber and Faber, 1968).

Jencks, C. *Modern Movements in Architecture* (Harmondsworth: Penguin, 1973).

Le Corbusier *Towards a New Architecture* (London: The Architectural Press, 1974).

Le Corbusier *The Decorative Art of Today* (Cambridge, MA: MIT Press, 1987).

Loos, A. *Spoken into the Void: Collected Essays 1897–1900* (Cambridge, MA: MIT Press, 1982).

Naylor, G. *The Bauhaus Re-Assessed: Sources and Design Theory* (London: Herbert Press, 1985).

Naylor, G. 'Swedish grace ... or the acceptable face of modernism', in Greenhalgh, P. *Modernism and Design* (London: Reaktion Books, 1990), pp. 15–20.

Pevsner, N. *Pioneers of Modern Design: From William Morris to Walter Gropius* (Harmondsworth: Penguin, 1960).

Schaefer, H. *Nineteenth-Century Modern: The Functional Tradition in Victorian Design* (London: Studio Vista, 1970).

Steadman, P. *The Evolution of Design* (Cambridge: Cambridge University Press, 1979).

Troy, N. *The De Stijl Environment* (Cambridge, MA: MIT Press, 1983).

Chapter 5 Designing identities

RECOMMENDED READING

A number of studies have focused on design as an ideological tool in the hands of nations. Paul Greenhalgh's *Ephemeral Vistas: The Expositions Universelles, Great Exhibitions, and World's Fairs 1851–1939* (Manchester: Manchester University Press, 1988) provides an overview of all the important exhibitions in the first half of the twentieth century at which design made an appearance. Wendy Caplan's collection of essays, entitled *Designing Modernity: The Arts of Reform and Persuasion 1885–1945* (Miami/London: Wolfsonian/Thames and Hudson, 1995) is a useful account of the ways in which a number of nations sought to exploit the links between design and modernity. In his book *Design in Germany 1870–1918* (London: Trefoil, 1986), John Heskett explores Germany's strategic relationship with modern design while, in *Designs on Modernity: Exhibiting the City in 1920s Paris* (Manchester: Manchester University Press, 1998), Tag Gronberg shows how France developed a quite different model of modernity through design.

FURTHER READING

Aynsley, J. *Graphic Design in Germany 1890–1945* (London: Thames and Hudson, 2000).

Burckhardt, L. *The Werkbund: Studies in the History and Ideology of the Deutcher Werkbund* (London: Design Council, 1980).

Bush, D. *The Streamlined Decade* (New York: George Braziller, 1975).

Calkins, E. 'Beauty, the new business tool' *The Atlantic Monthly* (14 August 1927), pp. 145–6.

Campbell, J. *The German Werkbund: The Politics of Reform in the Applied Arts* (Princeton: Princeton University Press, 1978).

Commune di Milano *L'anni trenta, arte e cultura in Italia* (Milan: Mazotta, 1982).

Crowley, D. *National Style and National State: Design in Poland from the Vernacular Revival to the International Style* (Manchester: Manchester University Press, 1992).

Crowley, D. 'Budapest: international metropolis and national capital', in Greenhalgh, P. *Art Nouveau 1890–1914* (London: V&A Publications, 2000).

Crowley, D. 'Finding Poland in the margins: the case of the Zakopane Style', *Journal of Design History* (vol.14, no.2, 2001), pp. 105–16.

Elliott, D. Introduction to *Devetsil: Czech Avant-GardeArt, Architecture and Design of the 1920s and 1930s* (Oxford and London: Museum of Modern Art, 1990).

Fell, S. 'The consumer and the making of the *Exposition des Arts Décoratifs et Industriels Modernes, 1907–1925*', *Journal of Design History* (vol.12, no.4, 1999), pp. 311–25.

Design, Process, Olivetti, 1908–1983 (Italy: Olivetti, 1983).

Gebhard, D. 'The Moderne in the USA, 1920–41', *Architectural Association Quarterly* (2 July 1970), pp. 33–40.

Gordon Bowe, H. (ed.) *Art and the National Dream: The Search for Turn of the Century Vernacular Design* (Dublin: Irish Academic Press, 1993).

Grief, M. *Depression Modern – the '30s Style in America* (New York: Universe Books, 1975).

Harrison, H.A. (ed.) *Dawn of a New Fay: The New York World's Fair, 1939/40* (New York: New York University Press, 1980).

Hobsbawm, E. *Nations and Nationalisms since 1780* (Cambridge: Cambridge University Press, 1990).

Johnson, P. and Hitchcock, H.R. *The International Style* (New York: W.W. Norton and Co. Inc., 1966).

Lamarova, M. 'The new art in Prague', in Greenhalgh, P. (ed.), *Art Nouveau 1890–1914* (London: V&A Publications, 2000).

Light, A. *Forever England: Femininity, Literature and Conservatism Between the Wars* (London and New York: Routledge, 1991).

Opie, J. 'Helsinki: Saarinen and Finnish Jugend', in Greenhalgh, P. *Art Nouveau 1890–1914* (London: V&A Publications, 2000).

Schwartz, F. *The Werkbund: Design Theory and Mass Culture before the First World War* (New Haven and London: Yale University Press, 1996).

Sheldon, R. and Arens, E. *Consumer Engineering: A New Technique for Prosperity* (New York: Arno Press, 1976).

Silverman, D.L. *Art Nouveau in Fin-de-Siècle France: Politics, Psychology and Style* (Los Angeles: University of California Press, 1989).

Tiersten, L. *Marianne in the Market: Envisioning Consumer Society in Fin-de-Siècle France* (Berkeley: University of California Press, 2001).

Troy, N. *Modernism and the Decorative Arts in France: Art Nouveau to Le Corbusier* (New Haven: Yale University Press, 1991).

Chapter 6   Consuming postmodernity

RECOMMENDED READING

A number of studies focus on the way in which the climate of mass consumption changed in the years after the Second World War. In *The Condition of Postmodernity: An Enquiry in the Origins of Cultural Change* (Oxford: Basil

Blackwell, 1989) the geographer David Harvey explores some of those changes. In his essay 'Towards a cartography of taste 1935–1962', in *Hiding in the Light* (London and New York: Routledge, 1988), pp. 45–76, the cultural critic Dick Hebdige, looks at the influence of American culture on Britain in the early post-war years, while Frank Mort's essay, 'Mass consumption in Britain and the USA since 1945', in Nava, M., Blake, A., MacRury, I. and Richards, B. (eds), *Buy This Book: Studies in Advertising and Consumption* (London and New York: Routledge, 1997), looks specifically at changing consumption patterns in those countries. Rob Shields' selection of essays in *Lifestyle Shopping: The Subject of Consumption* (London and New York: Routledge, 1992) show how the idea of lifestyle became linked to the acquisition of goods through the act of consumption in these years.

FURTHER READING

Attfield, J. 'Inside pram town: a case-study of Harlow House interiors', in Attfield, J. and Kirkham, P. (eds), *A View from the Interior: Feminism, Women and Design* (London: The Women's Press, 1989).

Baudrillard, J. *Simulations* (New York: Semiotext[e], 1983).

Bigsby, C.W. (ed.) *Superculture: American Popular Culture and Europe* (London: Paul Elek, 1975).

Boorstin, D. *The Americans: The Democratic Experience* (New York: Random House, 1973).

Carter, E. *How German is She? National Reconstruction and the Consuming Woman in the FRG and West Berlin 1945–1960* (Ann Arbor: University of Michigan Press, 1996).

De Grazia, V. 'Changing Consumption Regimes in Europe' in Strasser, S., McGovern, C. and Hudt, M. *Getting and Spending: European and American Consumer Societies in the Twentieth Century* (Cambridge: Cambridge University Press, 1998).

Du Gay, P., Hall, S., Janes, L., Mackay, H. and Negus, K. (eds) *Doing Cultural Studies: The Story of the Sony Walkman* (Milton Keynes: The Open University Press, 1997).

Eco, U. *Travels in Hyperreality* (New York: Harcourt Brace Jovanovich, 1986).

Entwhistle, J. '"Power dressing" and the construction of the career woman', in Nava, M., Blake, A., MacRury, I. and Richards, B. (eds), *Buy This Book: Studies in Advertising and Consumption* (London and New York: Routledge, 1997).

Galbraith, K. *The Affluent Society* (Harmondsworth: Penguin, 1958).

Gartman, D. *Auto Opium: A Social History of the American Automobile* (London and New York: Routledge, 1994).

Hebdige, D. 'Object as image: the Italian scooter cycle', in *Hiding in the Light* (London and New York: Routledge, 1988), pp. 77–115.

Hewison, R. *The Heritage Industry: Britain in a Climate of Decline* (London: Methuen, 1987).

Lewis, F.L. and Goldstein, L. (eds) *The Automobile and American Culture* (Michigan: University of Michigan Press, 1998).

Lowenthal, D. *The Past is a Foreign Country* (Cambridge: Cambridge University Press, 1985).

Lyotard, F. *The Postmodern Condition: A Report on Knowledge* (Manchester: Manchester University Press, 1984).

Marling, K.A. *As Seen on TV: The Visual Culture of Everyday Life in America in the 1950s* (Cambridge, MA: Harvard University Press, 1994).

Merkel, I. 'Consumer culture in the GDR', in Strasser, S., McGovern, C. and Hudt, M. (eds), *Getting And Spending: European and American Consumer Societies in the Twentieth Century* (Cambridge: Cambridge University Press, 1998).

Mort, F. 'Boy's own? Masculinity, style and popular culture', in Chapman, R. and Rutherford, J. (eds), *Male Order* (London: Lawrence and Wishart, 1995).

Reisman, D. *The Lonely Crowd: A Study of the Changing American Character* (New Haven and London: Yale University Press, 1970).

Samuel, R. *Theatres of Memory, Vol. 1: Past and Present in Contemporary Culture* (London: Verso, 1995).

Scranton, P. (ed.) *Beauty and Business: Commerce, Gender and Culture in Modern America* (New York and London: Routledge, 2001).

Urry, J. *The Tourist Gaze: Leisure and Travel in Contemporary Societies* (London: Sage, 1990).

Urry, J. *Consuming Places* (London: Routledge, 1995).

Warde, A. 'Consumers, identity and belonging: reflections on some theses of Zygmunt Bauman', in Kear, R., Whiteley, N. and Abercrombie, N. (eds), *The Authority of the Consumer* (London and New York: Routledge, 1994).

Williams, R. *Culture and Society 1780–1950* (London: Chatto and Windus, 1958).

Wilson, E. *Only Halfway to Paradise, Women in Postwar Britain 1945–1968* (London and New York: Tavistock Publications, 1980).

Wollen, P. and Kerr, J. (eds) *Autopia: Cars and Culture* (London: Reaktion Books, 2002).

Wright, P. *On Living in an Old Country: The National Past in Contemporary Britain* (London: Verso, 1985).

Chapter 7   Technology and design: a new alliance

RECOMMENDED READING

One important aspect of the years following the Second World War was the shift to what has been called 'post-industrialism'. One face of this was linked to the move away from standardised mass production. This is the subject of Charles Sabel's and Jonathan Zeitlin's *World of Possibilities: Flexibility and Mass Production in Western Industrialisation* (Cambridge: Cambridge University Press, 1997). Two important books appeared in 1999 – Alison Clarke's *Tupperware: the Promise of Plastics in 1950s America* (Washington and London: Smithsonian Institution Press, 1999), and Susannah Handley's *Nylon: The Manmade Fashion Revolution* (London: Bloomsbury, 1999), both of which focus on the important links between materials, culture and design. Paola Antonelli's *Mutant Materials in Contemporary Design* (New York: Museum of Modern Art, 1995), shows how new materials and design worked together at the end of the twentieth century.

FURTHER READING

Attfield, J. 'The tufted carpet in Britain: its rise from the bottom of the pile, 1952–70', *Journal of Design History* (vol.7, no.3, 1994), pp. 205–16.

Berger, S. and Piore, M.J. *Dualism and Discontinuity in Industrial Society* (Cambridge: Cambridge University Press, 1980).

Blaszczyk, R. *Imagining Consumers: Design and Innovation from Wedgwood to Corning* (Baltimore and London: The Johns Hopkins Press, 2000).

Dupont: The Autobiography of an American Enterprise (Wilmington, DE: E.I. Dupont de Nemours & Company, 1952).

Hogan, M.J. *The Marshall Plan: America, Britain and the Reconstruction of Western Europe 1947–1952* (Cambridge: Cambridge University Press, 1987).

Horowitz, R. *Boys and Their Toys? Masculinity, Class and Technology in America* (New York and London: Routledge, 2001).

Kron, J. and Slesin, S. *High-Tech* (New York: Potter, 1978).

Lash, D. and Urry, J. *The End of Organised Capitalism* (London: Polity, 1987).

Lupton, E. *Mechanical Brides: Women and Machines from Home to Office* (New York: Cooper Hewitt National Museum of Design, 1993).

Manzini, E. *The Material of Invention* (Milan: Arcadia, 1986).

Nichols, S. *Aluminum by Design* (New York: Harry N. Abrams, 2000), pp. 140–89.

Palmer, A. *Couture and Commerce: The Transatlantic Fashion Trade in the 1950s* (Toronto: UBC Press, 2001).

Pile, S. 'The foundation of modern comfort: latex foam and the industrial impact of design on the British rubber industry, 1948–1958', in *One-*

Odd: A Collection of Essays by Postgraduate Students on the V&A/RCA Course in the History of Design (London: Victoria and Albert Museum, 1997).

Postman, N. *Technopoly: The Surrender of Culture to Technology* (New York: Vintage Books, 1993).

Sabel, C.F. *Work and Politics: The Division of Labour in Industry* (Cambridge: Cambridge University Press, 1982).

Sparke, P. *Italian Design* (London: Thames and Hudson, 1988).

Sparke, P. 'Plastics and Pop culture', in Sparke, P. (ed.), *The Plastics Age: From Modernity to Postmodernity* (London: V&A Publications, 1990), pp. 92–104

Sparke, P. 'The straw donkey: tourist kitsch or proto-design? Craft and design in Italy, 1945–1960', *Journal of Design History* (vol.11, no.1, 1998), pp. 59–69.

Tevfik, B. (ed.) *The Role of Product Design in Post-Industrial Society* (Ankara: Middle East Technical University, 1998).

White, N. *Reconstructing Italian Fashion: America and the Development of the Italian Fashion Industry* (Oxford: Berg, 2000).

Chapter 8   Designer culture

RECOMMENDED READING

The maturation of designer culture that took place in the years after 1945 has still not been fully analysed from a cultural perspective. However, a vast body of literature exists about the designers themselves, which offers many insights into the phenomenon. Hugh Aldersey-Williams is among the few to address the subject directly in his essay 'Starck and stardom' in *Industrial Design* (34), pp. 46–51. Pat Kirkham's *Charles and Ray Eames; Designers of the Twentieth Century* (Cambridge, MA: MIT Press, 1995), is one of the best of its kind, while Andrea Brabzi's study of twentieth-century design in Italy – *The Hot House: Italian New Wave Design* (London: Thames and Hudson, 1984) shows the importance of designer culture to that country. P. Kunkel's *Digital Dreams: The Work of the Sony Design Center* (New York: Universe Publishers, 1999) shows how, in contrast, Japanese industry sought to promote its products through the names of its corporations rather than its designers.

FURTHER READING

Alessi, A. *The Dream Factory: Alessi Since 1921* (Milan: Electa/Alessi, 1999).

Ambasz, E. (ed.) *Italy: The New Domestic Landscape, Achievements and Problems of Italian Design* (New York: The Museum of Modern Art, 1972).

Caplan, R. *The Design of Herman Miller* (New York: Whitney Library of Design, 1976.

Dormer, P. Introduction to *Jasper Morrison: Designs, Projects and Drawings 1981–1989* (London: Architecture and Technology Press, 1990).

Drexler, A. *Charles Eames: Furniture from the Design Collection* (New York: Museum of Modern Art, 1973).

Ferrari, P. *Achille Castiglioni* (Milan: Electa, 1984).

Fossati, P. *Il design in Italia* (Milan: Einaudi, 1972).

Gere, C. *Digital Culture* (London: Reaktion Books, 2002).

Ive, J. 'Apple bites back', *Design* (no.1, autumn 1998), pp. 36–41.

Jackson, L. *The New Look: Design in the 1950s* (London: Thames and Hudson, 1991).

Jackson, L. *The Sixties: Decade of Design Revolution* (London: Phaidon, 2000).

Jackson, L. *Robin and Lucienne Day: Pioneers of Contemporary Design* (London: Mitchell Beazley, 2001).

Kelley, T. *The Art of Innovation: Lessons in Creativity from Ideo, America's Leading Design Firm* (New York: Doubleday, 2001).

Kenneth Grange at the Boilerhouse; An Exhibition of British Product Design (London: Boilerhouse Project, 1983).

Kirkham, P. (ed.) *Women Designers in the USA 1900–2000: Diversity and Difference* (New Haven and London: Yale University Press, 2000).

Larrabee, E. and Vignelli, M. *Knoll Design* (New York: Harry N. Abrams, 1989).

McCarty, C. *Marion Bellini, Designer* (New York: Museum of Modern Art, 1987).

Papanek, V. *The Green Imperative: Ecology and Ethics in Design and Architecture* (London: Thames and Hudson, 1995).

Pulos, A. *The American Design Adventure 1940–1975* (Cambridge, MA: MIT Press, 1988).

Sudjic, D. *Ron Arad* (London: Lawrence King, 1999).

Sweet, F. *Philippe Starck: Subverchic Design* (London: Thames and Hudson, 1999).

Chapter 9 Postmodernism and design

RECOMMENDED READING

Numerous writings exist that deal with the subject of 'postmodernism'. Not so many, however, relate that broad-based cultural phenomenon to the world of material culture and design. Anne Massey's *The Independent Group: Modernism and Mass Culture in Britain, 1945–1959* (Manchester: Manchester University Press, 1995) outlines ideas showing that modernism was in crisis in the 1950s in Britain, while Nigel Whiteley, *Pop Design: Modernism to Mod*

(London: Design Council, 1987), showed where this crisis led in terms of material culture. In the USA Eobert Venturi diagnosed a similar crisis in American architecture in *Complexity and Contradiction in Architecture* (New York: Museum of Modern Art, 1966). Michael Collins and Andreas Papadakis documented its effect on design production in the 1980s, in *Post-Modern Design* (New York: Rizzoli, 1989).

FURTHER READING

Banham, R. 'A throw-away aesthetic', in Sparke, P. (ed.), *Reyner Banham: Design By Choice* (London: Academy Editions, 1981), pp. 90–3.

Boorstin, D.J. *The Image* (London: Wiedenfeld and Nicholson, 1962).

Featherstone, M. *Consumer Culture and Postmodernism* (London: Sage, 1983).

Dorfles, G. *Kitsch* (London: Studio Vista, 1969).

Foster, H. *Postmodern Culture* (London: Pluto Press, 1990).

Gablik, S. *Has Modernism Failed?* (London: Thames and Hudson, 1984).

Giddens, A. *Modernity and Self-Identity: Self and Society in the Late Modern Age* (California: Stanford University Press, 1991).

Hebdige, F. 'In poor taste: notes on Pop', in *Hiding in the Light* (London and New York: Routledge, 1988), pp. 116–43.

Hochschule für Gestaltung, Ulm: Fie Moral der Gegenstande (Berlin: Ernst & Sohn, 1987).

Horn, R. *Memphis: Objects, Furniture and Patterns* (New York: Simon and Schuster, 1986).

Jameson, F. 'Postmodernism, or the logic of late capitalism', *New Left Review* (vol.146, 1984), pp. 53–92.

Kauffmann Jr, E. *Introduction to Modern Design* (New York: Museum of Modern Art, 1969).

Jencks, C. *The Language of Post-Modern Architecture* (London: Academy, 1973).

Massey, A. and Sparke, P. 'The myth of the Independent Group', *Block* (10, 1985), pp. 48–56.

Moles, A. *Le Kitsch* (Paris: Maison Mame, 1971).

Packard, V. *The Hidden Persuaders* (Harmondsworth: Penguin, 1957).

Packard, V. *The Waste-Makers* (London: Longmans, 1961).

Packard, V. *The Status Seekers* (Harmondsworth: Penguin, 1963).

Sparke. P. (ed.) *Reyner Banham: Design by Choice* (London: Academy Editions, 1981).

Sparke, P. *Ettore Sottsass Jr* (London: Design Council, 1982).

Sweet, F. *Alessi: Art and Poetry* (London: Thames and Hudson, 1998).

Thackera, J. (ed.) *Design after Modernism: Beyond the Object* (London: Thames and Hudson, 1988).

Venturi, R., Scott-Brown, D. and Izenour, S. *Learning from Las Vegas: The Forgotten Symbolism of Architectural Form* (Cambridge, MA: MIT Press, 1972).

Chapter 10   Redefining identities

RECOMMENDED READING

The globalism of the late twentieth century gave rise to a number of studies. They include Celia Lury's analysis of Benetton – 'The United Colours of Diversity: essential and inessential culture', in Franklyn, S., Lury, C. and Stacey, J. (eds), *Global Nature, Global Culture* (London: Sage, 2000). At the same time, with the destruction of the Berlin Wall, new nationalisms came into being and design was used to demarcate them. Studies of this new phenomenon include David Crowley's *Design and Culture in Poland and Hungary 1890–1990* (Brighton: Brighton University Press, 1992), and Gert Selle's 'The lost innocence of poverty: on the disappearance of cultural difference', *Design Issues: History; Theory; Criticism* (vol.8, no.2, spring 1992), pp. 61–73.

FURTHER READING

Aldersey-Williams, H. *Nationalism and Globalism in Design* (New York: Rizzoli, 1992).

Aynsley, J. *Nationalism and Internationalism in Design* (London: V&A Publications, 1993).

Banham, M. and Hillier, B. *A Tonic to the Nation: The Festival of Britain* (London: Thames and Hudson, 1976).

Breward, C., Conekin, B. and Cox, C. (eds) *The Englishness of English Dress* (Oxford and New York: Berg, 2002).

Bullig, M. *Banal Nationalism* (London: Sage, 1995).

Council of Industrial Design *Design in the Festival* (London: HMSO, 1951).

Erlhoff, M. (ed.) *Designed in Germany since 1949* (Munich: Prestel, 1990).

Ernyey, G. *Made in Hungary: The Best of 150 Years in Industrial Design* (Budapest: Rubik Innovation Foundation, 1993).

Falk, P. 'The Benetton-Toscani effect: testing the limits of conventional advertising', in Nava, M., Blake, A., MacRury, I. and Richards, B. *Buy This Book: Studies in Advertising and Consumption* (London and New York: Routledge, 1997).

Heskett, J. *Philips: A Study of the Corporate Management of Design* (London: Trefoil, 1989).

Julier, G. 'Barcelona design, Catalonia's political economy and the new Spain', *Journal of Design History* (vol.9, no.2, 1996), pp. 117–28.

Klein, N. *No Logo* (London: Flamingo, 2001).

Lury, C. *Consumer Culture* (Cambridge: Polity, 1996).

Marling, K.A. *Designing Disney's Theme Parks: The Architecture of Renaissance* (Paris: Flammarion, 1997).

McDermott, C. *Made in Britain: Tradition and Style in Contemporary British Fashion* (London: Mitchell Beazley, 2002).

Miller, D. 'Coca-Cola: a black sweet drink from Trinidad', in Miller, F. (ed.) *Material Cultures: Why Some Things Matter* (London: UCL Press, 1998).

Narotzky, V. *An Acquired Taste: The Consumption of Design in Barcelona, 1975– 1992* (unpublished PhD thesis, Royal College of Art, London, 2003).

Oliver, T. *The Real Coke: The Real Story* (London: Elm Tree, 1986).

Pavitt, J. (ed.) *Brand New* (London: V&A Publications, 2000).

Sparke, P. (ed.) *Did Britain Make It? British Design in Context 1946–1986* (London: Design Council, 1986).

Sparke, P. *Japanese Design* (London: Michael Joseph, 1987).

Sparke, P. '"A home for everybody?": design, ideology and the culture of the home in Italy, 1945–72', in Greenhalgh, P. (ed.), *Modernism in Design* (London: Reaktion Books, 1990), pp. 185–202.

Vukic, F. *A Century of Croatian Design* (Zagreb: Meander, 1998).

Zukin, S. *Landscapes of Power: From Detroit to Disney World* (Berkeley: University of California Press, 1995).

Zukin, S. *The Cultures of Cities* (Cambridge, MA: Blackwell, 1995).

INDEX

B